AF556357

ENCYCLOPAEDIA OF BIOTERRORISM-V

TERRORISM AND BIOTERRORISM

By

Dr. S.K. Prasad

School of Studies of Zoology & Biotechnology

Vikram University

Ujjain

DISCOVERY PUBLISHING HOUSE PVT. LTD.

NEW DELHI-110 002

First Published-2009

ISBN 978-81-8356-389-5

Published by:

DISCOVERY PUBLISHING HOUSE PVT. LTD.
4831/24, Ansari Road, Prahlad Street,
Darya Ganj, New Delhi-110002 (India)
Phone: 23279245 • Fax: 91-11-23253475
E-mail: dphbooks@rediffmail.com
dphtemp@indiatimes.com

Printed at:
Sachin Printers, Delhi

Preface

The present title "*Terrorism and Bioterrorism*" aims to bring historical context to present concerns about biological weapons, biological agents, chemical weapons and the potential for bioterrorism. The lack of use of biological weapons in war advocates for using biology to create a new class of weapons initially envisioned delivery systems for pathogenic aerosols that mimicked those for chemical weapons, which were mainly bombs that generated aerosols intended to kill or disable troops in a local area. This vision was quickly replaced by the concept of creating huge clouds of germs that would drift with the wind and infect people over areas of thousands of square miles. The scientists and civil and military leaders who believed in the future of biological weapons saw their potential for fulfilling the goals of total war, for the mass killing or debilitation of enemy civilians. It is often asked why biological weapons are different from any other means of destruction. The answer is that they are the only ones devised expressly to kill defenseless humans and animal and plant life, with little real battlefield potential in modern war.

When biological weapons were developed for possible retaliation against an enemy thought to be similarly armed, they fit this model of restraint. Nevertheless, germ weapons were developed and laws and political circumstances offered no guarantees against their use. Historians may seek neat explanations, but the element of uncertainty was always there. Political and military authorities differed unpredictably when it came to calculating the consequences of using biological weapons. This book also describes the new subject of bioterrorism and traces at least the beginnings of the present era, in which domestic preparedness and homeland security are major policy issue. One of the major homeland security directives is to use technology derived from medical research to protect civilians against bioterrorism. The use of biology to defined civilians against any and all biological agents is a daunting project that imposes new security restrictions more familiar to physicists in the defense establishment than to biologists.

The study of biological weapons combines knowledge from disparate fields: biology, medicine, military history, politics, law, and ethics. This book intends to give the reader a basic literacy in this complex area. The entire subject of biological weapons is characterized by an unusual degree of misinformation and even disinformation. Almost every fact in this book has several page backstory, with greater nuance and depth than a brief overview can provide. As scholars continue their work, more information and analysis will likely turn today's accepted wisdom on its head. This progress will be a healthy sign for the field, whose subject matter has often been exploited for the frightening and sometimes entertaining effect it has on the imagination.

There can be no claim to originality except in the manner of treatment and much of the information has been obtained from the books and scientific journals available in the different libraries.

The author expresses his thanks to his friends and colleagues whose continue inspirations have initiated him to bring out this book.

The author expresses his gratitude to Mr. Wasan and staff of M/s Discovery Publishing House Pvt. Ltd. for their whole hearted co-operation in the publication of this book.

Author

CONTENTS

1

INTRODUCTION

As the Cold War was ending, new hopes emerged for a strengthened *Biological Weapons Convention* through a protocol with strong compliance measures. The 1993 *Chemical Weapons Convention* offered a model of team inspections, mandatory verification procedures, and a standing organization, located in The Hague. Why not similar fortifications for the BWC?

From the beginning, the country proved wary of multilateral accord that would require transparency and subject it to international law. In 1991, it requested that a range of verification measures should be reviewed before protocol negotiations began. Two years later the Ad Hoc Group of Governmental Experts produced a technical and scientific report evaluating offsite measures (such as declaration of facilities, surveillance of publications, legislation, and trade, remote sensing and tests of physical materials) and onsite measures (exchange visits, inspection of buildings and key equipment, collection of relevant medical data, and continuous observation of certain facilities, whether by instruments or by experts). In this 1993 Verex Report, onsite measures were seen, especially by the United States, as a threat to the *commercial proprietary information* (CPI) of pharmaceutical and biotechnology companies and to the US defensive biological program. Russia and China also expressed resistance.

Still, since compliance was the goal, not radical transparency, it was agreed that common ground among participating nations might be found. In 1994, an *Ad Hoc Group* was established to start the negotiations for a BWC protocol that would strengthen compliance measures. U.S. President Bill Clinton supported a protocol for the treaty. But in 1995, after Republicans took control of Congress, the United States became increasingly antagonistic to international treaties, including the 1993 Chemical Weapons Convention, which President George H. W. Bush had promoted and signed. Senate leaders, especially the powerful Jesse Helms, continually objected to the compliance measures being proposed in the Ad Hoc Group negotiations. Although Russia and China also maintained their hesitancy, in the seven years of negotiations their delegates moved toward concessions while the United States introduced a series of proposals that would restrict declarations and inspections in favour of secrecy.

During this same time, *biological weapons* began taking on new significance for their potential use by terrorists in attacks on American cities. There was enough evidence from the *Cold War* years to indicate that small states, whether allied or neutral, could develop secret biological weapons and should be integrated into the larger world community that sanctioned *biowarfare*. National defenses against terrorism in general and bioterrorism in the specific were not necessarily in conflict with the BWC protocol. But bioterrorism soon enough became a diversion fro a multilateral agreement to curb state programs. Analysts began describing how America's enemies might acquire nuclear, biological, and chemical weapons (NBC), the unconventional weapons developed by the major powers, through the global marketplace and pose an asymmetrical national security threat to unprotected civilians.

This reconfiguration of national defense was part of the US struggle to position itself as the lone superpower with vast military resources in the globalized post—Cold War world, with no Soviet adversary Regional conflicts in the Balkans, Africa, and the Middle East were generating unpredictable military and political risks, including genocide in the former Yugoslavia and in Rwanda. Nuclear deterrence had a reduced significance in this complex world, as did a US army positioned for Cold War hostilities.

No bioterrorist assault on an American city occurred in this unsettled period. Terrorist attacks, though, were real and demanded new policies. The scale of bomb attacks at home and abroad drew no distinctions between political figures and innocent bystanders, including children. In conjunction with fears of terrorism, anxieties about the risks of bioterrorism increased and, in imagination, mass killings were magnified by epidemic scenarios. Few people had worried about biological weapons in years, yet gradually their potential, refitted to terrorists, generated federal policies that presumed that a state of emergency preparedness should be normal. As the millennium approached, influential politicians and consulting experts broadcast apocalyptic visions of thousands, even hundreds of thousands of Americans dying from unnatural, intentional epidemics of anthrax, smallpox, or some newly devised disease, in visibly inflicted by barbarous foreigners.

Civil Defense against WMD

Government emphasis on the vulnerability of civilians to *weapons of mass destruction* (WMD) raises the difficult question of how and if officials expect to protect the population and whether they intend to do this by technology or political initiatives. In a 1961 televised address, President Kennedy warned that the United States was on the brink of a nuclear war with the Soviet Union. To reassure the public, he promised that every American household would receive a pamphlet on how individuals could protect themselves by stocking food and water and seeking fallout shelters. By the time the pamphlet was mailed a year later, the White House and Soviet leaders had confronted and resolved the Cuban missile crisis, to the public's relief. Soon after, in 1963, the United States, the United Kingdom, and the Soviet Union signed the Limited Test Ban Treaty. This accord failed to halt proliferation, but Americans became less anxious about imminent world destruction.

During the early Reagan administration, withdrawal from the Strategic Arms Limitation Talks (SALT II) with the Soviet Union, discussion of prospects for limited nuclear warfare, and proposals to renew civil defense evacuation plans, plus presidential rhetoric characterizing the USSR as the uncontrollable "*Evil Empire*," fueled public fears of a nuclear holocaust and contributed to an international nuclear freeze movement. As an alternative to nonproliferation, in 1983 President Reagan turned to technology and proposed research on the *Strategic Defense Initiative* (SDI), a computerized system of ground and space-based interceptors. Also called "*Star Wars*;' this system was intended to sense and destroy attacking missiles. The president represented SDI as a national "*insurance policy*" against ultimate aggression by the Soviet Union and "a shield that could protect us from nuclear missiles just as a roof protects a family from rain?' As the Soviet Union collapsed, this technological defense, widely criticized as ineffective and politically risky, became irrelevant although it was later revived.

During the Clinton administration, officials at the highest level, including the president, publicly expressed their deep fears of bioterrorism, with little evidence that anti-American terrorists were interested in germ weapons. The United States had no single and equal political adversary with which it could negotiate to reduce risks, like the Soviet Union, and it was reluctant to subject itself to multilateral agreements with lesser powers. In this phase, the United States gradually lost its long-range perspective on the importance of states in preventing proliferation, for example, in restraining terrorist acquisition of biological weapons as well as secret state programs.

As it was imagined, bioterrorism reduced the technology of offensive biological weapons to the level of sabotage attacks on urban neighbourhoods, sports arenas, malls, or transportation systems, like subways or airports. These limited scenarios became the basis for exercises for local "*first responders*," the police, firefighters, and paramedics on the local scene. Unlike nuclear, chemical, or large-explosive attacks, the effects of an intentional epidemic would be slow to emerge and last for weeks or longer. Any bioterrorist event would put great demands on public health and hospital resources. The term "*dual use*" came into new use in reference to public health resources that might be mobilized in domestic preparedness plans. For a while it was hoped that, like the British in 1938, the government would decide that the best defense against biological weapons was a healthy population with good, publicly supported medical care. Instead, the American approach in the 1990s emphasized decentralized civil defense plans and broad technological solutions, such as improved electronic communication and federal antibiotic stockpiles, geared to emergency response.

Biological Weapons Threats from States

Over the years, the list of nations suspected by the United States of having biological weapons programs has emphasized what are often called "*niche states*, " ones that lack the conventional power to challenge the United States, but "possess the resources and know-how to possibly resort to WMD, especially biological or chemical weapons?" Cuba and North Korea, for instance, have been listed regularly, along with Iran and, until 2003, Iraq and Libya. On other lists, not all suspects are hostile to the US; some, like Taiwan, have American support. Nor are they necessarily small nations with limited military force. China, Pakistan, and India, each with nuclear weapons, have been cited as perhaps supporting offensive biological weapons programs.

Israel also appears on most lists compiled by analysts and arms control organizations. Little is known about the history of its biological weapons program and its alliance with the United States, which includes military aid, seems to have protected it from American inquiry about its present activities. After the 1948 war, Israel established a biological research unit, called Hemed Beit, which then moved to its permanent location on seventy acres outside the town of Ness Ziona, near Tel Aviv. Known since 1952 as the Israeli Institute of Biological Research (IIBR), the center was sponsored by the Ministry of Defense and staffed by civilian scientists who often had academic appointments and published in scientific journals.

Israel stands apart from other democracies in its refusal to become a party to either the Biological Weapons Convention or the Chemical Weapons Convention. It is a party to the Geneva Protocol, with the reservation that the Protocol would cease to be binding "as regards any enemy State whose armed forces, or the armed forces of whose allies, or the regular or irregular forces, or groups or individuals operating from its territory, fail to respect the prohibitions which are the object of this Protocol Syria, Jordan, and Libya have long maintained similar reservations specifically allowing retaliation against Israel.

Much more is known about the biological weapons programs of Iraq and apartheid South Africa than any comparable states. Each made different treaty commitments during the Cold War, when their programs were started. Iraq was party to the Geneva Protocol; it signed but did not ratify the Biological Weapons Convention (BWC) until required to do so as part of the 1991 United Nations cease-fire agreement, and it was not a party to the Chemical Weapons Convention (CWC). South Africa was party to the Geneva Protocol and the BWC and, after a regime change, joined the CWC in 1995.

Threat from Iraq

Before the Gulf War, the lawless characteristics of Saddam Hussein's Iraq were largely overlooked by the United States. Its conventional military force, built up during the Cold War with US and Soviet and other assistance, was a threat to the region. It was known to have used chemical weapons (tear gas, mustard gas, and nerve gas) against Iranian troops, and in 1987 and 1988 it used chemical weapons in attacks that killed Kurdish villagers. Its invasion of Kuwait, to reclaim what it contended were traditional lands, precipitated the

1991 Gulf War, the cease-fire agreement, and the eventual end of Saddam's power.

In 1991, United Nations Security Council Resolution 687 required Iraq to reaffirm its commitment to the 1925 Geneva Protocol, to ratify the BWC, and to accept, under international supervision, the destruction, removal, or rendering harmless of: "(a) all chemical and biological weapons and all stocks of agents and all related subsystems and components and all research, development, support and manufacturing facilities related thereto; (b) all ballistic missiles with a range greater than 150 kilometers and related major parts and repair and production facilities."

The United Nations Special Commission (UNSCOM), chaired by Swedish Ambassador Roif Ekeus, was assigned to facilitate the elimination of chemical and biological weapons, while the IAEA (*International Atomic Energy Agency*) was in charge of investigating possible nuclear weapons and succeeded in discovering and destroying Iraq's preliminary efforts in this area. UNSCOM had a double purpose, to disarm Iraq and to continue ongoing monitoring and verification to prevent its reacquisition of the prohibited weapons.

From 1992 to 1995, the UNSCOM team accumulated solid evidence of an Iraqi offensive biological program. Its detailed tracking of purchases of bacteriological growth media by Iraq's Technical and Scientific Materials Import Division showed that thirty-nine tons had been imported in 1988 and several more tons arrived later, with a shelf life of four to five years. This amount was far beyond what Iraqi hospitals, medical laboratories, and pharmaceutical industries could need in that time.

In July 1995, faced with UNSCOM's findings, the Iraqi government was forced to admit it had developed an offensive biological weapons program and to provide information on the amounts of various biological agents it had produced. The Iraqis claimed that all its biological agents had been destroyed and denied ever having placed them in munitions.

In August, Gm. Hussein Kamal, Saddam Hussein's son-in-law and a former top government official, departed for Jordan and there briefly described to Ekeus the development and production of biological agents and asserted that the program had ended. Iraqi officials reacted by arranging for UNSCOM to receive more documentation, at Kamal's farm where, in a chicken house, investigators found a box of written reports, along with microfiches, computer diskettes, videotapes, and photographs of prohibited hardware. Iraqi officials then admitted it had filled munitions with biological agents: five SCUD missile warheads with *anthrax*, sixteen with *botulinum toxin*, and four with *aflatoxin* (which is something of a puzzle, since aflatoxin is a slow-acting carcinogen). They also admitted that bombs and drop-tank aerosol generators for airplanes were part of Iraq's biological weapons arsenal. UNSCOM then intensified its monitoring, making over a hundred site visits, twenty of these to the declared biological production facility at Al Hakam, which the Iraqis, under UN supervision, destroyed in 1996.

According to Iraq's own declaration, as early as 1974, it began exploring the creation of a biological weapons program. Microbiologist Nassir al Hindawi, an anthrax specialist, has been represented as its founding father. Iraqi scientists and technicians were well educated in Western universities, as undergraduates and graduate students. Rihab Rashid Taha, a microbiologist with a doctorate from the University of East Anglia in the UK, was the main contact with United Nations inspectors.

In 1984 a group of biologists began research within one of the chemical weapons complexes, following the pattern of biological weapons program development in the United Kingdom, the United States, and the Soviet Union. Then, in 1988, Iraq established the Al-Hakam facility for mass production of anthrax, botulinum toxin, and later viruses. With its oil revenues, Iraq had the resources to build or buy the necessary technology, from fermenters to bombs, missiles, and aircraft.

During the 1980s, Iraq was able to purchase four strains of anthrax from the American Type Culture Collection, with the approval of the US Commerce Department. Other pathogens and toxins explored by the superpowers appeared in records of the Iraqi arsenal: *tularemia*, *botulinum toxin*, *brucellosis*, *wheat rust*, *aflatoxin*, and *ricin*. The Iraqis also investigated camel pox, rotavirus, hemorrhagic conjunctivitis, and trichothecene mycotoxin, the alleged "*yellow rain*" of the 1980s.

According to General Kamal in his August 1995 interview in Jordan, all this activity had ended. Kamal stated that, intimidated by the arrival of UNSCOM, he had ordered the destruction of Iraq's chemical and biological weapons programs in 1991. About biological agents and weapons, his assertion was, "*nothing remained.*"

According to Richard Butler, the Australian ambassador who became the UNSCOM chair in 1997, both Iraq's failure to cooperate fully and internal politics at the United Nations undermined the verification procedure. Russia and France in particular lobbied for approval of Iraqi disarmament efforts and the end to economic sanctions. The resignation in protest of one American inspector, Scott Ritter, raised suspicions that the United States tried to use UNSCOM to further its intelligence agenda, which Butler denied. 19 By December 15, 1998, relations with Iraq had deteriorated and the UNSCOM team was evacuated. Immediately after, the US and UK commenced a punitive four-day bombing raid on Iraq (Operation Desert Fox). The final UNSCOM report on Iraq pointed to missing documentation of compliance, "Iraq has not provided evidence concerning the termination of its offensive BW programme. The evidence collected by the Commission and the absence of information from Iraq, raises serious doubts about Iraq's assertion that the BW programme was truly 'obliterated' in 1991 as it claims."

Despite their varying levels of experience and the obstacles posed by the Iraqis, the UNSCOM teams had been energetic in their site searches. Over nearly eight years, dozens of teams of experts conducted and recorded hundreds of detailed inspections. Until 1995, UNSCOM reported, the Iraqis attempted to conceal the entirety of their biological weapons program and used "*outright lying*, evasiveness, intimidation, forging of documents, misrepresentation of sites and personnel, the denial of access to individuals and the issue of successive FFCDs [Full Final, and Complete Disclosures] that were fraudulent." By 1998, though, the "*absence of information*' not any material evidence of biological weapons, made Iraq suspect.

South Africa

Important information about the South African biological weapons program was acquired after a regime change that brought democracy and the franchise to the majority black African population. The new government voluntarily undertook the public disclosure of the combined chemical and biological weapons program, and its courts commenced legal proceedings that provided more information. UNSCOM and US leaders often compared Iraq's lack of cooperation to South Africa's willing exposure of its past. The South African process was, in fact, less than ideal and much more remains to be known about the program and its activities, both national and across national borders. Although unlike the Japanese program in China, the South African venture was also marshaled against a civilian population considered racially inferior, with the intent of subjugating or exterminating them.

In 1978, P. W. Botha, the former minister of defense, was elected president of South Africa. In the name of national security, he increased military, police, and special operations forces to promote a "*total national strategy*" against the "*total onslaught*" of terrorist attacks by the African National Congress and Rhodesian insurgents, and by guerrillas from neighbouring states. Soon after, Wouter Basson, a young military physician, was sent overseas to educate himself on chemical and biological weapons.

In 1981 South Africa initiated a combined chemical and biological weapons program in reaction to political threats to its apartheid government and its policies of segregation, which had already distanced it from the Common wealth and the West. As the Soviet Union, Cuba, and China supported black liberation movements in Angola, Mozambique, Rhodesia (now Zimbabwe), and South West Africa (now Namibia), South Africa identified itself as an anticommunist stronghold and used the South Africa Defense Force (SADF), assisted by chemical and biological weapons program officials, to support the last colonial regimes in Africa. In 1981, Botha appointed Basson the head of the new program, code-named Project Coast.

Although Project Coast was under the South African Defense Department's Surgeon General's office, Basson was subject to little supervision. The project involved South African universities and private industries in covert research projects. It likely had communication about biological weapons with Israel, which shared South Africa's sense of siege and cooperated with it on nuclear and conventional weapons programs. The project's growth years were from 1982 to 1987, when it developed a range of biological agents (such as those for *anthrax*, *cholera*, and the *Marburg* and *Ebola viruses* and for *botulinum toxin*) and had plans, probably never met, to build a large, secret production facility.

Counterinsurgency agents were a specialty, from tear gas to sedative drugs to the hallucinogen BZ, which the US had produced and stockpiled in the 1960s and then abandoned. Such "*incapacitants*" were used to facilitate the killing of hundreds of prisoners from South West Africa, whose bodies (unmarked by overt violence) were then dumped from airplanes into the sea. Project Coast reportedly had research plans, however dubious, for a "*black bomb*" that would selectively kill or weaken black insurrectionists in troubled, mixed-race areas. The covert sterilization of black people with drugs or vaccines was apparently another project goal.

The end of the Cold War, the 1989 election of F. W. De Klerk to the presidency, and the 1994 political ascendancy of Nelson Mandela and the African National Congress ended the South African chemical and biological weapons program, along with its nuclear one.

In the final years of the apartheid government, British intelligence discovered that Wouter Basson was traveling to Libya as a consultant; he also had made frequent trips to Eastern Europe and Iran and cultivated contacts with racist militia sympathizers in the United States. Basson was the kind of wild-card scientist that US and UK intelligence agencies feared would sell information to hostile states and terrorists. The United States and the United Kingdom urged the Mandela government, which lacked the legal means to restrain Basson, to rehire him.

In 1997, President Mandela asked that the history of Project Coast be considered for hearings before the Truth and Reconciliation Commission. Encumbered by some government restrictions, the hearings proceeded and former program scientists and administrators gave precise, disturbing accounts of their work and its use for sabotage and war. Basson, delaying his appearance to the final hours of the last day, kept his testimony short and evasive.

A subsequent criminal trial of Basson commenced in October 1999 and lasted until April 2001. The judge, who openly approved of Project Coast, finally cleared Basson of all charges. The prosecutors immediately appealed for a new trial with a new judge, which led to years of judicial deliberations, still inconclusive. Nonetheless, both public processes, the Truth and Reconciliation testimonies and Basson's trial, disclosed important information about the secret program.

Administration and Terrorism

During the 1990s, widespread fatal epidemics were seriously disrupting sub-Saharan Africa, South Asia, South America, and the Caribbean, especially Haiti, and making inroads in Russia and Eastern Europe. Most people in the United States felt little connection to the risks of disease, poverty, and violence afflicting much of the rest of the world. In the 1980s, the AIDS epidemic had introduced Americans to a devastating emerging infectious disease; with new medical cocktails, HIV infection became more like a chronic disease than a fatal epidemic. Medical technology had contained the threat of collective death. If there was a worry, it was that federal withdrawal from medical and social welfare programs would leave Americans prey to for-profit hospitals, managed care, and drug companies.

In this context, terrorist attacks of increased scale and daring opened the door to thinking that biological weapons attacks would be next, if not nuclear weapons or nerve gas. The 1993 bombing at the New York World Trade Center, planned and executed by international terrorist Ramzi Yousef, was the first event that demonstrated how easy foreign attack might be. Only chance prevented it from having its planned catastrophic impact, that one of the Twin Towers would topple against the other.

In 1995, the Oklahoma City bombing again demonstrated US vulnerability, this time from within, from an American, Timothy McVeigh, a Gulf War veteran inspired by militia extremism and the Christian Identity movement. The violence of the event shocked the nation with its scale of destruction and death (168 killed, including 19 children). In response, President Clinton issued *Presidential Decision Directive* (PDD-39), which laid out an agency-by-agency national strategy for preventing and responding to terrorist at tacks. PDD-39 was the first high-level, major policy document to address the problem of large-scale terrorism with centralized federal controls. The increase in the federal counterterrorism budget went from $5. billion in 1995 to $11.1 billion in 2000.

The US Congress reacted with bipartisan legislation to bolster preparedness against WMD terrorism in state and local communities. Senators Sam Nunn and Richard Lugar, who had sponsored legislation to reduce the post- Soviet threat, were joined by Senator Pete Domenici in sponsoring the 1997 National Defense Organization Act, which established the Domestic Preparedness Program. Although the United States was not at war, the theme of decentralized civil defense was popular in Congress; it meant that funds would flow to cities and states to reinforce emergency police, firefighter, and medical resources. The Nunn-Lugar-Domenici legislation gave the Defense Department the lead in allocating grants to the nation's 120 largest cities for training, equipment, and exercises to prepare them for WMD attacks.

Two minor links between militia extremists and the possession of dangerous pathogens surfaced in the 1990s. One was the 1994 case of the Minnesota Patriots Council, in which four members derived ricin from castor beans with the intent to kill government officials. The other was the case of Larry Wayne Harris, arrested in 1995 and again in 1998 on suspicion of planning to create a biological weapon using anthrax spores. Harris, who received extensive media coverage, was released both times. The Minnesota militia members were sentenced to jail in 1994 and 1995 for violation of the 1989 Biological Weapons Antiterrorism Act, which extended the prohibitions in the BWC (including possession) to federal law. Both these cases, along with Iraq's earlier purchase of anthrax strains, sounded the alarm about the commercial availability of dangerous pathogens. Still, foreign terrorists appeared a much more substantial threat of WMD attacks than America militias.

Foreign Terrorists

A month before the Oklahoma City bombing, members of the Aum Shinrikyo (Shining Truth) cult released nerve gas in an attack in the Tokyo subway. The delivery system was little more than multiple plastic bags with holes poked in them by umbrellas. In addition to the twelve people who were killed, a thousand were hospitalized and thousands more sought care. Eight months earlier, in the town of Matsumoto, the cult had released a sarin cloud that killed seven. The event, although reported in the press, went largely unnoticed in the United States. Further investigation revealed that the cult had experimented unsuccessfully in Japan with dispersing anthrax spores in public places. It also had a New York City office and plans to attack there and in Washington, DC.

The FBI had already had a brush with a cult group's hostile use of a pathogen. In 1984, the Oregon members of the Indian Rajneeshee cult covertly sickened 751 people by contaminating ten local restaurant salad bars and coffee stations with *Salmonella typhimurium* purchased from a US medical supply company. The following year, after the cult had dispersed, a former member voluntarily confessed the plot, saying it was part of a plan to keep local voters from impeding Rajneeshee expansion. Until the confession, the outbreak was attributed to poor restaurant sanitation.

Aum Shinrikyo's organization was global. In post-Soviet Russia, it recruited thirty thousand members and had twenty thousand or more in Australia, Germany, Taiwan, and the former Yugoslavia. Its war chest, conservatively estimated at $20 million, reflected its support by members. Unlike other active terrorist organizations, Aum Shinrikyo attracted scientists and explored the possibilities of other lethal agents and perhaps nuclear weapons. Its goal was apocalyptic, the destruction of the corrupted world order in order to create a new, pure society.

Much of the cult's success in attacks resulted from the Japanese government's reluctance to intrude on any of its many religious sects. Japan also had to create new laws to prosecute individuals for WMD possession and use. Nine of the Aum's members were given death sentences by the Japanese courts in a slow legal process that kept Asahara Shoko, the group's leader, in jail for nearly ten years before he received the same sentence. Aum Shinrikyo and its chemical and biological activities strongly influenced how the US government perceived the global terrorism threat: apocalyptic, international, equipped with the financial assets and scientific skills to develop and use weapons of mass destruction.

Postmodern Terrorism

Since the 1980s, US troops and embassies in the Middle East and Africa had been the targets of terrorist attacks. The globalization of Islamic extremist terrorism was a new phenomenon, epitomized by Al Qaeda (the Base) and its leader, Osama bin Laden, a son of a Saudi millionaire. Bin Laden was along-time sponsor of Sunni Islamic extremism in Afghanistan, where during the 1980s the United States had supported his guerrillas against Soviet troops.

In August 1998, Al Qaeda operatives coordinated the bomb attacks on the US embassies in Dares Salaam, Tanzania, and Nairobi, Kenya. In the first explosion, eleven were killed and seventy-four injured. In the second, in a congested downtown area, 213 were killed and 4,500 were treated for injuries. The Al Qaeda coordination of the embassy bombings, which involved terrorists from Egypt, Jordan, Saudi Arabia, a US citizen, and several Africans, supported bin Laden's claim of control over an international network united in an Islamic jihad against Israel and against American military "*Crusaders*" in the Middle East. As Secretary of State Madeleine Albright commented in reaction to the bombings, they seemed to indicate "a clash between civilization itself and anarchy—between the rule of law and no rules at all."

The Aum Shinrikyo attacks and the Al Qaeda bombings lent credence to theories that terrorism had entered a new postmodern age of violence, driven by religious fanaticism. Or, as some hypothesized, the conflict between the Western civilization and fundamentalist Islam would define future wars.

In reaction to the embassy bombings, President Clinton responded with military force against two targets. Following a CIA report of a chemical precursor (called EMPTA) to the nerve agent VX found near a Sudanese factory, Clinton ordered the factory bombed. The president also ordered the bombing of six terrorist training camps in Afghanistan, where around sixty people were killed. Critics of these strikes and of the December 1998 Desert Fox attacks on Iraq suggested that President

Clinton, beset by a perjury and sex scandal, was creating a political diversion. Others felt he did not go far enough in attacking the terrorist camps. Clinton's resort to punitive military force to counter terrorism had a precedent. Earlier, in 1994, President Clinton had authorized cruise missiles against an Iraqi intelligence center in retaliation for its attempt to assassinate former President Bush while he was in Kuwait. Even before that, in 1986, President Reagan had ordered an air strike against Libya in retaliation for the terrorist bombing of a West Berlin disco frequented by US soldiers. Like Reagan's air strike, Clinton's air attacks were intended as a warning blow to a lesser nation that might encourage anti-American terrorism. That Clinton relied on a scientific test, later disputed, to justify bombing Sudan was the unusual aspect of that decision.

In the aftermath of attacks on the United States abroad and at home, "*a permanent crisis mode*" dominated the White House. At the National Security Council Richard Clarke made Al Qaeda his principal target and worked on strategies to destroy the network with the CIA, Defense Department, Justice Department, and the FBI.

Visions of the Apocalypse

The first high-level Clinton appointee to promote biological weapons as a national security threat was Secretary of the Navy Richard Danzig Danzig, a Yale Law School graduate like Clinton, closely followed the Aum Shinrikyo case and considered it a likely model for future WMD terrorism. He was optimistic about Defense Department programs for a range of technologies (from biosensors to test air to improved vaccines) and for defensive troop training and the development of doctrine to preempt and respond to biological attack.

In 1997 President Clinton, concerned about the possible terrorist use of genetically altered biological agents, turned to microbiologists for advice. Like Danzig, Clinton relied on Nobel laureate Joshua Lederberg. For decades Lederberg had consulted for US intelligence and defense agencies. In addition, he had long warned of the possibility of devastating epidemics of exotic infectious diseases. In 1968, in reaction to a small epidemic of just such a disease (Marburg fever), he wrote in the Washington Post of the "*global pandemic*...that hangs over the head of the species at any time." In 1997, in the same apocalyptic mode, Lederberg adjusted his warning to the times: "Visualize the World Trade Center [in 1993] or an Oklahoma City—style attack complicated by the inclusion of a kilogram of anthrax spores as a kind of microbiological shrapnel along with the explosives. And its implications for salvage and rescue, public health, panic. If I just mention the word Ebola, you have some idea of what I am talking about."

Another science advisor to the president was Craig Venter, founder of the Institute for Genomic Research and of Celera, the company that first sequenced the human genome. Venter urged sequencing the genomes of dangerous pathogens as a possible way to design improved measures against them. Like Venter, Lederberg advocated a technological solution, the use of basic research to develop new drugs and vaccines, which could also protect against emerging infectious diseases.

In November 1997, Secretary of Defense William Cohen appeared on national television to make the viewing public conscious of an imminent mass biological weapons threat. Holding up a five-pound bag of sugar, Cohen stated that an equivalent amount of anthrax, if sprayed by plane over Washington, DC, would kill half its population. Having articulated the possibility of this horrible attack, Cohen could offer for protection the Nunn-Lugar Domenici bill, the decentralized domestic preparedness program the Defense Department would administer.

The other part of Cohen's speech announced a pharmaceutical solution to protect US troops abroad. Through a new Anthrax Vaccine Inoculation Program (AVIP), all 2.3 million American military personnel would be vaccinated against the risk of a biological weapons attack by a hostile nation such as Iraq or by a foreign terrorist group. This vaccination campaign was Secretary Danzig's idea, and he had enlisted Lederberg to overcome the reluctance of Pentagon leaders. Anthrax vaccinations were already standard for soldiers about to be deployed to high-risk areas, such as the Middle East or the Korean Peninsula. This new program was tied to federal support for a private company that was to be the army's sole supplier. The former head of the Joint Chiefs of Staff, Adm. William Crowe, sat on its board and had testified before Congress on behalf of the venture.

To advertise the vulnerability of the public to mass biological attack was in itself a risky approach, especially when few safeguards were in place. Who knew what ideas such an announcement would stimulate? The Cohen speech was followed by a precipitous rise in anthrax hoaxes, with hundreds of envelopes of sugar or other white powders posted to individuals, schools, offices, and churches and causing anxiety and disruption. Another result was media exploitation of fears of "*intentional epidemics*" on television, in films, and in the press, with political and medical authorities warning the public that a bioterrorist attack was not a matter of if but when.

In 1999, after several years of low funding, the annual budget for WMD domestic preparedness programs reached $10 billion. Seventy percent was al located to the Department of Defense and most of the rest went to the Justice Department and the Department of State.

Although Secretary Danzig called for an "*enhanced cooperative relationship*" between the military and federal agencies charged with civil defense against biological weapons, the scope of that cooperation remained undefined. In 1994, Clinton had supported the National Defense Authorization Act, which gave the Defense Department the responsibility for preparation and response to domestic nuclear, chemical, or biological attacks. In the remote event of an enormous catastrophe, such as a nuclear strike, the military was prepared to evacuate survivors. Its role in response to chemical or biological attack was uncertain. Afterward, Congress funded a dozen of what Cohen dubbed RAID (*Rapid Assessment* and *Initial Detection*) National Guard units, for integration into local response plans, which proved unsuccessful in practice. In mid- 1998, the Pentagon proposed establishing a national military command to coordinate a National Guard and other military responses to emergencies. It then retreated when the American Civil Liberties Union and influential members of the press protested. They argued that, if crossed, the line between military and police enforcement, established after the Civil War with the Posse Comitatus Act, could lead to violations of civil rights.

In 1998, in a new directive (PDD-62), President Clinton further delineated the federal counterterrorism responsibilities and placed them squarely within civilian agencies. Within the Department of Justice, the FBI would handle "*crisis management*": frustrate or stop a terrorist attack, arrest terrorists, and gather evidence for criminal prosecution. FEMA (the *Federal Emergency Management Agency*) would be in charge of "*consequence management*": the provision of medical treatment, evacuation of populations in danger, and the restoration of government services. These two task distinctions would later be reformulated as the number of federal agencies and offices potentially mobilized by a grand-scale terrorist attack increased to more than forty.

Civil Biodefense

In major cities across the country, the federal government helped stage simulated biological, chemical, and radiological ("*dirty bomb*") attacks to mobilize local officials for emergency response. Police, firefighters, and emergency medical teams rehearsed the rescue of afflicted civilians, played by community volunteers. "*Domestic preparedness*" was far from standard. Local government leadership determined the degree of participation, the plans for mobilization, and what resources would be requested from the federal government—whether new computers or police cars or ambulances or support for personnel and training.

In 2000, to test if domestic preparedness legislation was improving national readiness, Congress asked the Justice Department and FEMA, together with the National Security Council, to stage an exercise that would mobilize top government officials in a simulation of an attack response. The exercise, called TOPOFF (for "top officials"), was directed by an established defense contractor, SAIC (Science Application International Corporation). Costing around $10 million, TOPOFF simulated a mustard gas attack in Portsmouth, New Hampshire, where the response went smoothly, and a scripted plague aerosol attack in Denver, Colorado.

The Denver exercise produced chaos (locating mortuaries to store fictive cadavers was a major problem) and brought out the difference between a limited chemical attack and one with a contagious disease. This difference was important. An explosion or chemical attack would be immediately evident and localized. A disease outbreak, though, could be undetected at first and then last over weeks. Patients could leave the attack locale without realizing they were infected, fail to understand the gravity of their illness, and, if the disease were contagious, perhaps spread and prolong the epidemic.

In July 2001, another bioterrorist simulation, called "Dark Winter emphasized the contagious disease threat, even more strongly, on the scale of war. Held at Andrews Air Force Base, Dark Winter was a tabletop exercise, based on a fictional pandemic of smallpox; the scenario condensed the events of thirteen days into two. The invited participants or actors were Washington political insiders. For example, Senator Sam Nunn, a key sponsor of domestic preparedness legislation, played the part of the president. The script, written largely by staff at the Johns Hopkins Center for Civilian Biodefense Studies, illustrated a worst-case scenario in which smallpox spread across the nation, where insufficient vaccine was available to stop it. The US military had to intervene to curtail violence and social breakdown. Then a worldwide pandemic was added.

The Dark Winter scenario was later criticized by scientists at the Centers for Disease Control (CDC) and other infectious disease experts for its exaggerated contagion rates and its lack of emphasis on proven simple ways to curtail epidemics, such as home care, wearing face masks, hand washing, and, perhaps most important, avoiding hospitals where transmission rates would soar. In fact, the exercise served well as political rhetoric. Two weeks later, its organizers and participants testified before Congress in support of increased funding for stockpiling smallpox vaccine and for domestic response training. The exercise showed that the scale of an imagined bioterrorist attack could vary greatly, according to the scriptwriters and their intents.

During 2002, as polls indicated, the American public became more intimidated by the possibility of a nationwide smallpox outbreak. Among experts, concern about a future smallpox outbreak with perhaps a new strain had a direct impact on indefinitely delaying the WHO scheduled date (December 31, 2002) for destroying the US and Russian reserves of the virus, the last known in the world. Following the WHO smallpox eradication campaign, no case of the disease had been recorded since 1979.

Experts who saw basic science as the key to defense against bioterrorism envisioned the development of antiviral drugs to replace current vaccines, which, although valuable, were already contraindicated for people with compromised immune systems. Political justification for the delay was found in fears that Saddam Hussein might use smallpox in a last-stand attack or that North Korea's Kim Jongil would do the same. By this reckoning of future threats, it could be argued that the smallpox stocks should be preserved for research purposes.

Donald A. Henderson, a leader of the WHO smallpox eradication campaign and founder of the Johns Hopkins unit that organized Dark Winter, disagreed. His solution was for the government to destroy the virus and stockpile enough smallpox vaccine to counteract an American pandemic. The smallpox virus itself is not used in making the present vaccine; better vaccines, Henderson argued, could be developed without retaining the virus.

A report from the Institute of Medicine disputed the wisdom of destroying the virus. In agreement, the WHO delayed the extinction of smallpox. Developing nations most vulnerable to smallpox reemergence protested. At the same time, the US government moved forward with the production and stockpiling of the smallpox vaccine in the event of a bioterrorist attack on America.

Public Health and Bioterrorism

If bioterrorism posed a collective infectious disease threat, public health seemed the obvious response. The United States, though, had only inconsistently supported public health, which was often seen as a way in which government might curtail individual liberties and the operation of a free market. In the 1990s, the low-status and underfunded American public health system was charged with disease prevention and health care for the disadvantaged, such as AIDS and hepatitis testing, prenatal care, childhood vaccinations, drug abuse prevention, annual influenza shots for the elderly, and the laboratory monitoring of disease outbreaks. Its professional organizations and schools were also oriented to international infectious disease problems; national security was a limited and even unrealistic framework for risk reduction in a world with accelerated global travel, trade, and movement of populations.

In 1999, the Clinton administration heralded the integration of public health and national security to fight the threat of bioterrorism. But this integration was oriented not toward a reinforcement of, say, Medicaid, the nation's most comprehensive public health program, but toward technological solutions such as electronic disease surveillance and reporting, better medical diagnostic tests, and improved surveillance of water supplies and food production.

Public health physicians became concerned about the impact that "*civilian biodefense*" and its emphasis on emergency response could have on their role in providing routine services and protecting patients' rights. Victor Sidel, the public health leader who advocated the elimination of the US biological weapons program, saw a conflict between what were fundamentally national security goals and professional responsibilities to patients. He made the point that "military, intelligence, and law enforcement agencies and personnel have long histories of secrecy and deception that are contrary to the fundamental health principles of transparency and truthfulness. They may therefore be unsuitable partners for public health agencies that need to justify receiving the public's trust."

Troubling issues of military deception and secrecy had already tainted the Department of Defense's universal anthrax vaccination program, AVIP. Side effects were being underreported or suppressed by the Pentagon. The private pharmaceutical company had failed to win FDA approval for vaccine production and was relying on old, faulty stocks inherited from the last manufacturer, the State of Michigan.

Soldiers refusing the vaccination were being dishonorably discharged. Much of this information was released only because independent critics, such as Dr. Meryl Nass and Victor Sidel, and the families of soldiers had pressured Congress for investigation.

Sidel and others who emphasized trust and openness in disease management spoke from practical experience. In all outbreaks, accurate information—about the source of the disease, its nature and trans about who might have been exposed and why and where, and about how the victims can be quickly helped—is crucial to local public awareness and mobilization and, on clinical level, to early diagnosis and saving lives. The 1979 Sverdlovsk outbreak provided a worst-case example on a small scale of how military and government secrecy can have deadly consequences for the public. A larger outbreak similarly fraught with misinformation and disinformation would be a true catastrophe.

The millennium ended without the predicted bioterrorism event. The perceived threat of biological weapons, rather than diminishing after the end of the *Cold War*, continued to increase.

2

Framing the Threat

Well before October-November 2001, the spectre of "*bioterrorism*" benefited from an extremely successful sales campaign. Between 1995 and 2001, the most common portrayal of the potential for "*bioterrorism*" was the facile catchphrase, "It's not a matter of whether; just when." This proved to be one of the most successful catchphrases since the old soap-powder advertisement, "Duz Does Everything." But, of course, it was a matter of both "whether" and "when," or at least it might have been in this initial period. Those calling for preparation and preventive measures certainly believed, at a minimum, that the imagined sequel to whether and when, "...and with what consequences," could be affected. That was the purpose of the wake-up calls. But "whether" and "when" were modifiable also, depending on the policies chosen. It depended most particularly on how the threat was portrayed, and how that portrayal was broadcast to potentially interested parties around the world. Perhaps bioterrorism is a given between whenever "now" is and decades hence, but lots of things can intervene between now and then. The inflated predictions that were common were certainly not realistic. Much worse, in addition to being wrong, inflated predictions were counterproductive. They induced interest in BW in the wrong audiences.

One immediate problem was the conflation of biological weapons and "*bioterrorism*" (and even between biological "*agents*" and "*weapons*"). Biological weapon use had been possible in the entire 20th century. Now the entire subject became subsumed under "*bioterrorism.*" That simple switch in language made it easy to transfer levels of state capability to "*terrorists.*" Everything became and was referred to as "*bioterrorism.*" This wiped out any discrimination, or attempt to discriminate, between the relevant capabilities of state programs and existing terrorist groups as they are known to date. The possibility of incidents involving low numbers of casualties evolved in 2 or 3 years to "*mass casualty*" terrorism, and in several more years to "*Apocalyptic Terrorism.*" Generic terrorist groups (excluding the perpetrator of the U.S. anthrax events)—none of which had yet shown the ability to master their microbiological A, B, C's in the real world—were endowed with the prospective ability to genetically engineer pathogens. Yet the resources and capabilities available to states and to terrorist groups are vastly different.

If we go back 10 years or so, we can look at a series of portrayals of the threat. A 1997 U.S. DoD Defense Science Board report grouped the characteristics of both chemical and biological warfare agents:

1. They are relatively easy to obtain (certainly compared to nuclear), and potential users do not need access to large and expensive facilities to achieve potent capabilities.
2. They can be developed and produced in laboratory or small scale industrial facilities, which makes them difficult to detect. Also, the technologies required to produce them often have commercial applications as well, so their "dual use" can be plausibly denied.
3. They can be extremely lethal, so small quantities can be very effective.
4. They can be delivered by a variety of means.

The paragraph went on to add that "A few kilograms of a biological agent could threaten an entire city." Summations of this kind were grossly oversimplified even further. Former Secretary of the Navy Richard Danzig's 1997 and 1999 papers contain an example: "...a kilogram [of anthrax], depending on meteorological conditions and means of delivery, has the potential to kill hundreds of thousands of people in a metropolitan area...biological weapons are so potent and so cheap ...the technology is readily available...so many of our adversaries have biological warfare capabilities..." They do have "the potential," but they might also kill only few, or none at all. More correctly, not 1 kilogram but some 50 kilograms could kill anywhere between 0 and 95,000 people, depending on the initial population number, the quality and nature of the *anthrax preparation*, the meteorological conditions, and the means of delivery if distributed over a city.

More recent model studies by Dean Wilkening at Stanford University have demonstrated the difficulties in releasing biological agents so that they are infective in large airborne releases. The model studies show very wide ranges of variability, over five log units (orders of magnitude).

The years between 1995 and 2000 were characterized, then, by:

1. spurious statistics (hoaxes counted as "*biological*" events);
2. unknowable predictions;
3. greatly exaggerated consequence estimates;
4. gross exaggeration of the feasibility of successfully producing biological agents by nonstate actors, except in the case of recruitment of highly experienced professionals, for which there still was no evidence as of 2000;
5. the apparent continued absence of a thorough threat assessment; and,
6. thoughtless, ill-considered, counterproductive, and extravagant rhetoric.

Nonetheless, these descriptions were considered realistic and taken seriously by people responsible for public safety in various sectors: the Director of the World Trade Center in 2001 reported that "What the security people and others were telling us was that the threat was chem-bio.... We felt this was the coming wave." He acted on that information, purchasing protective suiting and training programs for his own security personnel. The very day after 9/11, former Secretary of Defense Cohen predicted that the next attack by al-Qaida would involve biological weapons.

There were authoritative assessments during the same period that were substantially different, offering more sophisticated accounts of impediments to successful "*bioterrorism.*" Some of these were made by Colonel David Franz, then Deputy Commander of USAMRIID; John Lauder, then Special Assistant to the Director of Central Intelligence; and Dr. Steven Block, Chair of a U.S. DoD Defense Science Board "Summer Study on *Biological Weapons*"—as well as Dr. Brian Jenkin's critique of "*fact-free analysis.*" All these went by the board after 9/11 and the anthrax events that followed in October and November 2001.

Five essential requirements must be mastered in order to produce biological agents:

1. One must obtain the appropriate strain of the disease pathogen.
2. One must know how to handle the organism correctly.
3. One must know how to grow it in a way that will produce the appropriate characteristics.

4. One must know how to store the culture, and to scale-up production properly.
5. One must know how to disperse the product properly.

A U.S. military field manual dating back to the 1960s remarks on the attributes of a desirable BW agent, that in addition to its pathogenicity, "means must be available for maintaining the agent's virulence or infectivity during production, storage, and transportation." One should add, most particularly during its dispersal as well. Two members of Sweden's biodefense program stress methods on how to optimize formulations of BW agents as the most critical step of all: "They key competence is... how to formulate the organisms to facilitate aerosolization of particles that cause severe disease by inhalation."

It is interesting that the classified 1999 DIA report quoted earlier in the section on state programs contained a single sentence regarding the possible use of BW agents by terrorist groups: "Terrorist use should also be anticipated primarily in improvised devices, probably in association with an explosive." No anticipation of the capability for aerosol distribution was mentioned, no overflight of cities, sports stadiums, etc.

In a recent BW "*Risk Assessment*" published elsewhere, a group of authors from the Sandia National Laboratory listed a series of factors closely paralleling the above as "Technical Hurdles to Successful BW Deployment": acquisition of a virulent agent; production of the agent in suitable form and quantity; and, effective deployment of the agent.

This was summed up in simple words as "obtaining a pathogen or toxin..., isolation, amplification, protection against environmental degradation, and development of an effective dissemination method." They concluded that "Even a low-consequence event requires a considerable level of expertise to execute." Dr. Steven Block, Chair of the U.S. DoD Defense Science Board Summer Study on biological weapons in the late 1990s explained the same requirements.

A lesson from the Aum Shinrikyo case is that any group bent on developing offensive *bioweapons* capabilities must overcome two significant problems, one biological and the other physical. First, it must acquire and produce stable quantities of a suitably potent agent. For a variety of reasons, this is not the trivial task that it is sometimes made out to be. Second, it must have an effective means of delivering the agent to the intended target. For most, but not all, bioweapon agents, this translates into solving problems of dispersal. Programs in both the United States and the USSR devoted years of effort to perfecting these aspects.

Unfortunately, a recent example provides the sort of grossly uninformed description that is more frequently provided to the general public. Speaking at the Harvard Medical School on June 1, 2005, and trading on his training as a medical doctor as he frequently does, Senator Frist claimed that "...a few technicians of middling skill using a few thousand dollars worth of readily available equipment in a small and apparently innocuous setting [could] mount a first-order biological attack. It is even possible to synthesize virulent pathogens from scratch, or to engineer and manufacture prions..." He repeated that this was "the single greatest threat to our safety and security today." The remarks are a travesty: "...a few *technicians* ... middling skill ... few thousand dollars," leading to a "*first-order*" a biological attack, and additionally extending this to "*synthesizing virulent pathogens*" in the same breath.

To bolster his argument, Senator Frist larded his presentation with other gross inaccuracies, claiming that "During the Cold War, the Soviet Union...stockpiled 5,000 tons *annually* of biowarfare-engineered anthrax resistant to 16 antibiotics." The only source in the world for the tonnage of anthrax stockpiled by the USSR is Dr. Ken Alibek. He has never quoted a figure higher than 200 tons, and he has never claimed that the 200 tons was produced "*annually*," or in any single year. The USSR's anthrax stockpile consisted of a genetically unmodified classical strain (or strains). The antibiotic resistant strain which was developed by Soviet BW laboratories in the mid- to late-1980s was not resistant to 16 antibiotics, but to half that number, and had not yet reached the point of being stockpiled by the time that the Soviet BW program began to be cut back in 1989. Finally, the 5,000-ton figure is the approximate sum of the annual production capacities of all Soviet-era BW mobilization production facilities that would have initiated production only with the onset of, or just prior to a (nuclear) war with the United States. No such quantities of BW agents were ever produced in the USSR.

Scenarios and Exercises

If one looks at the scenarios used in various exercises carried out by U.S. Government agencies or private institutes, one finds the following:

1. [Unnamed], March 1998, Mexico-Texas border: smallpox chimeric viral agent (following Alibek).

2. Top Off I, May 2000: aerosolized plague, FEMA and U.S. Department of Justice.
3. [Unnamed], July 2000: aerosolized pneumonic plague, U.S. Department of Justice and DoD DTRA.
4. Dark Winter, June 2001: aerosolized smallpox, Johns Hopkins Center for Biosecurity and three collaborating groups.
5. Sooner Spring, April 2002: smallpox, National Memorial Institute for the Prevention of Terrorism (MIPT), Oklahoma.
6. Top Off II, May 2003: aerosolized plague, U.S. DHS and U.S. Department of State.
7. Atlantic Storm, January 2005: Aerosolized dry powder smallpox, Center for Biosecurity (now affiliated with the University of Pittsburgh Medical Center).
8. Top Off III, April 2005: aerosolized pneumonic plague, U.S. DHS.

The Dark Winter exercise used a person-to-person secondary transmission rate (RO) of 10, three times the historical average of three. Pneumonic plague has a historical average transmission rate of one. Nevertheless, there are indications that the Top Off 2 and 3 exercises used values five times as high, and the July 2000 exercise used a value of 10. Such inflated transmission rates, of course, make it next to impossible for the game players to do very much to contain the outbreak, and assure a disastrous outcome irrespective of whatever control measures the players may attempt to carry out.

Plague is known to microbiologists who routinely work with it as a "*difficult*," "*skittish*" agent, "*fragile* and *fastidious*" in the laboratory. That a terrorist group would be likely to manage that seems very unlikely. In addition, plague organisms die very quickly when aerosolized, and both the United States and the UK failed for years in attempts to aerosolize plague. Both the British and U.S. BW programs in the 1950s field tested plague in open air field trials using animals, and the tests failed. The USSR BW program, with many more man-years of work, apparently did succeed in producing an aerosolizable plague agent. Did the Top Off scenario builders know of the efforts of the British and American BW programs to aerosolize plague and the outcome of those efforts? Did they know of the negative results, or decided to simply disregard them in any case? In the first case they could be accused of ignorance, in the second case of incompetence. They finessed the problem, however, by saying that the terrorists "*obtained a sample*" of the plague. But what kind of sample? Was it aerosolizable? From whom did they get it? In what quantity? Did they have to culture it? If so, how did they manage that? How was it dispersed? The scenario is not meant to answer these questions, which, of course, would all be crucial in the real world to determining whether a terrorist group was capable of producing and dispersing plague. Its purpose is simply to present a situation for the responders to deal with, without bothering with the question of how the situation came about, its likelihood, or in fact if it could take place at all.

In an influential August 2003 monograph, Richard Danzig suggested four cases that he recommended for "*near term planning premises.*"

1. A large-scale outdoor aerosol anthrax attack.
2. A large-scale outdoor aerosol smallpox attack.
3. An attack that disseminates botulinum toxin in cold drinks.
4. An attack that spreads foot and mouth disease among cattle, sheep, and pigs.

Danzig adds that "...these cases ... are real, possibly imminent, and very substantial dangers. Virtually all experts and policymakers agree with this." Despite that, he added "...in the immediate future, most attacks are likely to be versions, often lesser version, of these cases." Nevertheless, at the same time Danzig routinely speaks of "*reloads*," and of terrorists producing sufficient quantities "that can be used again and again" in a series of attacks crossing the United States. That is scarcely "a *lesser version.*" Casualties resulting from Case #3 would be identified almost immediately and would be quickly limited. Case #4 would have serious economic consequences, but not human public health ones. Cases #1 and #2 are the significant ones, and comparable to the exercise scenarios listed above.

The same holds for the BW cases among the official "*Planning Scenarios*" of the U.S. DHS. Of 15 selected scenarios, four concerned BW:

#2. Biological Attack, aerosolized anthrax, in five cities in succession;

#4. Biological Attack, aerosolized plague in three locations in a single city;

#13. Biological Attack, liquid anthrax placed in ground beef in a factory, resulting in intestinal anthrax, mortality in the low hundreds; and,

#14. Biological Attack, Foot and Mouth Disease; economic loss, no human mortality.

Again, it is the first two of these four scenarios that are of prime concern since they are the ones capable of producing mass casualties.

However, the capabilities that would have to be posited for the above scenarios are far beyond the present and "near term" capabilities of any known terrorist group. That is particularly the case for smallpox. The counter argument, even by those who accept that fact, is obvious, and was presented by Dr. Gerald Epstein in Congressional testimony in February 2005.

Exactly how close terrorist groups are right now to the capability to conduct a major biological attack matters if we want to know how likely it is that such an attack will take place in the near future. However, looking out over the several years that our defensive preparations will take to implement, the details of today's threat are less important than the realization that the rapidly increasing capability, market penetration, and geographic dissemination of relevant biotechnical disciplines will inevitably bring weapons capabilities within the reach of those who may wish to use them for harm.

"*Inevitably*" is longer than "*several*" years.

Atlantic Storm

An excellent example of grossly misleading assumptions underlying the more advanced scenarios and base cases was provided by the seventh exercise listed above, "*Atlantic Storm*," which took place on January 14, 2005. The comments below concern *only* the assumptions used by the producers of the exercise to argue that the terrorist group they envision would have obtained, produced, and distributed a dry-powder preparation of *smallpox*. These comments do not concern at all how the scenario unfolded once the hypothesized preparation had been released.

The group responsible for producing and releasing the smallpox was defined as a "*Radical al-Qaida Splinter Group*." In contrast, as best is known from the declassified documents and all the other materials obtained by U.S. military forces in Afghanistan in November and December 2001:

1. No al-Qaida capacity for culturing viruses has ever been identified.
2. No al-Qaida group has yet been able to obtain a pathogenic strain of anthrax.
3. The group operating in Afghanistan in 2000-01 had apparently not yet reached the stage of attempting to culture vaccine strain anthrax. It had been provided with U.S. and UK microbiological journal literature from the 1950s and 1960s. The "*methods*" sections of those papers would have provided some aid for understanding

culturing requirements for anthrax. They would not have assured success in doing it.

4. Al-Qaida affiliated groups apparently either have not yet been able to synthesize ricin, or have not yet attempted to do so. As indicated earlier, the "*traces*" of ricin reported as having been found in London several years ago turned out to be false positives. No ricin was found when the United States overran the al-Qaida affiliated Ansar al-Islam camp in Northern Iraq in March 2003.

The scenario posits that "Seed stocks of Variola major [smallpox] virus...were obtained...from a bioweapons facility in the former Soviet Union. This strongly implies that the "*facility*" suggested would be one of the former premier institutes of the Soviet Biopreparat system, Vector, located in Koltsovo near Novosibirsk, Russia. When the Iranian government made overtures to Vector scientists in the years around 1994, offering very generous payment to come and work and/or teach in Iran, they failed to convince a single member of the institute to come to Iran. These facilities are in better shape now than they were 10 years ago, both in their financial circumstances and in their biosecurity arrangements. At a first approximation, it therefore seems highly unlikely that an al-Qaida affiliated group would be able to obtain a smallpox sample from Vector. A U.S. Government official with frequent contact with this facility thought that "the probability was low."

The Atlantic Storm scenario attempts to prop up the basic implausibility of this point in its assumptions by a gratuitous "*Intelligence Briefing*" which states that "information from U.S., UK, French, and German intelligence" corroborated that the *al-Qaida group* "has made contacts with former Soviet bioweaponeers." If it were the case that no less than four Western intelligence agencies had been informed of the "*contacts*" by the al-Qaida group, it would seem that there would have been a good chance to abort the activities of the group. The scenario organizers point out that smallpox is also assumed to be located in Russia in another institute besides Vector, one belonging to the Ministry of Defense (MOD). That may very well be the case, but if Vector has, to date, not been penetrated by "*terrorist*" groups, it is still less likely that a Russian MOD facility would be successfully penetrated.

The scenario posits that the *al-Qaida* group's scientists received microbiological training at Indian and U.S. universities. These scientists received additional training when the group hired a scientist who was part of the former Soviet Union's offensive biological weapons program. This scientist taught the [al-Qaida group] scientists how to grow a number of biological agents, including *Variola major* [smallpox], *Bacillus anthracis*, *Ebola virus*, and *Burkholderia mallei* [glanders]. The terrorist group combined this knowledge with publicly available technical information to develop dry powder preparations of the viruses. Then, with their own microbiology training, the terrorist group was able to acquire all the required laboratory equipment to grow and process the Variola major seed stock they had acquired into a relatively high-quality dry powder that was then used in the attacks.

In the real world, *Al-Qaida* had one single individual who had received a BS degree in Biology "with a clinical concentration" at a U.S. college. He could in no way be described as a "scientist." Furthermore, he was arrested in December 2001. The individual with more advanced training who supplied al-Qaida with its microbiological literature was unwilling to himself do any laboratory work for them. The few pieces of standard equipment obtained by the group in Afghanistan were rudimentary in the extreme.

The USSR's BW program and the organization of its relevant institutes would make it extremely unlikely that a single former Soviet BW scientist would know how to grow and work with both *Variola* (smallpox) and *Ebola* viruses, as well as *B. anthracis* and *B. mallei* bacteria. Even the Soviet virologists who worked with Ebola and with Variola were in separate teams. Even more significant, growing the viruses in tissue culture requires knowledge of tissue culture growth and maintenance. Soviet institutes such as *Vector* had very sizable teams of specialists simply to do the tissue culture preparations on which the viruses could grow. These individuals would never have had experience growing *B. anthracis* or *B. mallei*. In addition, not even the Soviet BW program succeeded in making a dry-powder preparation of *Ebola*, the second virus that the scenario includes.

When the former director of a Western national BW defense laboratory was asked how long it would take a fully competent professional group of experienced microbiologists who had never before worked with viruses or tissue culture to successfully grow *Variola* in tissue culture, he estimated 5 years. When asked how long he thought it would take a group of not very competent individuals to do it, he estimated 10 years to never. Smallpox can also be grown on the *Chorioallantoic* membrane of fertilized chicken eggs. While Soviet scientists grew vaccinia in eggs in their process of making vaccine against smallpox, even that requires experience and careful, tedious technical work.

In response to some of these criticisms of the Atlantic Storm scenario, two of its principal creators, Colonel Randall Larsen and Dr. Tara O'Toole have both invoked, ...a once-secret Defense Department experiment called Project Bacchus [sic], which was conducted in the late 1990s to assess whether terrorists could create a biological terror weapon using commercially available equipment.

The project "demonstrated quite persuasively that about four people, only one of whom had any biological training at all--and that was not with the U.S weapons program; that was a degree in biology—could, using materials bought through the Internet, set up shop, undiscovered, and create a *Bacillus anthracis* look-alike," O'Toole said.

The statement is wrong on numerous grounds. First, the description of the Biotechnology Activity Characterization by Unconventional Signatures (BACUS) project that has been publicly available and is repeated by O'Toole and Larsen is essentially misleading. Its purpose was *not* to see "whether terrorists could create" but to be certain that the experimental group *did* successfully "*create*," in order to see if detectable signatures would result that could subsequently be used by U.S. forces in the field hunting for such sites. To that end, the group was composed of much more than "about four people, only one of whom had any biological training at all." The on-site portion of the team was composed of 8-10 people, many of whom had postgraduate degrees and experience. One held a Ph.D. in microbiology from Oak Ridge National Laboratory. Another had a masters degree in engineering, while another served in Special Forces intelligence, and so on. The team had been specifically selected so that all the aptitudes considered necessary to complete the project successfully would be represented. They were to produce a harmless bacterial anthrax simulant; no work with viruses or with any lethal pathogen comparable to smallpox was involved. In addition, this on-site group was backed up by four or five highly experienced biological weapons specialists acting as consultants, whose role it was to oversee their work to be certain that *no* errors were made, to the point of correcting a decimal place in a calculation.

In addition, the same group had gone through this exercise in an earlier classified project named BITE SIZE. The two projects differed primarily in their physical location—underground and above ground—and the purpose of both projects was to serve as a test for new detection methodologies. They were *not* experiments to see "whether" the group could succeed. The claim that the experience of the BACUS group proves the legitimacy of the Atlantic Storm scenario is completely unsupportable.

Location of preparatory work by the *al-Qaida* splinter group: The scenario describes the group's laboratory as having been "disguised as a small brewery in Klagenfurt, Austria." With all the years of claims that the production of biological agents could take place "*in breweries*," it would not be surprising if readers of the extensive media coverage of the *Atlantic Storm* exercise might have thought that the smallpox was being grown in the fermenting vats of a brewery. For various technical reasons, that would be virtually impossible. Viral bioreactors are, in contrast to brewery fermenting vats, relatively small. The scenario, in fact, does not explain by which method the group would have been able to produce its smallpox. It says only "*Smallpox virus* can be grown in embryonated eggs and a variety of tissue culture systems." Work with viruses and cell culture is very much more difficult than growing bacterial cultures, and the difficulties of cell culture for the putative group have been referred to above. Embryonated chicken eggs must be special-ordered.

The suppliers are limited, and the customers are limited and usually well-known to the suppliers. If the group ordered the thousands and possibly tens of thousands of embryonated eggs and the egg incubators that would be required for this method of growing smallpox virus, local suppliers might wonder why an ostensible brewery needed thousands of embryonated eggs, since only yeast, hops, and grain would be ordered by a brewery. Suppliers therefore would be likely to report such information to local authorities, offering another opportunity to abort the group's activities. Operating breweries in Austria are very highly regulated and routinely inspected. Even construction of a brewery requires government licensing, design approval and construction inspections. Applications for ownership or operation are also regulated. Inspectors who would chance on masses of incubating embryonated eggs would immediately be alerted to the covert operation.

The group would also have to prevent the escape of the grown *smallpox virus* in liquid and solid waste effluents. Incineration, water sterilization and air-handling equipment are not normally installed in "a *small brewery*." These auxiliary systems alone are relatively large, and the ability for them to be housed together with the laboratory facilities "in a building as small as a 3-car garage," which the scenario suggests would be possible, is extremely unlikely. More probably, it is impossible. These auxiliary systems must also be custom-installed by specialists, and then tested. Depending on how or where the smallpox vaccinations for the terrorist group were obtained, that too could run the risk of being noted.

The Atlantic Storm scenario involved the distribution of a dry-powder smallpox preparation from "a commercially available dry powder dispenser" by vaccinated individuals in six different cities over a span of 4 days. As regards preparation of the smallpox powder, the scenario says only that "several sources for information on methods" are available, and that "*Variola virus* can be processed to a stable dried form just as vaccinia virus is dried to make a vaccine."

Such work was never carried out in the British government's BW program. Work with virus culture in the British program was extremely rudimentary overall. It did advance further in the pre-1969 U.S. BW program, but some years ago one of the individuals involved in that work, Dr. William Patrick, offered the judgment that "*Only a state-sponsored* group of terrorists with a lot of money and connections would be able to acquire the smallpox virus and the means for wielding it as a weapon." The Atlantic Storm scenario producers knew this quotation, since they have elsewhere used an accompanying sentence by Patrick as a source.

Speaking at a conference on April 22, 2005, after the details of *Atlantic Storm* were known, Dr. Ken Alibek, the former Deputy Director of the Soviet-era Biopreparat BW research and development program, commented that he could "not understand why some people make these scenarios using dry powder smallpox." He explained that "no one"—that is, the Soviet BW program—"wanted to or could develop dry powder smallpox." He gave two reasons for that: first, that the Soviet BW program had been able to develop a preparation that kept smallpox stable in liquid; and second, that it was much too dangerous for their own staff to prepare dry powder smallpox preparations, even working in facilities with elaborate and advanced containment systems. The claim in the Atlantic Storm scenario that, nevertheless, this could have been achieved by a small inexperienced group has absolutely no chance of being credible.

As for "*Sources for Information*" on methods, simply having them on paper would certainly not be sufficient, though it is the necessary first step. Even vaccinia is grown under conditions of containment, but there is one critical difference: drying variola would have to be carried out under extremely rigorous conditions of containment of the opposite nature, that is, under negative air pressure, rather than positive. The necessary air-handling equipment is sizable and is not part of the infrastructure of a brewery. It is also not simply purchasable from catalogues and, as indicated, would have to be custom installed.

Elsewhere, Dr. Patrick has written, a dry product with these [desired] properties requires serious development with skilled personnel and sophisticated equipment.... [While] Iraq successfully produced high quality liquids of anthrax and botulinum toxin A in quantity, their efforts to weaponize their agents were crude and far from successful. ... By analogy, if a dedicated nation such as Iraq had problems with agent delivery and dissemination, it follows that terrorists would also experience these problems, and at a higher level of intensity.

Dispersal of the dry-powder preparation took place over a period of several hours in each location. Does a "commercially available dry powder dispenser" produce the particle size distribution required for human aerosol infection? Is it battery-powered or gas cartridge-powered to operate noiselessly? The device that the Aum Shinrikyo group had made but never used in a Tokyo subway was designed to distribute a liquid and would have worked for only a short period.

Spread of the Smallpox Epidemic

The *Atlantic Storm* scenario uses rates of first generation person-to-person transmission of 1:3, and 1:0.25 for second generation transmission. This is a major correction from the value of 1:10 used by the same exercise sponsor in "Dark Winter," its previous smallpox exercise in June 2001. As recently as the spring of 2004, a member of the University of Pittsburgh group still defended the 1:10 estimate in a briefing given in Washington, DC.

Adding anthrax production by the same "*al-Qaida* splinter group," presumably at the same brewery location. Several months after the initial *Atlantic Storm* exercise, its creators were able to repeat the exercise with 28 of the 34 members of the Homeland Security Committee of the U.S. Congress. After replaying the *Atlantic Storm* scenario (which followed a separate simulation of a terrorist attack using a 10 kiloton nuclear device), this time yet another component was added: "...[a] few days into the disaster, terrorists followed up with anthrax attacks in major cities." No other details were provided. This adds an entire additional layer of implausibility regarding the ability of an "*al-Qaida* splinter group" to produce anthrax, the delivery of growth media to the "brewery," and so on, not to speak of the technical requirements of producing *both* anthrax *and* dry-powder *smallpox*. Brewery fermenters are not useful for growing *anthrax*, just as they are not useful for growing smallpox.

The individuals who played the roles of "*World Leaders*" in the exercise. These took the roles of purely political figures, presidents and prime ministers of their respective countries, except for one who played the role of Director-General of the World Health Organization (WHO). Of the 12 individuals, one had been the former Director-General of WHO, and a second had been a Minister of Health. Nevertheless, none had any experience with issues regarding biological weapons. This point is mentioned only to note that none apparently raised any questions regarding the basic plausibility of the scenario. According to those responsible for the exercise, the players were not even informed of the antecedent assumptions that are being discussed here. Two members of a European advisory panel to the Atlantic Storm exercise recommended that it should deal with an outbreak of pandemic flu rather than smallpox, but the suggestion was rejected. Had pandemic flu been chosen, references to a "radical al-Qaida splinter group," invoking "bioterrorism," and so on would all have had to be discarded.

Media Response

As best is known, not a single report of the exercise raised any questions whatsoever regarding the plausibility of the basic assumptions of the scenario. Dr. O'Toole, Director of the Pittsburgh group that produced the exercise, stated that "The scenario we posited is very conservative.... This could have been much worse. The age of engineered biological weapons is here. It is now." Portions of the scenario once it was in play may have been conservative; however, "*engineered biological weapons*" are not relevant to an "*al-Qaida splinter group*," and they are not "now" in relation to "terrorist" groups. Dr. O'Toole has also claimed that the scenario antecedents were made "as scientific as possible." The preceding discussion demonstrates that they were very far from "*scientific*," and were a combination of unrealistic and implausible imaginings. A *Washington Post* editorial ended with another O'Toole quote: "This is not science fiction. The age of Bioterror is now," and an enthusiastic *Washington Post* columnist described the exercise as an "*eminently plausible scenario*." Rather, it *was* science fiction because the scenario antecedents are not "now," and they were not in the least plausible.

Botulinum Toxin

Substantial controversy surrounded the recent publication of a model study examining the consequences of the postulated addition of botulinum toxin to the U.S. milk supply. Publication of the paper in the *Proceedings of the National Academy of Sciences* (PNAS) had been delayed for a month due to a request by an official in the U.S. Department of Health and Human Services (DHHS). During that interval, the author, Dr. Lawrence Wein, released his conclusions in a guest editorial in the *New York Times*. Dr. Wein, a mathematical modeler at the Stanford University School of Business, posited that "a *terrorist*"—that is, a single individual—could produce, variously, a "*few grams*," ten grams, or even as much as a kilogram of botulinum toxin, "using a 28-page manual called '*Preparation of Botulinum Toxin*' that has been published on several jihadist websites, and [could buy] toxin from an overseas black-market laboratory." He estimated that ten grams of the toxin might poison 568,000 people, of whom as many as 60 percent might die.

It was possible to obtain a copy of the manual, which appeared to be composed of the linked reproductions of the methods sections of several journal papers. The manual did not explain how to obtain "a producer strain" of clostridium botulinum in the first place, other than suggesting trial and error from sources in the wild. There are seven serotypes of *C. botulinum*, each containing around 100 strains. Many strains of *C. botulinum* produce no toxin at all, or very little. It took the pre-1969 U.S. biological weapons program many man-years of work by competent professionals to find a reliable toxin producing strain. The manual required the use of a walk-in cold room, a refrigerated vacuum centrifuge, highly specific reagents, etc. None of these, as well as many other necessary components, would likely be found in "*jihadist*" camps. More importantly, having the manual, or having the books or journals from which it is derived, does not confer on anyone the ability to make botulinum toxin. That requires knowledge and experience, and it is not the simplest procedure. Producing ten grams would be a feat even for an experienced professional. It is useful to remember that the Japanese Aum Shinrikyo group, with no constraints on funds for purchasing equipment and supplies, spent 3 to 4 years attempting to produce botulinum toxin and failed. It is now known that the Aum had never even been able to obtain a culture of the organism to work with. The author of the model introduced "an overseas black market" as an obvious deus machina to evade these difficulties, but no international black market for botulinum toxin is known to exist. The author also appeared to be unacquainted with the journal literature regarding the purification of Botulinum toxin, which would indicate what some of the difficulties are.

The author admitted in the PNAS paper that three variables in his model "each contain several orders of magnitude of uncertainty." They appear to each contain at least three orders of magnitude of uncertainty. Cumulatively, the author's calculations could therefore be off by as much as nine orders of magnitude—a billion times—which could mean that not a single person would be poisoned or die. If a mathematical model is widely divergent in its assumptions from reality, all the mathematics in the world will not improve the accuracy of its predictions.

One of Dr. Wein's two main recommendations was that the milk industry increase the temperature and duration time for milk pasteurization. Over a period of several years, the International Dairy Foods Association (IDFA) had, in fact, already done this, developing new procedures which result in 99 percent inactivation of any botulinum toxin present. By mid-2004, the IDFA had recommended to its affiliated milk distributors that such changes be instituted, although there was no legal statute that required that the steps be followed by all producers. Dr. Wein had learned of this in 2004 while giving seminar presentations of his model, but it apparently did not alter his calculations.

Efforts to arrive at realistic assessments have frequently been unwelcome. In 1998, D. A. Henderson wrote that: Four points of view prevalent among national policy circles and the academic community at various times have served to dismiss biological terrorism as nothing more than a theoretical possibility. (i) Biological weapons have so seldom been deployed that precedent would suggest that they will not be used. (ii) Their use is so morally repugnant that no one would deign to use them. (iii) The science of producing enough organisms and dispersing them is so difficult that it is within the reach of only the most sophisticated laboratories. (iv) Like the concept of a "*nuclear winter*," the potential destructiveness of bioweapons is essentially unthinkable and so to be dismissed.

Henderson concluded that "Each of these arguments is without validity." Three of them certainly are: I have seen no one arguing the first, second, or fourth of these parodies. The closest approximation to the second are those studies by terrorism experts that seek to understand whether real terrorist groups might or might not consider using BW in light of their political interests, the potential responses of the publics whose support they seek, etc. Examples of such analyses by Parachini, Schweitzer, Simon, and others, based entirely on years of study of real international terrorist groups and not the result of abstract speculation, were referred to earlier. Only the third "*point of view*" which Henderson refers to, with some modification, is at issue. More recently, Jill Dekker-Bellamy, Biodefense Consultant to a new European defense policy interest group, the New Defense Agenda, wrote:

We shouldn't be stuck in the box debating the lack of sophistication terrorists have yet employed; the feasibility question or which pathogen they will use, be it in a material or weaponised form. Our focus instead would be better placed considering the stated intent of terrorists to do so and preventing and denying them access to all the means to conduct their terror campaign. ...

Much debate has gone into whether or not terrorists or states pose the greatest threat in the use of disease as a weapon. These debates over whether or not terrorists are capable of successfully conducting a biological attack normally get bogged down in a number of areas related either to acquisition, technical areas (i.e., feasibility/dispersal/capacity) or areas related to kill ratios and casualty numbers as if this is the Geiger counter of successful biological terrorism. This may be of interest in ranking weapons of mass destruction but not necessarily in ranking a successful bioterror campaign. Contemporary threat assessments, even more than 2 years ago, point to smaller groups as now being more likely to succeed in a bioterrorism event, utilizing a diversity of agents.

The "*contemporary threat assessments*" referred to remained unidentified, and no one is "stuck in [a] box" or "*bogged down.*" The intellectual "*know-nothingism*" in the above comment is palpable, and harks back to Brian Jenkins' 1999 description of "*fact free analysis*" in the area of bioterrorism assessment. There is no incompatibility between seeking the best preventive measures and having a moderately realistic threat assessment. A statement by U.S. Department of State Anti-Terrorism Coordinator William Pope that "Europe should expect biological, chemical, and radiological terrorist attacks at any time" is an example of the inadequacy that is so common in many cases. In contrast, one recent thorough study carried out for the UN WMD ("Blix") Commission rendered a considered assessment without fear of getting into "*boxes*" or "*bogged down,*" and without contrived scenarios carried out in a show-business atmosphere.

This brings us to some anticipation of the future. A very brief 2-page statement released in November 2003 by the U.S. CIA titled "The *Darker Bioweapons Future*" was limited to very general remarks:

A panel of life science experts convened for the Strategic Assessments Group by the National Academy of Sciences concluded that advances in biotechnology, coupled with the difficulty in detecting nefarious biological activity, have the potential to create a much more dangerous biological warfare threat. The panel noted:

1. The effects of some of these engineered biological agents could be worse than any disease known to man.
2. The genomic revolution is pushing biotechnology into an explosive growth phase. Panelists asserted that the resulting wave front of knowledge will evolve rapidly and be so broad, complex, and widely available to the public that traditional intelligence means could prove inadequate to deal with the threat from these advanced *biological weapons*.
3. Detection of related activities, particularly the development of novel *bioengineered pathogens*, will depend increasingly on more specific human intelligence and, argued panelists, will necessitate a closer—and perhaps qualitatively different—working relationship between the intelligence and biological sciences communities.

In the last several decades, the world has witnessed a knowledge explosion in the life sciences based on an understanding of genes and how they work. According to panel members, practical applications of this new and burgeoning knowledge base will accelerate dramatically and unpredictably.

Growing understanding of the complex biochemical pathways that underlie life processes has the potential to enable a class of new, more virulent biological agents engineered to attack distinct biochemical pathways and elicit specific effects. The same science that may cure some of our worst diseases could be used to create the world's most frightening weapons. The know-how to develop some of these weapons already exists.

Others have filled in what this may evolve into in future decades in more detail. Papers by James Petro, *et al.*, Robert Carlson, Raymond Zilinskas, Aleksandr Rabodzey, and others are recent examples which were published prior to the brief CIA item above. These projections are not discussed further here. The purpose of this monograph has been to present a *current* threat assessment of "*Bioterrorism*" and what one may expect "in the near future." Advanced genetic engineering capabilities are not likely to become available to real-world nonstate actor/terrorist groups in the near future. Judgments based on the prevalence of genetic engineering competence in the general academic molecular research community are still not useful guides to terrorist capabilities. A classified U.S. Defense Intelligence projection prepared in July 1999 looking ahead to 2020 presented the following anticipation of developments in future national BW programs:

An increasing number of countries with biological warfare programs will be able to develop infectious agents such as anthrax and plague, as well as toxins such as botulinum and ricin.... New types of agents, such as modified infectious organisms, low-molecular weight physiologically active substances that disrupt body function, and synthetic modified toxins, are also in development.

Given that this was written when the number of existing states with offensive BW programs was still considered to be higher and that the "*new type of agents*" referred to had all been available for decades, this was a relatively low keyed assessment. Speaking in 2001, Dr. Joshua Lederberg, probably the most highly qualified expert in this field, said "I don't think we're going to leapfrog to the second or third generation without seeing some of the more primitive efforts in the first instance." In response to a statement by an official of the DHS in June 2005 that the Department had "developed a strategy to address the potential for a *bioengineered attack*," Dr. Richard Ebright commented that "There is no—zero—current likelihood that a terrorist organization would construct '*bioengineered*' viral pathogens, or would construct '*bioengineered*' bacterial pathogens other than antibiotic-resistant bacterial pathogens."

3

CHALLANGE OF BIOLOGICAL TERRORISM

Over the last several years, a confluence of events—the *World Trade Center* bombing, the Tokyo subway sarin gas attack by the Aum Shinrikyo, and the bombing of the Murrah Federal Building in Oklahoma City—focused attention on the growing threat of terrorist use of chemical, biological, radiological, or nuclear (CBRN) weapons in the United States. These developments gave rise to a set of perceptions—among policy makers and the public alike—that the United States is vulnerable to terrorist attack; that such attacks could entail the use of CBRN weapons; and that the United States has not been well prepared to deal effectively with such a challenge.

This set of perceptions promoted a sense of urgency among lawmakers and other policy makers that the United States must act. Over the last five years, the U.S. Congress has provided substantial financial support to many government agencies that have initiated programs to address the CBRN terrorism problem.

The rapid emergence of the perceived threat and the urgency of the U.S. government's response did not provide an opportunity for full development of a systematic analysis of the CBRN terrorism problem. In particular, programs were begun without a strategic framework to guide program definition and resource allocation. Such a framework can serve several critical functions: defining objectives and relating means to ends; identifying key functions of an effective response; creating awareness of trade-offs among those key components; determining their priorities; and establishing the basis for sustained support of the most critical components over time. The need for a strategic framework to address the threat of terrorist use of *biological weapons* (BW) is especially critical. Biological weapons unique instruments of violence, and many of their characteristics could make them particularly attractive for terrorists contemplating the use of mass casualty weapons. As a result, biological weapons could become the mass casualty weapon of choice among terrorists in the years ahead.

Terrorist use of biological weapons could produce widespread, devastating, and tragic consequences. According to the Office of Technology Assessment, if used under optimal conditions, biological weapons could have an impact similar to that of a small nuclear device. A single attack using a sophisticated biological weapons in a major metropolitan area such as Washington, DC could kill as many as 3 million people. Even if casualty levels from a biological attack do not achieve their theoretical maximum, *any* terrorist use of biological weapons in the United States could have profound effects.

Bioterrorism differs from other types of CBRN terrorism in that it would impose particularly heavy demands on the nation's public health and health care systems. Although a chemical attack would also tax these systems, bioterrorism would impose especially stressful burdens. Yet, that same public health system is the crucial factor in an effective response. A highly effective public health system should make an important contribution to deterring the threat by demonstrably diminishing the gains of a potential attack. It also constitutes the "*first line of defense*" in the event deterrence or prevention fails. Ultimately, it will be the public health system that will be called on to mitigate and ameliorate the consequences of a bioterrorist attack.

A number of programs are underway to improve the health and medical dimensions of the national response to the threat of bioterrorism. Uncertainty exists, however, as to whether current programs are those that are most needed or whether they are being implemented in the most effective way possible. This uncertainty exists because to date there have been insufficient means to judge the efficacy of existing programs. This lack of criteria is the product of not having an analytic framework that establishes national requirements for an effective response derived from a comprehensive threat assessment. The development and application of a strategic framework is urgently needed. Making a contribution to the development of that framework is the purpose of this project. This report analyzes the requirements for an effective health and medical component of the overall bioterrorism response system and assesses where the United States stands today in meeting those requirements. It does so in the context of an evaluation of the current bioterrorism threat. What is the link between the two? It is simple: a better and more sophisticated understanding of the threat—which emerges from this analysis as a complex, multidimensional phenomenon—better informs decisions about needed response capabilities, helps establish priorities, and more effectively guides resource allocations. The report also includes a series of recommendations, both general and specific, that could strengthen current and future health and medical response capabilities.

Shortcomings of Vulnerability Assessments

One might ask why there is a need for such a study, given that several analyses of terrorism with biological weapons have already been conducted. The reason is that most of the studies done in relation to health and medical requirements of a response to bioterrorism have focused on what biological weapons could do, not on what they are most likely to do. They are vulnerability assessments, which, as suggested by terrorism expert Brian Jenkins, suffer from a number of drawbacks in guiding policy and establishing resource priorities.

First, the vulnerabilities of the United States to a bioterrorism attack are virtually infinite. As a result, no definitive catalogue of problems can be developed against which to plan and allocate resources. Defining the bioterrorism problem as virtually limitless can also instill policy paralysis. Confronted with an enormous range of potential disasters, it is hard for policy makers and those who lead response efforts to know where to begin.

Second, vulnerability assessments lead to worst-case analysis. Emphasizing vulnerabilities promotes a focus on catastrophic events, regardless of their likelihood. Indeed, as terrorism expert Brian Jenkins argues, "focusing on only the most horrendous events overwhelms any estimates of their likelihood. The possibility of occurrence becomes irrelevant unless the threat can be dismissed with a high degree of confidence—of course, it cannot." In fact, the possibility of occurrence, the likelihood, of an event is a critically important factor in planning efforts. It does little good to engage in elaborate preparations for an event that is not likely to happen to the exclusion of addressing those contingencies that are. Moreover, as the Gilmore Commission and others have argued, the assumption that lower consequence/higher probability events can be treated as "lesser included cases" of more catastrophic contingencies is not necessarily warranted.

Worst-case analysis, therefore, can skew resource allocation. It can shift limited resources—money, manpower, and time—toward high consequence, low probability events and away from those events that are lower consequence, but higher probability. The danger, of course, is that without proper preparation, even so-called "*lower consequence events*" could produce results with significant impact both locally and nationally.

Third, vulnerability assessments create a mentality that tends to reify "*what ifs*" into imminent risks. In the way that high consequence scenarios are discussed and approached, theoretical possibilities are too often transformed into real contingencies. The result is to give such possibilities more credence than they deserve.

Vulnerability assessments, therefore, while identifying the potential scope of the challenge, provide no sense of whether or not those vulnerabilities can and will be exploited by a terrorist. As a result, they can produce a misdirected planning process, inadequately defined policy choices, and distorted resource allocations.

Vulnerability assessments, however, are not without value. It is natural for policy makers and lead responders to focus on vulnerabilities and the high, indeed catastrophic consequences that could ensue if theoretical possibilities did become reality. No policy maker could accept ignoring the possibility of such consequences even if they were highly unlikely. To do so is politically unacceptable. Vulnerability assessments, therefore, identify contingencies that, while perhaps not central to the planning process, nevertheless constitute possibilities against which some "*hedging*" is necessary so that, if the unlikely happens, the system is not totally unprepared.

An effective response to the bioterrorism threat, then, includes both threat and vulnerability assessments—the former to determine the most plausible threat against which the majority of planning and resources should be directed, and the latter to identify those outcomes whose consequences are so severe that they demand some preparatory action and some resources. Of course, what the balance will be between core planning and hedging and how resources will be divided among them is often hard to determine.

Need for a Strategic Approach

Successfully meeting the challenge of bioterrorism requires a multifaceted response. No single approach will, in and of itself, be successful. It must also be a response that is *strategic* in nature. Clausewitz defined strategy at the military level as "the combination of individual engagements to attain the goal of the campaign...[It is] the employment of battles as a means to gain the object of war." At the level of national policy, a strategy is the intellectual construct that marshals all appropriate resources and guides them toward the achievement of the objective. For the response to bioterrorism to be genuinely strategic, it must integrate all critical policy tools in an approach in which those elements of policy are mutually reinforcing, support the same objectives, do not work at cross purposes, and provide a flexibility that is responsive to changing circumstances and different conditions.

A strategic response to the BW terrorism challenge, therefore, is one in which:

1. Each element of policy is as strong as possible.
2. Those elements of policy are brought together in a framework marked by
   - Clearly defined objectives;
   - Awareness of pitfalls and potential contradictions; and
   - Emphasis on reinforcing strengths of individual policy tools and compensating for shortcomings.
3. The U.S. government is organized to facilitate strategic thinking and action, including
   - Mechanisms for the effective exchange of information and interaction of key players; and
   - Flexibility and responsiveness to change.

Need for Flexible Response

This report emphasizes the need for a strategic approach to the development of public health and medical response capabilities. It places particular emphasis on the need for flexibility. To be successful, any strategy must be agile; it must be flexible enough to adapt to the full range of potential contingencies that can cause harm.

Strategic flexibility derives, most importantly, from having more than a single response option that allows for tailoring responses to the specifics of the event and the severity of the crisis. It diminishes the prospect of wasting resources by not incorporating elements that are marginal or irrelevant to the challenge at hand. Furthermore, it improves the chances of avoiding unintended consequences.

In the military realm, an analogy that provides important insights is the evolution of NATO strategy. In the late 1960s, NATO shifted from a strategy of massive retaliation to a strategy of flexible response.

It did so because the alliance did not want to depend on the threat of a major nuclear retaliation as its only response to a wide range of potential contingencies, from a limited "*land grab*" by Warsaw Pact forces to their full-scale invasion of Western Europe using conventional forces alone. The catastrophic scenario, a strategic nuclear attack by the Soviet Union against the United States or Western Europe—the "*bolt out of the blue*"—was one for which the threat of massive retaliation was deemed appropriate. But it was also considered highly unlikely. For those events considered more likely but of lesser consequence, the implications of only having the ability to respond with a major nuclear attack were not acceptable to alliance political leaders. As a consequence they improved NATO's "*front-end*" capabilities, particularly allied conventional forces. If those capabilities proved insufficient, then NATO would move to ever more dramatic options to deal with an escalating crisis. In essence, NATO strategy came to depend on having a range of effective potential options that could be applied in ways appropriate to the crisis at hand.

The NATO experience suggests a number of lessons for developing a strategic response to the threat of bioterrorism. First, a single, massive response option has serious drawbacks with respect to both resource allocations and unintended consequences. If the only response available to a bioterrorism incident—particularly those that are most likely but of consequences below catastrophic levels—is mobilization of a massive federal apparatus, resources may be unnecessarily expended because more limited capabilities, perhaps local resources augmented in selected areas, are all that are needed to deal with the problem. Moreover, such a massive mobilization could create unnecessary public panic, media scrutiny, and political repercussions. A strategic response should be viewed as drawing on a spectrum of capabilities that can be tailored to the event, organized to be implemented in a phased or tiered manner in increasingly demanding circumstances.

Second, along this spectrum, enhancing "*front end*" capabilities—surveillance, detection, and assessment—is likely to yield disproportionate dividends. The better the deployed initial capabilities are to meet the crisis, the less likely the crisis will escalate. In the bioterrorism context, this "*lesson*" suggests paying special attention to improving surveillance and epidemiological capabilities as much as possible. Robust surveillance, epidemiology, and laboratory capacity could lead to fewer demands on medical treatment—and all of the tasks that entails—by limiting the number of victims.

Third, creating flexible response options is neither easy nor cheap. An effective flexible response capability creates more demanding planning requirements in that it entails the coordination of more policy areas and more actors, requires extensive and ongoing training and exercising, and can involve complex communication requirements. It depends on organizational adaptability, which is not always a hallmark of government bureaucracies. A flexible response strategy also relies on high levels of cooperation among a range of independent actors, which is not always easy to promote. Moreover, it absorbs significant resources in an effort that must be sustained over time. Shifting to Flexible Response was expensive for NATO because developing effective conventional forces was costlier than relying on a limited arsenal of nuclear weapons. Similarly, implementing an effective flexible response strategy to deal with bioterrorism could entail significant expenditures over time. The alternative is to rely on a limited number of response options that may or may not be appropriate to the specifics of a crisis and that may or may not provide the right kinds of hedges against the less likely but potentially catastrophic contingencies.

This report addresses these issues and provides recommendations on means by which the U.S. government can enhance its strategic approach to improving the health and medical dimensions of the response to the challenge of bioterrorism. The recommendations are offered as a contribution to promoting effective national responses to a challenge that deserves sustained attention, adequate resources, and unflinching political will.

Biological Terrorism Threat: A Multifactor Assessment

Biological agents are living organisms, or the by-products of living organisms, that cause diseases that lead to incapacitation or death. The most pervasive characteristic of the threat of terrorist use of such biological agents is its uncertainty. An enormous range of possibilities exists in terms of the character and impact of a bioterrorism attack; the variety of scenarios that could be elaborated is virtually unlimited. Anything can happen. Popular culture is suggestive in this regard. It has produced movies and books using bioterrorism as their major plot device, describing situations from a lone scientist genetically modifying diseases to strike against major urban populations to fanatic ethnoseparatist or religious groups exploiting agents that have been researched for biological warfare to hold cities or governments hostage.

These fictional accounts, however, may be divorced from reality, and they may have contributed to fostering an impression of biological terrorism as easy and effective that does not square with the facts. With respect to biological terrorism, the formulation that "it is not a matter of if, but when," also is not helpful. Something may never happen. The historical incidence of successful biological terrorism is very, very small, and, while the past is not always prologue, history should not be ignored. With respect to the threat, therefore, we just do not know with any certainty.

A threat assessment is needed precisely to reduce the uncertainty that currently permeates the debate over *bioterrorism*. Undertaking a threat assessment is particularly important in the current environment in which government investments in programs to combat terrorism with chemical, biological, radiological, and nuclear (CBRN) weapons are increasing significantly. We will be able to ensure that society is prepared in the event of a bioterrorism incident—and to do so in a way that ensures that taxpayers' money is wisely spent—only if the nature of the threat is systematically addressed, and its complexity is understood and appreciated.

A good threat assessment will create a "*threat envelope*" that describes the most plausible contingencies and identifies those possibilities that fall within it and those that lie outside. Defining a plausible threat envelope also provides a means to identify those contingencies that require hedging, in that, due to the severity or enormity of their consequences, some preparation for them should be undertaken, even if they are relatively unlikely. The combination of the threat envelope and the hedging contingencies should give policy makers some measure for making decisions regarding policy priorities and resource allocations.

A framework is needed for thinking about the *bioterrorism threat*. That framework should cast the threat more in the nature of a forecast than a prediction; that is, it should identify the ranges of probability of something happening, while recognizing that those ranges can sometimes be quite wide. Expecting certainty creates a standard that will never be achieved, and it implies a greater precision in the analysis than, in fact, can be achieved given the complexity of the subject matter.

An analytical framework for thinking about the *biological terrorism* threat will also highlight the fact that the threat is not unidimensional; it does not come from only one factor. Rather, it is composed of several elements. For purposes of this study, the key elements of the bioterrorism threat have been identified as the *who* (the actor), the *what* (the agent), the *where* (the target), and the *how* (the mode of attack). Each of these elements, in turn, entails a significant array of possibilities. The different kinds of actors who might try to exploit biological weapons, the large number of potential agents, and the variety of possible dissemination methods are some examples of the complexity of each element of the threat. The endless scenarios and contingencies that have been described as potential bioterrorism events represent the plausible or fanciful combination of the many facets of these factors into particular configurations.

The key to a successful bioterrorism threat assessment, therefore, is disaggregating the threat into its component elements and assessing the relationships among them. Only by doing so can one examine comparative likelihood of various contingencies. With the ability to make those comparisons, policy makers will have a better means by which to determine those contingencies that are more important. It is the introduction of likelihood into the analysis that distinguishes a threat assessment from a vulnerability assessment, a distinction of critical importance, as already discussed.

The goal of this assessment, then, is not to provide a detailed examination of every possible bioterrorism scenario or contingency, but to suggest an analytical framework about the biological terrorism threat that facilitates making judgments about effective responses—especially in the public health and medical arena. In the last several years, the analytical community has given considerable attention to the bioterrorism threat. This assessment is not intended to "*reinvent the wheel*" by replicating these existing studies, but to take the best of that work and integrate it into a coherent, holistic framework.

Integrating the Components

The key components of the threat assessment—who, what, how, and where—must be pulled together into an integrated assessment that provides the basis for formulating policy and program requirements for an effective national response. The analysis that constitutes such an integration, however, must be informed by several important considerations.

Impact of change

In looking to the future of the threat of biological terrorism, three sets of changes are especially important to note: technological change, the changing socio-political context, and the changing face of terrorism.

Changing technology will have an impact on future terrorist options. People have described the next hundred years as the "*century of biology*," and incredibly rapid and profound changes in biotechnology in particular are likely to have a major influence on the prospects for bioterrorism. Genetic modification, biomolecular engineering, and enhanced bioproduction technologies, for example, may make it easier for terrorists to overcome the barriers that inhibited acquisition of biological weapons in the past. Technological change, however, should not be considered only for what it might do to make the threat more severe, but such change must also be evaluated for what it can do to facilitate responses to the threat. Advances in biotechnology and materials sciences, for example, may underpin the development of rapid and effective detection and identification devices. Breakthroughs in understanding of human physiology may provide new approaches to improving the immune response to pathogens. Evaluating the future terrorism threat demands that we pay attention to both positive and negative aspects. It requires a balanced appreciation of the impact of technology, not just a focus on what may capture the headlines.

Technological change is only one aspect of the evolving context within which the new terrorism will have to be confronted. That context involves the interplay of political, economic, social, ethnic, and religious factors, not just in one country but around the world. The terrorism of the future will be in response to broad trends such as globalization, accelerating interconnectedness, and population dynamics, but it is also likely to entail narrow psychological elements from marginalization to techno-rage to revenge for real or imagined wrongs. As motivations move away from the traditionally political, the more important the special mindsets of potential terrorists become. Refining understanding of the threat of bioterrorism demands special attention to these distinctive mental topographies. Equally important is the requirement to understand how these unique psychologies interact with circumstances, capabilities, and opportunities, to take potential terrorists down particular paths, including one path (among many) at the end of which may be the use of *biological weapons*.

A third aspect of the evolving environment is the changing *face of terrorism* itself. In part, it is a question of the change in the actors. Of the current watch list maintained by the U.S. Department of State of terrorist groups of concern to the United States, more than half were not on the list at the end of the *Cold War*. The structure of terrorist actors, however, is also changing, as more transnational, network based entities join traditional organizational hierarchies, a development exemplified by Osama bin Laden's al-Queda. Terrorist tactics also appear to be evolving, with more indiscriminate attacks and less acceptance of responsibility for those attacks that do occur.

"Lessons" of history?

Finally, much of the skepticism about the severity of the bioterrorism threat derives from the fact that, historically, not only have few terrorist attacks with biological weapon been attempted, but those few that can be identified have either been unsuccessful or have produced only limited results with respect to casualties. Looking to history for answers to the *bioterrorism threat*, however, provides mixed results. This is the case for several reasons. First, the historical record in fact identifies relatively few data points, especially with respect to BW use. Second, while developments in the years ahead must be expected to combine continuity and change, which one will dominate? It is not necessarily the case that, in all things, the future will resemble the past. History provides few precedents, clear indicators, or discernable trends to instill confidence that looking at history will alert us in advance to what will happen in the future, particularly given the nature of the changes mentioned above and the variety of factors involved in shaping the bioterrorism threat.

Evaluating bioterrorism "pathways"

The project team used a "*matrix-pathways*" approach to integrate the components—actor, agent, method of attack, and target—into a representation of the complex nature of the bioterrorism threat. Given the importance of the actor in shaping the threat, the team decided to break the question of "who?" into two distinct but related elements suggested by the questions: "what are the motivations for a group to use a biological weapon?" and "what capabilities must an actor possess to develop and use a biological weapon?" These five components provided the starting point for constructing the matrix.

A bioterrorism pathway is produced by systematically identifying plausible relationships between factors and outcomes. For example, a group seeking to produce over 500 casualties will need certain connections between its internal group dynamics, technical expertise, dissemination technique, and target to reach its desired goal. Working through the complete set of factors generates a bioterrorism pathway. In many cases, a pathway cannot be completed because logical connections between factors and desired outcomes cannot be made. For example, a group seeking to create disruption or illness without actually killing anyone is not likely to follow the path of an aerosolized anthrax attack. Using the threat matrix in this way produced the set of possible bioterrorism pathways. Combining these pathways with judgments regarding the comparative likelihood of each pathway produced the "*plausible threat envelope*" for bioterrorism.

The first example represents a pathway that successfully produces a middle range attack using anthrax that infects a total of 500 people. The second example has two variants in which an attempt to produce a mass casualty anthrax attack (over 5000 people infected) ultimately fails. In the red variant, the group plans to carry out numerous small aerosol releases of anthrax slurry in a large metropolitan city. The attack fails due to a lack of microbiological expertise within the group. The group possesses the resources to illicitly acquire a sample of anthrax, a large fermenter (500 L), and sufficient quantities of growth media. However, the type of growth media obtained is not ideal for growing anthrax and the particular strain of anthrax does not grow rapidly. The group is consequently not able to produce sufficient quantities of viable anthrax slurry to execute a successful attack. The green variant of this example shows that the group, while possessing many of the technical requirements, is not large enough to enjoy the full set of skills necessary to conduct a successful attack.

These two examples are *hypothetical*. The project team also examined the historical record to inform its pathways analysis. It did so in two ways. First, it examined cases of bioterrorism to determine the pathway that was exploited. Figure represents the case of Aum Shinrikyo which, despite having a large manpower pool, scientific expertise, major financial resources, technical equipment and so on, was nevertheless unsuccessful in conducting several biological attacks aimed at producing large casualties because it did not have the appropriate agent. Figure represents the case of the Rajneeshee cult in which the motivation to achieve a limited impact through the use of biological materials produced a less sophisticated, but ultimately successful pathway.

Second, the project team turned the question around and asked whether the historical record could offer analogs to some of the pathways deemed more probable than others by the project team because of the logical relationship between factors and outcomes. Given the paucity of historical data, however, this step in the analysis had limited utility.

Threat of Biological Terrorism: Key Findings

The application of the "*pathways*" methodology yielded several important findings that should inform efforts to develop an effective health and medical dimension to the nation's overall capabilities to respond to bioterrorism.

A key relationship exists between the degree of risk and the level of casualties desired in an attack. That relationship, however, is not the straightforward one that higher risk is associated with catastrophic casualty scenarios. Indeed, the degree of risk declines as the level of desired casualties increases, insofar as it becomes less likely.

In essence, as a terrorist seeks higher casualties, fewer pathways are available to achieve that objective, and those that remain are more difficult. There are several reasons:

1. Few terrorist actors have the necessary combination of size, resources, skills, facilitative ethos (e.g., willingness to experiment and accept failure), or appropriate organizational structure to achieve mass casualty capabilities.
2. Traditional agents capable of inflicting mass casualties are either difficult to acquire, cultivate and produce, or disseminate effectively. The relationship between agent and dissemination technique is especially important in that if the dissemination process is less than optimal (due to the device, the method, or the environment), the terrorist must compensate through meeting more demanding technical requirements such as producing greater volumes or better quality agent to achieve the same effect. Producing and disseminating more agent also increases the possibility of detection and capture.
3. Likely targets for bioterrorism attacks do not necessarily facilitate mass casualty outcomes given the other requirements for conducting an effective attack against such targets, including technical knowledge (of air flows in large arenas, for example) or operational skills (surveillance, planning, finance, etc.).

Despite the low probability of catastrophic bioterrorism, there is still ample cause for concern. We do not know how "*massive*" a mass attack has to be; worst-case scenarios may not need to happen.

Bioterrorism attacks that produce levels of casualties below those considered catastrophic constitute a significant problem for two key reasons:

1. We do not know at what point the response system will become overburdened and stressed to the point of collapse. Some officials involved in response preparation, particularly at the local level, suggest that the threshold is not very high.

2. Use of unconventional terrorism for other than massively destructive purposes is consistent with the historical record, which suggests that such events have often been designed to achieve more discriminate goals, including assassination and financial gain.

The danger and harm inherent in the bioterrorism threat is not limited to physical fatalities and casualties. Psychological impact and social disruption could also be severe if effective preparations are not made and useful responses are not developed.

Terrorism expert Brian Jenkins has argued that "Frightening millions may exceed the desire to kill thousands." Terrorists might seek leverage and advantage from provoking a number of psychological reactions to even limited use of bioterrorism: panic that would magnify the attack; hysteria that would stimulate untoward behaviour among the population; futility that could create momentum for responding to terrorist demands; depression that could make it more difficult to shape an effective strategic reaction; lack of confidence in government that would be seen as incapable of meeting its fundamental purpose of safeguarding its citizenry. One could argue that the Aum Shinrikyo attack, while a failure in terms of achieving mass casualties, nevertheless had a profound impact on the way we look at the world and the problems society now confronts. Targets may be selected, therefore, more for their symbolic value than for the number of people that can be killed.

Beyond the psychological impact, even a lower scale bioterrorist attack could disrupt civil society on a significant scale, both in the locale of the attack and more broadly. Experience with natural disasters or conventional terrorist attacks suggests that it could take a community considerable time for its life to return to some kind of "*normalcy.*"

Although many terrorists either will not be interested in using biological weapons or not able to do so, two categories of non-state actors—those with relationships with national governments and those outside the traditional scope of governmental scrutiny—warrant particular attention.

Terrorism analysis tends to exclude violent acts by non-state actors allied with foreign governments in times of conflict because such actions are considered acts of war. In terms of national bioterrorism response planning, this is short-sighted for three reasons:

1. The consequences of such an attack would be no different than if it occurred as an isolated incident and the response needs would be the same.

2. State-sponsored terrorists are among the few actors who could assemble the requisite resources, skills, and materials to conduct a successful attack that produces significant levels of casualties.
3. Countries who see themselves potentially in a conflict with the United States are demonstrating an increasing interest in "*asymmetric strategies*" to obviate the overwhelming U.S. advantage in conventional military power. When combined with a perception of the United States as a country that insists on "*casualty-free*" conflicts, enjoys only limited credibility in terms of its commitments to friends and allies overseas, and retains little consensus on when and how to use its military power, the appeal of asymmetric strategies that include terrorism with unconventional weapons could increase.

This is not to argue that an adversary of the United States would share biological weapons technology with a non-state actor or allow such an entity to "set off" a biological weapon in isolation from a major confrontation. The potential costs will generally prevent those countries from giving the United States "a poke in the eye with a sharp stick" just for the sake of doing so. But the United States should not expect that its future will be free of conflict with adversaries in other parts of the world, and if that conflict entails interests great enough for the other party—for example, regime survival—they may be willing to "*bring the conflict home*" to the United States through domestic attacks by non-state actors using unconventional means.

The second category of actor that bears particular attention includes those who may not have been a regular focus of scrutiny either because they are new to the scene or they have not been considered part of the terrorism universe. Among the actors who now define contemporary terrorism—which itself is a combination of old and new dimensions—recent analysis suggests that those who might be most attracted to the use of biological agents include:

1. Non-state actors inspired by religious ideals;
2. Groups from the Right of the political spectrum;
3. Actors with millennial world views that combine with notions of the "cleansing" value of violence;
4. Transnational networks that are less constrained by central authority; and
5. Radical single-issue groups.

Few of these actors will have the requisite skills to perpetrate bioterrorist attacks that produce catastrophic casualties. Cults, for example, tend to be insular, paranoid, smaller groups that lack the full range of skills necessary to carry out a mass attack. The diffusion of transnational networks could make it hard for them to assemble all of the necessary requirements. The concept of "*leaderless resistance*" that is a value of the right-wing in the United States may leave it without the organizational discipline to conduct successful attacks. Despite all of these shortcomings, however, these groups must continue to be of concern regarding future bioterrorism, if only because smaller-scale events in terms of casualties could still produce significant negative impacts.

Uncertainty Surrounding Bioterrorism

The threat is not static and will continue to evolve. Changing actors and evolving technology - especially in biology-related areas—will be major drivers of such change but not the only ones. Globalization and the Information Revolution will shape the terrorism environment just as they will most other forms of social organization and interaction. Specific events outside the bioterrorism realm will intrude to influence terrorists' goals, perceptions, and modes of operation. The impact of individual personalities should not be discounted.

Two points in relation to the uncertainty about the bioterrorism threat by ongoing change are important for those who must respond to the challenge. First, the assumption is usually made that such change will make the threat more severe. Such an assumption is not necessarily warranted. Change should also benefit those who must respond to the threat, not only in the tools they could have available, but in terms of the broader social, political, and psychological context. Whether terrorism waxes or wanes at any particular time depends on a confluence of factors that is not always in the terrorist's favour. Part of the overall objective of those responsible for dealing with terrorism must be to promote an environment in which the elements that support or facilitate terrorism find expression difficult.

Second, uncertainty is created by the constant adjustment in the dynamic between terrorists and those who fight them. Like the offense-defense relationship in military affairs, the relationship between terrorists and responders is constantly in flux, and uncertainty arises because it is not possible to state precisely at any given point in time how the balance stands between them. The important point, however, is that both elements are necessary to create that dynamic relationship. In the case of responding to the threat of bioterrorism, certainty will only be achieved if we take ourselves out of the game and do nothing.

In that case, we can be confident that the terrorists will prevail. Otherwise, a measure of threat and a degree of risk must be accepted. The challenge is to reduce that risk to manageable, and acceptable, levels. In the case of bioterrorism, the health and medical dimension of the overall response system will play an important role in achieving that objective.

An analytical framework for assessing the threat of biological terrorism is needed to reduce the uncertainty that currently permeates the national debate over an issue that has forced its way on to the national agenda. A good threat assessment creates a "*threat envelope*" that describes the most plausible contingencies and identifies those possibilities that fall within it and those that lie outside. Defining a plausible threat envelope also provides a means to identify those contingencies that require hedging, in that, due to the severity or enormity of their consequences, some preparation for them should be undertaken, even if they are relatively unlikely. The combination of the threat envelope and the hedging contingencies should give policy makers some measure for making decisions regarding policy priorities and resource allocations.

An analytical framework for thinking about the biological terrorism threat will also highlight the fact that the threat is not unidimensional; it does not come from only one factor. Rather, it is composed of several elements. Each of these elements, in turn, entails a significant array of possibilities. The key to a successful bioterrorism threat assessment is disaggregating the threat into its component elements and assessing the relationships among them. Only by doing so can one examine comparative likelihood of various contingencies. It is the introduction of likelihood into the analysis that distinguishes a threat assessment from a vulnerability assessment. For purposes of this study, the key elements of the bioterrorism threat have been identified as the *who* (the actor), the *what* (the agent), the *where* (the target), and the *how* (the mode of attack).

The key components of the threat assessment—who, what, how, and where—were integrated into a "*matrix-pathways*" approach to develop a representation of the complex nature of the bioterrorism threat. Given the importance of the actor in shaping the threat, the team decided to break the question of "who?" into two distinct but related elements suggested by the questions: "what are the motivations for a group to use a biological weapon?" and "what capabilities must an actor possess to develop and use a biological weapon?" These five components provided the starting point for constructing the matrix.

Bioterrorism pathways were produced by systematically identifying plausible relationships between factors and outcomes. Combining the pathways with judgments regarding the comparative likelihood of each pathway produced the "*plausible threat envelope*" for biological terrorism.

The project team also examined the historical record to inform its pathways analysis. It did so in two ways. First, it examined cases of bioterrorism to determine the pathway that was exploited. Second, the project team turned the question around and asked whether the historical record could offer analogs to some of the pathways deemed more probable than others by the project team because of the logical relationship between factors and outcomes. Given the paucity of historical data, however, this step in the analysis had limited utility.

The application of the "*pathways*" methodology yielded several important findings that should inform efforts to develop an effective health and medical dimension to the nation's overall capabilities to respond to bioterrorism.

1. A key relationship exists between the degree of risk and the level of casualties desired in an attack. That relationship, however, is not the straightforward one that higher risk is associated with catastrophic casualty scenarios. Indeed, the degree of risk declines as the level of desired casualties increases, insofar as it becomes less likely.
    - Few terrorists have the necessary combination of size, resources, skills, facilitative ethos, or appropriate organizational structure to achieve mass casualty capabilities.
    - Traditional agents capable of inflicting mass casualties are difficult to acquire, cultivate, and produce, or disseminate effectively.
    - Likely targets for attacks do not necessarily facilitate mass casualty outcomes.
2. Despite the low probability of catastrophic bioterrorism, there is still ample cause for concern. We do not know how "*massive*" a mass attack has to be; worst-case scenarios may not need to happen.
    - We do not know, for example, at what point the response system will become overburdened and stressed to the point of collapse.
    - The danger and harm inherent in the bioterrorism threat is not limited to physical fatalities and casualties. Psychological impact and social disruption could also be severe if effective preparations are not made and useful responses are not developed.

- Use of unconventional terrorism for other than massively destructive purposes is consistent with the historical record.

3. Although many terrorists will not be interested in using biological weapons or not able to do so, two categories of non-state actors – those with relationships with national governments and those outside the traditional scope of governmental scrutiny – warrant particular attention.

Terrorism analysis tends to exclude violent acts by non-state actors allied with foreign governments in times of conflict because such actions are considered acts of war. In terms of national bioterrorism response planning, this is short-sighted for three reasons:

- The consequences of such an attack would be no different than if it occurred as an isolated incident and the response needs would be the same.
- State-sponsored terrorists are among the few actors who could assemble the requisite resources, skills, and materials to conduct a successful attack that produces significant levels of casualties.
- Countries who see themselves potentially in a conflict with the United States are demonstrating an increasing interest in "*asymmetric strategies*" to obviate the overwhelming U.S. advantage in conventional military power. When combined with a perception of the United States as a country that insists on "*casualty-free*" conflicts, enjoys only limited credibility in terms of its commitments to friends and allies overseas, and retains little consensus on when and how to use its military power, the appeal of asymmetric strategies that include terrorism with unconventional weapons could increase.

The second category of actor that bears particular attention includes those who may not have been a regular focus of scrutiny either because they are new to the scene or they have not been considered part of the terrorism universe. Among the actors who now define contemporary terrorism—which itself is a combination of old and new dimensions—recent analysis suggests that those who might be most attracted to the use of biological agents include:

- non-state actors inspired by religious ideals;
- groups from the Right of the political spectrum;
- actors with millennial world views that combine with notions of the "cleansing" value of violence;

- transnational networks that are less constrained by central authority; and
- radical single-issue groups.

Few of these actors will have the requisite skills to perpetrate bioterrorist attacks that produce catastrophic casualties. These groups must continue to be of concern regarding future bioterrorism, however, if only because smaller-scale events in terms of casualties could still produce significant negative impacts.

4. The environment of uncertainty surrounding bioterrorism will remain.

The threat is not static and will continue to evolve. Changing actors and evolving technology—especially in biology-related areas—will be major drivers of such change but not the only ones. Globalization and the Information Revolution will shape the terrorism environment just as they will most other forms of social organization and interaction. Specific events outside the bioterrorism realm will intrude to influence terrorists' goals, perceptions, and modes of operation. The impact of individual personalities should not be discounted.

Two final points in relation to the uncertainty about the bioterrorism threat by ongoing change are important for those who must respond to the challenge. First, the assumption is usually made that such change will make the threat more severe. Such an assumption is not necessarily warranted. Change should also benefit those who must respond to the threat, not only in the tools they could have available, but in terms of the broader social, political, and psychological context.

Second, uncertainty is created by the constant adjustment in the dynamic between terrorists and those who fight them. Like the offense-defense relationship in military affairs, the relationship between terrorists and responders is constantly in flux, and uncertainty arises because it is not possible to state precisely at any given point in time how the balance stands between them. The important point, however, is that both elements are necessary to create that dynamic relationship. In the case of responding to the threat of bioterrorism, certainty will only be achieved if we take ourselves out of the game and do nothing.

4

Training and Education

Early recognition of a biological attack depends on two critical resources: warning networks, such as those within hospitals and public health agencies, and individual clinical expertise of medical personnel. A central defense against bioterrorism will be the astute emergency clinician or laboratory technician who spots a suggestive epidemiological pattern early and sounds the alarm.

Medical personnel, lab technicians, public health officials, and hospital administrators can clearly play a key role in helping to ensure that hospitals and communities are prepared to respond to bioterrorism. However, in order to do so, they must receive adequate training and education on a variety of issues related to bioterrorism response, including agent and outbreak recognition, treatment of casualties, protection of personnel and hospital staff, resource acquisition, and response plan implementation.

Requirements

Training requirements can be broken into two distinct but connected categories: content and organization. Content addresses what trainees need to know; organization provides the medium through which training can be carried out most effectively.

Content

Education and training for physicians and nurses on bioterrorism should encompass several important elements essential to a comprehensive medical response. These elements include recognition of an unusual outbreak or uncommon *syndrome*, treatment of *casualties*, protection of hospital staff, *resource acquisition*, and the implementation of an integrated, community-based plan.

Outbreak and disease recognition

Because diseases like *anthrax*, *plague*, and *tularemia* are given scant attention in medical school and daily practice, most doctors would have difficulty recognizing cases appearing in their hospitals and offices. Furthermore, many of these diseases have nonspecific, flu-like symptoms until their advanced stages. An effective training program should incorporate not only extensive clinical analysis of agent presentation, but should also highlight basic surveillance and epidemiological warning signs and signals. Moreover, training should encompass both traditional biological agents and non-traditional, more common agents. Dr. Paula Krapf, writing in *Illinois Medicine*, recommends specific education to teach the medical community how to distinguish between common disease outbreaks and those resulting from intentional poisoning. Some warning signs that should be stressed include a strongly suspected case of a disease in a patient with no risk history, a cluster of patients who present with a similar syndrome, an unusual disease or a disease uncommon to a particular geographic area, and an unexplained increase in a common syndrome, such as influenza. *Recognition* of the signs of a bioterrorist attack by physicians will be critical to early treatment and saving lives.

Treatment of casualties

Medical personnel must also be educated about treatment guidelines in the event of a *biological attack*. Many doctors, nurses and technicians who have previously received HAZMAT training assume that the triage and decontamination procedures that accompany chemical weapons exposure also apply to biological weapons; however, biological agents require specific forms of treatment and mitigation.

Training programs to date have emphasized decontamination procedures as part of a comprehensive response to bioterrorism. The emerging consensus, as explained by Nicki Pesik and Mark Keim in "Do U.S. Emergency Medicine Residency Programs Provide Adequate Training for Bioterrorism," and Christopher Richards in "*Emergency Physicians and Biological Terrorism*," is that decontamination of persons exposed to a biological agent is unnecessary; at most, clothing removal and a soap and water shower are adequate to prevent secondary exposure. Similarly, reaerosolization of an agent from clothing or skin is not a major issue and does not pose a risk to health care providers.

Another important component of treatment training should be basic *prophylactic guidelines*. Most physicians or nurses have neither sufficient clinical knowledge of many of the agents commonly associated with bioterrorism, such as *smallpox* or *anthrax*, nor familiarity with the antibiotics or special forms of treatment necessary in the event of a biological attack. For example, during an informal anthrax scenario conducted by John Bartlett, Chief of Infectious Diseases at the Johns Hopkins University School of Medicine, several physicians did not know the size of Baltimore's standing supply of ciprofloxicin, a common antibiotic used against anthrax. Many physicians and nurses also do not know the prophylactic schedule for antibiotics associated with biological agents. Medical training should couple clinical analysis of agent manifestations with their appropriate prophylactic and treatment strategies.

Protection of hospital staff and patients

A bioterrorist event will unfold in an environment populated with primary care workers and *immunosuppressed patients*. As doctors and nurses are key caregivers in the event of an attack, they must take care to ensure their own health. Consequently, while treating victims of an attack will be important, training should also be geared toward the protection of the hospital staff, patients, health facility and its environment, and the victims, in that order.

While full NBC protective suits are not necessary, it is important that hospital personnel implement standard infection control measures until definitive laboratory confirmation is received that the agent is noncontagious. These measures include the use of surgical masks, eye protection, gloves, and barrier gowns, as well as the thorough disinfection of medical instruments. Previous use of these protective measures during large disease outbreaks has proven effective at diminishing disease transmission; notably, emergency department staff in New Mexico pointed to protective gear as an important tool in the confinement of the Hantavirus outbreak of 1994.

If the agent is determined to be contagious, a more comprehensive set of infection control measures are necessary, including separate isolation wards, negative airflow rooms, and respirators. In this case, training medical personnel to take proper precautions in evaluating and treating victims will stem the transmission of a biological agent while protecting the "*front line*" defenders—hospital staff.

Resource acquisition

A bioterrorist attack will strain the infrastructure of an already strapped hospital and public health system. Needed resources can range from personal protective supplies, such as *latex gloves* and *air masks*, to negative airflow rooms, respirators, and separate ventilation and waste collection systems. Further response requirements may include additional staff, direct communication tools, or vaccines.

It is critical for public health officers involved in consequence management to understand where and how to acquire resources quickly. Most medical personnel, however, do not know whom to contact at their local public health department for support or to request additional equipment or antibiotics. For example, during a 1998 test of Maryland's response system, John Bartlett discovered that no one knew the phone number to set into motion the state's bioterrorism response network, and the number itself was not in the hospital directory or 911 listings. Teaching medical personnel about reporting structure and resource acquisition is key to a comprehensive and rapid response.

Coordinated action and communication between response entities

Perhaps the most important, and often overlooked, element of a strong training program is relaying the intricacies of a complicated response system to medical personnel and instilling the need for clear and consistent communication among public health and medical workers and other response entities. In the past, training has addressed nuclear, chemical, and biological weapons response simultaneously, and has specifically stressed responding to chemical terrorism with HAZMAT-like procedures. As a result, the public safety community took the early lead role in shaping the WMD terrorism response. Training programs have provided little room for awareness of the role of public health departments or medical personnel.

A greater understanding is emerging that bioterrorism is largely a public health and medical issue and that hospitals and public health agencies will bear the brunt of the response, although local and state emergency management agencies, EMS services, fire and law enforcement agencies, and federal organizations will all play a role. Many of these entities are nontraditional partners for the public health and medical sectors, and as such, do not have previously established communication networks. The complex hierarchy of agencies and departments involved with a potential bioterrorist incident has often resulted in a lack of knowledge of who is in charge, what roles various entities play, or how they relate to each other, further complicating the response system.

For the public health officer attempting to respond to a suspicious outbreak of disease, being able to communicate early with these entities is critical because their resources and legal authority will be vital in containing the effects of an attack. In fact, getting the public safety and public health communities to understand their respective roles is a key factor in an effective response. Organizations like the Federal Bureau of Investigation will be important in evidence collection and preservation, while local and state public health agencies, the Centers for Disease Control, and the U.S. Army Medical Research Institute of Infectious Diseases may provide epidemiologic and laboratory diagnostics expertise. Because hospital and community response plans should indicate when these agencies should be involved and which agencies will be in charge, training should include an analysis of the federal, state, and local response structure. Similarly, encouraging tabletop exercises that integrate members of the public safety and medical community will allow both entities to better understand their distinct roles and how they will support each other in the event of an attack.

Implementing a bioterrorism response plan

As the first to recognize a potential attack, medical personnel must be familiar with the hospital plan and chain of command to be able to set into motion the local, state and federal response. Knowing when and how to begin an overall strategic response, which hospital departments to contact, and who is in charge is a critical aspect of medical preparedness. Training doctors, nurses and technicians to take an active role in creating and implementing their facility's response plan will allow for a stronger, more rapid, more integrated local response.

Organization

Training can be carried out through a number of different mediums, from classroom-style seminars to web-based teleconferences to tabletop scenarios. The choice of medium can have important effects on both the quality and quantity of information relayed, as well as on the ability of trainers to reach their target audience.

Classroom-style seminars

To date, *classroom-style* seminars have been the standard form of *bioterrorism* training available to medical personnel. Whether sponsored by national organizations such as the Department of Defense or the American Medical Association (AMA), or by state and local health departments, conferences usually unfold as intensive sessions that run from one day to one week addressing critical topics related to bioterrorism preparedness.

Seminars offer the opportunity to hear directly from issue experts, ask questions related to information presented, and interact with colleagues interested or involved in bioterrorism response. They further allow for a compact, generalized overview of the most salient response elements. However, because of their length, seminars often cannot address in detail large response issues, such as how a bioterrorism plan should be implemented. Moreover, because conferences are often off-site, multiple-day sessions, many doctors and nurses, who balance hectic schedules and work in chronically understaffed environments, do not make time to attend. Consequently, additional training is needed.

Web-based teleconferencing

Web-based teleconferencing combines the style and content of conferences and seminars with a more flexible, off-site approach. Teleconferencing allows doctors, nurses, and other medical personnel to attend pre-planned discussions or educational presentations by logging on to the Internet from their home or office computer. By eliminating the need for physical attendance, medical personnel can fit appropriate sessions into their schedule.

As previously discussed, one of the problems of classroom-style teaching is the inability of trainers to hold the attention of participants for a long period of time. Thus, in theory, the shorter, more frequent sessions associated with teleconferencing should result in greater focus, and thus better information retention. Because of the flexibility of the format, training managers can use an increased number of short sessions to provide more in-depth education on a larger variety of subjects.

However, the pick-and-choose format of teleconferencing means that many medical personnel may not receive training in areas essential to their ability to mount an effective response simply because they do not recognize that the topic is important. Similarly, because only a few of a series of sessions may be attended by a doctor, nurse, or infection control professional, those trained may fail to understand the larger response picture.

Continuing medical education materials

Continuing medical education (CME) offers great flexibility and potential breadth of information. CME materials can be provided in a variety of forms, from self-tests attached to published articles in medical journals, to full courses offered by professional organizations, newsletters, and web-based information. To some extent, medical personnel are expected to initiate educational efforts on their own; however, attaching increased knowledge about bioterrorism to additional educational credit has proven to be an incentive for many medical personnel who may not otherwise participate in training sessions. By using CME credit, an almost endless number of topics or response issues can be discussed, allowing trainers to access a large audience.

Because some form of test accompanies most CME materials, CME works to reinforce educational principles while providing a level of accountability for information learned. However, CME contains many of the same problems associated with web-based distance learning; by allowing medical personnel to pick and choose their topics, many participants will not receive training on important response issues simply because the issues are considered uninteresting or inapplicable. Moreover, because CME training is an individual exercise, participants will not benefit from the discussions or opinions of other colleagues involved in bioterrorism response.

Tabletop exercises

Tabletop exercises and scenarios aim to educate through hands-on experience. While a few important principles or response elements may be reviewed during the course of a tabletop exercise, training takes place largely by working through a scenario focused on a hypothetical attack. Participants learn through interaction and group discussion, and minimal written materials are provided. Tabletop exercises are most effective when participants have some prior knowledge of the subject being tested, and can put that knowledge to use in a problem-solving setting.

Tabletop exercises allow for new information to be rapidly incorporated into practical experience, as well as for reinforcement of important principles relayed in the course of training. In many ways, tabletop exercises promote an understanding of different entities' response roles, as well as an appreciation for the high-level coordination needed for a successful response. However, because of the fast-paced and immediate-problem-solving nature of tabletop exercises, longer-term problems or solutions are rarely addressed. Similarly, because exercises focus on scenarios rather than concrete information dissemination, important educational aspects may not be addressed. For example, in an exercise during which participants focus primarily on triage and *prophylaxis*, agent or outbreak recognition may not be effectively stressed.

Where Are We?

Training for Medical Personnel

Training to date has been conducted largely through the *Domestic Preparedness Program* (DPP) run by the Department of Defense that takes a "*train-the-trainer*" approach. According to this approach, a "*training hierarchy*" is established; those first trained are expected to train other emergency responders through follow-on courses. Training begins with national-level professionals and responders, and is then replicated at the state and local levels. While the training programs have reached countless emergency responders across the country, the number of medical personnel participating has been disappointing. Attendance by doctors, nurses and technicians has been consistently low, and the sessions themselves have concentrated heavily on agent recognition and treatment rather than on larger response issues.

The Nunn-Lugar-Domenici Domestic Preparedness Program was established in 1996. The Department of Defense was designated the lead agency but the program was also designed to stress DoD collaboration with the Federal Bureau of Investigation, the Federal Emergency Management Agency, the Department of Energy, the Environmental Protection Agency, and the Public Health Service. Designed as a "*train-the-trainer*" program to build on the existing knowledge and capabilities of local first responders, those trained are expected to train other emergency responders through follow-on courses. Training is to occur in over 120 cities, and, to date, the DPP has reached over 90 cities. Many of the cities that have received training have institutionalized various adaptations of that training program, primarily in their fire and law enforcement training academies.

The DPP's efforts to educate the medical community have been concentrated in its Hospital Provider course, a program emphasizing overall disaster planning skills and hospital-based decontamination. Specifically, the Hospital Provider course provides instruction to trainers of emergency department physicians and nurses. The course has focused primarily on those agents with the greatest morbidity and mortality rates, including *anthrax*, *smallpox*, and *plague*, and has also stressed the use of personal protective equipment and on-site triage. Most courses run as 8-hour, single-day workshops with NBC-unique demonstrations and individual case studies. As with other DPP efforts, the Hospital Provider course allows participants, upon completion, to instruct the technical aspects of bioterrorism and the defensive actions required for responders to protect themselves and their community to other first responders.

The *General Accounting Office* (GAO) has criticized the Domestic Preparedness Program for failing to take advantage of existing state emergency management structures, mutual aid agreements among local jurisdictions, or other collaborative arrangements for emergency response. By delivering the program to cities based on population size, GAO argues that a program conducted in one place often replicates training sessions in nearby cities that also qualified for the DPP and may be part of the same response system. According to the GAO, increasing mutual aid agreements, unified emergency service districts, councils of government, hazardous materials response regions, and traditional state roles in fire and emergency management training would allow the DPP to consolidate training and result in less training repetition.

Moreover, because the program is limited to 120 cities, training will not be provided to smaller cities that may, for reasons other than population size, face a higher threat index. Follow-on training is insufficient to address trainer turnover, and the program is perceived to have a strong chemical bias. Despite its one-day Hospital Provider course, the program is also geared towards the public safety community, resulting in limited involvement from public health or medical organizations.

Several problems specific to the organization and content of the DPP Hospital Provider course have also limited its effectiveness. Howard Levitin of Disaster Planning International, an organization that runs the course for the Department of Defense, has underlined that specific requirements for response have not been well defined, and no training currently exists on how to implement a bioterrorism response plan. Furthermore, training has not touched on many issues that will be essential to a comprehensive medical response, including implementing a community-based surveillance system, expanding the current capacity of the health care system, creating more bed space, accessing additional supplies and equipment, and providing an adequate number of staff. The program has focused heavily on traditional agent recognition and treatment, and as such, often fails to give the medical provider a complete response picture. Most practicing physicians and nurses possess a low level of awareness about the program, as well as about other training opportunities at the local and state level, resulting in diminished interest and low attendance. According to the Emergency Management Coordinator of a large metropolitan area, "participation by hospital and medical personnel has been minimal at best."

Education of Medical Students

There is currently no standardized curriculum for training emergency medical students and physicians about the health hazards related to biological weapons. Furthermore, opportunities for teaching this material remain limited. Indeed, the current emergency medicine core content and most popular training textbooks do not contain specific reference to the recognition, reporting, detection, or management of biological weapons disasters. In a survey distributed to 118 emergency medicine residency program directors participating in the 1997 National Resident Matching Program, the majority of respondents indicated that they felt inadequately prepared to manage casualties of a biological attack. While more than 50 percent had participated in a residency program that included formal training in bioterrorism, the most common form of training was through lectures, with only 6 percent incorporating training courses into their operational program. In contrast, over 85 percent had received formal training in HAZMAT.

Respondents to the survey also revealed a limited knowledge of how to access information regarding biological warfare agents; most listed *toxicologists*, poison control centers, and local health departments as reference sources, all of which would likely be unable to provide the appropriate information on *biological weapons*. Only 8 percent of respondents could claim access to more than three sources, and of all references available, the most prevalent were military manuals. Similarly, only slightly more than half of the respondents were aware of the appropriate protective equipment in their emergency departments. A lack of access to vital information represents a weak link in physician and health care training.

A multi-specialty Weapons of Mass Destruction Education Task Force organized by the American College of Emergency Physicians (ACEP) is currently developing curricula for emergency health care providers that should form the basis of ongoing educational efforts. To date, the Task Force has identified several key content learning objectives that will serve as the basis of an improved medical school and training curricula. The first category—*awareness objectives*—aims to increase general knowledge of terrorism, event types, index suspicion and event recognition, response systems and communications, and personal protection and safety. The second category—*performance objectives*—encompasses such themes as response support, decontamination, isolation and containment, evidence preservation, psychological effects, communication and agency interaction, triage, and fatality management. Once developed, these curricula should be incorporated into medical school course-work, residency training programs, disaster medicine and toxicology fellowships, and continuing education meetings and symposia.

Key Issues and Recommendations

Lack of Preparedness within the Medical Community

Most medical personnel are unprepared to respond to a bioterrorist threat. The experience of physicians who dealt with anthrax hoaxes over the last three years demonstrates that most medical personnel are unprepared to respond to a bioterrorist incident and generally rely on HAZMAT principles to guide their response. As Keim and Arnold Kaufmann chronicle, case management of *anthrax* hoaxes has varied from incident to incident. In some cases, patients were provided with no intervention and were sent home from a threat scene without accompanying documentation of care; in other incidents, people were removed from the workplace, disrobed, scrubbed down in portable decontamination units, and referred for *clinical evaluation* and *prophylaxis*. In a *bioterrorism* scenario carried out by John Bartlett at Johns Hopkins University Hospital, the chief emergency room physician, despite having completed an 8-hour training course on bioterrorism, confessed that an early case of *inhalation anthrax* would have been diagnosed as the *flu*. As a result, the patient would have been sent home without additional laboratory tests or treatment. Moreover, during planning for a possible CBRN terrorist incident during the 1996 Atlanta Olympics, it was discovered that only the FBI specialized assessment team had clinicians who were experienced in identifying the signs and symptoms of exposure to chemical and *biological agents*. The inconsistent response of public health and EMS organizations indicates that the proper training of medical, public health, and emergency personnel is essential to a comprehensive response framework.

Bias Toward Chemical/HAZMAT Training

As with most response plans, the programs currently in place to train medical personnel in weapons of mass destruction response have been built on the existing infrastructures of EMS and fire services' plans for hazardous materials response. While some of these procedures, including isolation and infection control, yield positive results when treating BW patients, the majority of HAZMAT responses are not optimized for biological agents and do not underline the distinct responses required for a biological event.

Specifically, HAZMAT responses rely on a sentinel event, the expectation of rapid agent detection and identification, and on-site decontamination, all of which may not be needed or helpful in a biological attack. As Christopher Richards points, the HAZMAT model does not address some essential components inherent to bioterrorism planning, including delayed emergence of disease and evolvement in a hospital setting. DoD's training program, which today represents the most widely available training forums for personnel involved with bioterrorism response, in particular retain a chemical focus. This is in part because the target audience of the DPP was initially the public safety community. Fire departments in particular were dubbed "*first responders*" because they go to the scene of an emergency and take control of the situation. The DP training initiatives built on the operational experience fire departments had in responding to HAZMAT incidents. As a result of their HAZMAT bias, training programs often leave the health care worker unprepared to respond to an event involving a biological agent release.

Even those training programs that have focused more specifically on the health response to bioterrorism, such as the DPP's Hospital Provider course, continue to emphasize procedures more in line with HAZMAT response. Moreover, these programs have not touched on a myriad of issues that are unique to responding to a biological event, including implementing a community-based surveillance system, expanding the capacity of the health care system, creating more bed space, and acquiring additional medical equipment. Consequently, even those physicians who have received training in bioterrorism response under existing programs may not have addressed the correct issues or treatment plans. The Domestic Preparedness Program should place a greater focus on health and medical response issues, and training should be adapted from HAZMAT criteria to focus more closely on procedures dealing specifically with biological weapons response, including agent and outbreak recognition and treatment measures. Training should focus on "*big picture*" response, incorporating integrated response issues, communication, surveillance, and reporting.

Poor Attendance by Medical Personnel at Training Sessions

The DPP courses have not been organized in a way to attract medical personnel. During a recent "*train-the-trainer*" session in Baltimore, only 5 emergency physicians attended, with no other medical representatives present. According to Levitin, interest in bioterrorism among medical personnel falls into four main categories, each representing a different level of commitment to the issue. Those in the "*immediate*" category possess a profound interest in the topic, and will thus attend training sessions regardless of location, cost, or availability. The second, or "*delayed*", category encompasses medical personnel who are casually interested in the issue and may attend training sessions, but will not get involved in planning unless they are convinced it is necessary. Medical personnel in this category are more likely to attend training sessions if they are convenient and continuing education credit is offered. Those nurses, doctors and technicians in the "*self-care*" category are not interested at all in learning about bioterrorism and will not willingly attend any training sessions offered. Consequently, they must be convinced that bioterrorism is truly a health priority. Finally, the "*dead*" category includes personnel who believe that if a bioterrorist incident does occur, there is no way to adequately prepare for it. As a result, medical personnel in this category will not attend a training session no matter how hard they are lobbied.

The difficulty in getting doctors and nurses to attend educational sessions related to bioterrorism highlights that training must be both marketed and flexible. Many doctors and nurses balance hectic schedules and multiple training priorities. Similarly, most hospitals and public health centers are chronically understaffed and unwilling to pay for additional training sessions. Consequently, attending a day-long session focused on a low-probability event is deemed neither feasible nor practical by most medical personnel. In order to attract doctors and nurses to bioterrorism training modules, sessions must be scheduled to better fit into a typical medical calendar. One option would be scheduling sessions in two four-hour periods on different days, which would allow doctors and nurses greater flexibility. Distance learning also provides a potential educational alternative. The satellite distance learning program established by USAMRIID and the Centers for Disease Control has had wider participation among physicians than the DPP, although there is a need to reach an even greater number of medical personnel. It is also important to make bioterrorism training a priority among medical personnel. Instead of focusing exclusively on clinical manifestations of certain agents, training programs should focus on medical surveillance, reporting requirements, identifying rare events, interaction with public health agencies, local hospitals, and infection control, and the applicability of training to daily practice. Efforts must be made to attract medical personnel to training sessions. A greater focus should be placed on flexible sessions that can accommodate the schedules of health care practitioners. A good first step is making DP training materials available through the Internet.

Lack of Involvement by Health Organizations

Health organizations have not been involved with creating or implementing training programs. Public health and medical organizations must play a greater role in shaping training guidelines and class content. The Nunn-Lugar-Domenici Domestic Preparedness Program courses, for example, were developed with insufficient input from national, state, or local medical organizations. As such, they have lacked guidelines for several critical components of medical response, including coordination and command issues, and have had trouble attracting medical and public health personnel.

Involvement by the Centers for Disease Control and the Department of Health and Human Services could improve the content of educational initiatives by incorporating a more concentrated medical approach into current training programs and placing a larger priority on bioterrorism preparedness among medical providers. Both the CDC and HHS have emphasized a more holistic method of medical training, one that involves a variety of organizations and extensive partnership development. According to this method, training must be applicable to a number of different medical response entities, from doctors and nurses to infection control professionals, public health officials, epidemiologists, and laboratory technicians. Training programs would thus focus not only on agent and outbreak recognition but also on the roles played by the different medical response entities, how these entities coordinate their actions in the event of an attack, and how the medical community should interact with other response entities, including the public safety community. Similarly, both CDC and HHS, by increasing opportunities for continuing education credit and distance learning, could make training available to a larger percentage of the medical population. The involvement of national medical organizations such as the American Public Health Association (APHA), the National Association of City and County Health Officials (NACCHO), the American Red Cross, the Joint Commission on Accreditation of Healthcare Organizations (JCAHO), and the Association of State and Territorial Health Officials (ASTHO) would give training activities an even greater reach; in fact, many of these organizations are currently campaigning to educate their membership on bioterrorism-related issues.

Local and state public health departments should also carry out training. Local health departments can do this internally, by educating health department personnel on bioterrorism recognition and informatics, as well as externally, by going directly to medical clinics and hospitals to promote awareness and access to available resources. In many ways, local and state training programs may have more success at reaching a greater number of medical personnel because they already have partnerships in place with local and regional hospitals and clinics, and will be able to use real examples based on local data. For example, the Chicago Department of Health has established a "*training through partnerships*" program that reaches local medical responders through a technical advisory group, a monthly newsletter covering timely local public health issues, conferences, grand rounds presentations at local hospitals, and on-site surveillance rounds. One of the most effective aspects of the program has been site-visits, which allow doctors and nurses to undergo training without spending time away from their hospitals or clinics. While Chicago's program serves as a potential model, training can also be carried out by more personnel-strapped health departments through distance learning classes and tabletop exercises, as well as by creating a clearinghouse of available information and resources that can be tapped by medical personnel involved with the issue. Medical personnel should be involved with the planning of local, state, and federal government response efforts.

5

Information and Communication

An effective response system depends in large measure upon providing the right people with the right information at the right time. Preparedness and response capabilities, therefore, will rely heavily on effective information dissemination and communication. As a result, information strategies underpin efforts to bolster the public health and medical response to bioterrorism and help to integrate various components into a genuine system. Effective communication "*mechanisms*" are comprised of human organizations using technology to share information. Both the technological and human dimensions must be addressed if requirements of communication and information dissemination are to be met.

Requirements for information and communication can be broken into two distinct, but closely connected categories. The first set of requirements is shaped by communication needs of the various government and non-governmental entities involved in bioterrorism preparedness efforts. The second set of requirements is defined by the communication and information needs during the course of responding to a bioterrorism incident itself.

Preparedness

Planning

The response planning function should be supported by two communication capabilities. The first is a *communication capability* among all the participants involved in local efforts. Different locales have organized their planning processes differently. Each, however, involves many players, and a shared frustration appears to be insuring that all those involved receive necessary information in a timely and effective manner. Local planning officials must have a mechanism for sharing their concepts for detecting and responding to *bioterrorism incidents*, assessing local response capabilities, and developing response capabilities.

The second *key communication capability* is a means through which plans and concepts can be shared among state and local jurisdictions across the nation. Few formal mechanisms or processes currently exist for local and state jurisdictions to exchange information and ideas on local preparedness and planning. The jurisdictions completing their Metropolitan Medical Response System and bioterrorism response plans, for example, need better methods of communicating and sharing ideas and concepts with colleagues in other jurisdictions. Most sharing has occurred through informal networking and previously established contacts, but the efficiencies of this system can be improved by more systematic information sharing.

Training

Bioterrorism training efforts will be best served by an effective, efficient, and low cost system for providing training materials to different communities of users. The most effective and efficient method of accomplishing this task is to exploit telecommunications and the Internet to provide tailored training.

Among the more frequently mentioned communication capabilities to support training are distance-learning capabilities, satellite broadcasting systems, and web-based learning courses. Distance learning requires the audience to have the technical capacities for participating. This means public health officers, doctors, and other care providers should have rapid and reliable Internet access in order to exploit web-based training opportunities. It also requires that satellite downlink and teleconferencing capabilities be available for satellite broadcast opportunities.

In order to exploit available training opportunities, either through distance learning technologies or by the traditional classroom techniques, information on how and when training is taking place must be made available early enough for the audience to schedule their participation. A central location or clearinghouse for providing bioterrorism training information would be an important step in identifying future training opportunities and distributing that information to relevant audiences.

Surveillance and Detection

As previously discussed, good information and effective communication are vital to *successful surveillance*. Various information suppliers and recipients must be connected to ensure effective monitoring of the health status of a population. In order to develop a national system for *health surveillance*, information linkages should be installed between providers of basic information and entities with the mandate and expertise to analyze that data. At the local level, this requires information infrastructure improvements to link the local public health agency or other monitoring entity with the various data providers, especially health care providers. It also requires improvements to connect other data providers— pharmacies, EMS systems, schools and employers, and so on—to the local public health department.

As already discussed, an improved *national surveillance* information infrastructure to integrate local systems into state systems and, ultimately, a national system should be a long-term goal. Possible methods of establishing these links are numerous. The type of link utilized would depend on the number, size, and type of care providers within a jurisdiction and should exploit previously established communications systems. Whatever type is chosen, it should balance cost-effectiveness with the need for sufficient capacity to allow continuous exchanges of surveillance information, disease reporting, and periodic communications and consultations between the health department and care providers. While it is possible to transmit this data between providers and users using other, less sophisticated systems, the slow operation times of such systems make them virtually useless in detecting bioterrorism incidents fast enough for effective intervention.

Laboratory Systems

The information and communication needs to support an effective laboratory response to bioterrorism are significant. They include extensive databases of agent characteristics, testing protocols for a range of organisms, and information on anti-microbial sensitivities of agent strains to evaluate the efficacy of treatment options. A number of laboratories exist across the country, each with a unique set of skills and capabilities—that together provide the expertise and knowledge necessary to provide sufficient support.

In order to effectively exploit available laboratory response capacity, however, a communications network is required to link public health and other clinical laboratories. Such a network would serve a number of important functions. First, it would provide a useful platform for training materials, laboratory protocols, and other forms of information from experts to clinicians. While a great deal of expertise and information resides with experts at federal institutions like the CDC and USAMRIID, an information network would allow for systematic information exchange between laboratories and laboratory clinicians, and also provide information back to the federal institutions. Second, this network would serve as a mechanism for disseminating standardized laboratory protocols and procedures. It could also provide a standard process for public health laboratories to order reagents.

Warning and Alert Systems

An important communication requirement in the bioterrorism response architecture is the ability to communicate warnings and alerts between the federal, state, and local levels and across functional areas. During a suspected or confirmed bioterrorism incident, a system is needed to provide broadcast alerts that raise awareness among those responsible for detecting additional cases and treating existing cases. Such a system should also provide information to the broader public on what types of precautions should be taken and points of contact to obtain further information or ask questions.

Possible mechanisms include broadcast fax capabilities, *listservs*, secure web pages, e-mail distribution lists, or pager gateways. To be successful, each of these systems requires contact information for all key agencies and their critical people. This contact information requires continuous updating for accuracy and relevance.

Cooperation with Law Enforcement

During suspected incidents of bioterrorism, both *epidemiologists* and *law enforcement* personnel will be conducting investigations. They will need some channel or mechanism for communicating—not just during an incident but on an ongoing basis. Such a channel can produce a better understanding of respective investigatory responsibilities and requirements between the law enforcement and epidemiological communities. From such an improved understanding can come agreed procedures for sharing information during bioterrorism investigations, a reduction in the chance of the two investigations working at cross-purposes, exchanges of best practices and new approaches to conducting investigations, as well as sharing information more generally.

Feedback Loops

Formal and informal communication channels should be available to local and state level public health and medical communities to provide federal entities with information, ideas, and critiques regarding ongoing preparedness efforts and programs. While federal entities like the DoD, DOJ, HHS, and CDC have considerable expertise and experience pertaining to CBRN weapons, counterterrorism, infectious disease control and prevention, public health practice, and other important issues, considerable expertise exists at lower levels as well. Moreover, it is at the local level that things must be made to work, and what looks good at the federal level may be seen quite differently by others. Because the HHS counterterrorism program has focused on bolstering the ability of the state and local public health and medical systems to respond to bioterrorism, feedback on how those programs are being implemented is extremely important for making the best decisions about future programmatic planning and execution. Local level input is an important evaluation tool for federal officials, both during preparation activities as well as during actual incidents.

In looking at candidate processes for this kind of needed feedback, a number of areas require particular focus. Public health officials at the local, state, and federal levels should interact and communicate as often as possible. In part, the national organizations of public health officials, like the National Association of City and County Health Officials (NACCHO) and the Association of State and Territorial Health Officials (ASTHO), fulfill this function by representing their constituencies in interactions with colleagues at CDC, HHS, and even Congress. State and local public health officials should also have opportunities to provide information, ideas, and critiques in a more direct fashion through telephone calls, e-mail, presentations at conferences and workshops, and by publishing articles and books. Importantly, CDC and HHS need to recognize and engage in these processes and exploit them as they make policy and programmatic decisions.

Response

Communication and information needs during an incident are quite different than those associated with on-going preparedness efforts.

Mass prophylaxis and medical treatment

The information and communication requirements to support the organization and implementation of a program to provide prophylaxis and therapeutics to a very large number of people are considerable and will demand effective coordination among many organizations and entities. The general public will need detailed information on the nature of the outbreak, procedures for acquiring medicines or vaccinations, time frames in which they must be obtained for maximum effectiveness, and procedures for acquiring treatment if they are sick. People directly participating in the distribution system will require information on their roles in receiving and distributing medicines and other material supplies—from the people responsible for receipt of the national pharmaceutical stockpile to those driving the delivery trucks and manning points of distribution. In addition, primary care providers need information on their responsibilities while they must provide incident coordinators with regular updates on their capabilities and requirements.

Coordinating this massive medical response requires effective communication, from the incident coordinator down to individual responders and back up. Predefined frequencies, equipment, and communication protocols shared among all local-level response entities —public health, fire, EMS, hospitals, etc—are clearly essential. In the end, each of these elements should be planned, tested, and constantly updated. A number of communication requirements are defined by the need to coordinate the logistical dimension of the medical response effort. First, responding to a bioterrorism incident requires clearly defined roles and relationships and effective communication systems for the local and on-scene public health officials, medical care providers, and the incident "*coordinator*." Importantly, all require access to and training on the use of emergency radio systems used by the public safety and emergency management agencies. The coordinator in particular requires a two-way exchange of information to assess the degree of effectiveness of certain response initiatives and make changes in the response activities.

Second, while the initial response will be a local activity, federal and national assets will arrive—some quickly, some more slowly—to support the response. Integrated communication systems will be one means to integrate federal resources into local efforts. This requires some level of standardization of communication equipment to insure interoperability between local and federal authorities. This is an important issue because those entities with the mandate to manage the response must have two-way communication with both local and federal response assets.

Third, improved inventory tracking systems are required both during an event, but also before. These systems are especially important for improving the transparency of medicine, material, and equipment stockpiles at the federal, state, and local level. Greater transparency allows supply managers to determine how much medicine and equipment is available on a regular basis before an incident. This information creates an ability to assess what is available at the local, state, and federal level, and to determine what the local responders require from national stockpiles.

In addition to tracking medicines and supplies, improved tracking systems would also be useful in managing the distribution of prophylaxis and medicines by recording who has received medicines, which medicines they have received, and when they received them. This type of system could be constructed using paper and pen. The size and arrival time of shipments to distribution points or care providers would be recorded on paper and then called or *faxed* into the central distribution point. Points of distribution could also use paper-based systems to record the name, address, social security number, and time of prophylaxis of people receiving medicines. But these systems would be slow and prone to inaccurate records. Electronic systems similar to the scanning systems used by parcel companies like UPS and FedEx could be applied to track movement of supplies and their distribution.

Fourth, it is extremely important for epidemiologists and laboratory personnel, typically assumed to be part of the detection and assessment but not response function, to remain in communication with response coordinators to provide information on how the event is progressing and how the response may have to be modified. Detecting changes in the numbers affected, their location, perhaps even in the symptoms presented by patients is a necessary aspect of assessing how well the response is meeting the event. As the event changes, the response may have to change as well. Another issue is the possibility of additional attacks. This requires the involvement and consultation of both epidemiologists and laboratories throughout the event.

Finally, these systems of communication, both people and technologies, must be used on a regular basis, either through simulations and testing or by incorporating key systems into normal operations. Regular use ensures that systems are both available and effective and also helps to ensure that the necessary people are part of the communication system, have access to the various communication technologies, and know how to use them. Without regular use, the social communication constructs will wither and become ineffective, and the technical systems may fail.

Where Are We?

Through various bioterrorism related initiatives, a number of successes have been achieved in meeting the requirements discussed above. In spite of these successes, however, more work is still required in a number of areas.

Through the *Health Alert Network* (HAN) Program, the CDC is providing grants to state and local public health departments to bolster their information technology infrastructure. This program has provided the resources necessary for localities to improve computer capabilities, establish telecommunication networks between public health departments, bolster distance learning and teleconferencing capabilities, and improve alert and warning capabilities through improved e-mail, broadcast fax, and pager systems. In addition to the grants to develop the physical infrastructure, HAN is also developing bioterrorism-related training materials and other information packages to be made available to state and local public departments.

HAN has provided an excellent first step in developing a national public health information network. But this effort needs to be followed with important next steps. First, *funding* should be extended to all 50 states and territories. To date, HAN funding has been provided to 37 states and the three largest U.S. cities. Second, HAN needs to be integrated with other public health bioterrorism networks, most notably the Laboratory Response Network (LRN). To date, little funding has been provided to the public health laboratories to improve their information infrastructure. Improved communication capabilities between laboratories and public health departments will bolster coordination of surveillance, epidemiology, laboratory assessment, and response. This requires linkages and integration between information provided through the HAN and the LRN. Third, HAN focuses on interconnecting national, state, and local public health departments through information technologies. Both the network and funding for the network stops at the local public health department. No funding is provided to link local public health departments with other local entities.

A second issue that must be addressed is the uncertain capacity of emergency response communication capabilities in many cities. Importantly, the extent to which state and local public health departments have been integrated into state and local emergency communications systems is uncertain. As mentioned previously, public health authorities must help shape disaster management plans and preparations, including effective, robust emergency communication capabilities. It is one thing to agree on a communication plan for bioterrorism response. It is another thing to make sure sufficient radios and telephones are available before an event, test the adequacy of communication procedures and hardware, and test the system to see if it can withstand increased loads and deliberate disruption attempts.

There are several opportunities for improvement. Fire departments and public safety agencies often lead the bioterrorism response planning process at the local level. While many local public safety personnel recognize the centrality of public health and medical capabilities in detecting, assessing, and responding to bioterrorism incidents, this understanding is not universal. Localities should ensure local public health officials are fully integrated into emergency communication systems by ensuring their involvement in local planning efforts and by working with them to ensure they have communication hardware compatible with public safety systems.

The necessary "*feedback loops*" do not appear to exist, at least in any systematic sense. One salient example is a consistent complaint by local officials that the federal government entities responsible for response planning do not provide them with citywide emergency response plan templates, press release templates, and hospital emergency plans, etc., that have been written in other locales. On a number of occasions local officials have said, "It's not a good use of our time and funds to reinvent the wheel when many cities before us have already written templates." While it is understandable that some locales are concerned about providing these templates to other cities for fear they may get criticized for shortcomings in their preparedness plans, it is clear that some mechanism should be put in place to facilitate communication flows from locales back to federal entities as well as between states and locales directly.

With respect to information systems to support detection and assessment, a major gap in local communication capabilities remains the link between the local public health agency and area medical care providers. Such connections are vital not only for establishing real-time surveillance and disease reporting networks, but also for developing distance learning capabilities and communications between the public health agency and care providers during an event. Even in major municipalities the physical communication infrastructure between area medical care providers and the local public health department is inadequate. Too often, the telephone remains the only method of communication between public health officials and care providers According to many local officials and representatives interviewed during the project, many doctors and nurses still do not know how to contact their local public health agency.

Lastly, federal activities related to building communication infrastructure preparedness and response have been marked by a lack of coordination and frequent disconnects. This lack of connectivity is not specific to the communication issue, but is indicative of the broader lack of coordination among various counterterrorism programs, most notably between public safety programs administered by DoD and DoJ and the public health and medically oriented programs administered by HHS and CDC. If Justice is going to manage state and local public safety preparedness programs and Health and Human Services in partnership with CDC is going to manage state and local public health and medical preparedness, then these entities must coordinate their efforts better to build communication and information infrastructure. Integrating federal programs to build the necessary infrastructure will determine how well local entities will be able to integrate their communication systems. Without this federal coordination, it is possible for DoJ to provide local fire and EMS systems with communication systems incompatible with systems provided to local health departments through CDC grants. To date, insufficient coordination has taken place at the federal level.

Key Issues and Recommendations

CDC and other federal agencies should further emphasize the need for improved infrastructure and actively work to provide state and local partners with both the necessary financial resources and the consultative expertise to build a truly national public health information network that includes traditional local public health agencies, as well as other key bioterrorism preparedness and response partners like federal and local law enforcement entities. The Bioterrorism Preparedness and Response Program Office, with the advice of the Public Health Practice Program Office, needs to have increased responsibility for making program allocation decisions for building public health information infrastructure at the state and local level. States should also be provided with consultative information and advice on the types of hardware and telecommunication systems they should acquire with grant funds and the types of software and protocols they should utilize.

Developing a new national information infrastructure for *bioterrorism preparedness* and response would be neither cost-effective nor efficient, given the number of communication and networking initiatives already underway. The keys to developing a national BT preparedness and response information infrastructure are making sure the individual components and initiatives already in train are able to meet key requirements, defining and implementing new initiatives where gaps exist, and then working to integrate the various technical communication systems into an effective network.

Based on the requirements listed above, this network can be divided into three layers. The first layer should provide a platform for the bioterrorism preparedness effort. Federal, state, and local agencies require communication technologies to move expertise from those who have it to those who need it and exchange ideas on where programs might need adjustments or changes. A single infrastructure should improve local level efforts at developing detection and response capabilities by facilitating communication between local level entities, easing regular consultation between local and national organizations, and providing a mechanism for coordinating and sharing ideas between different cities and states. It should also provide the infrastructure for efficiently and effectively delivering training materials tailored to specific audiences using distance-learning technologies. This layer should exploit the internet as much as possible to support planning, training, and information exchanges. Current internet technologies can support these activities in a way that adequately balances cost efficiency and security.

The second layer of the system would focus on supporting detection and assessment capabilities in the areas of *surveillance*, *epidemiology*, and *laboratory response*. Such an infrastructure could provide the capability for real-time data exchange between surveillance data sources and local health monitoring entities as well as between those local health monitoring entities and state and federal public health agencies. The infrastructure should also provide national, state, and local microbial laboratories with real-time communication and data exchange capabilities. This includes information exchanges, consultations, and training before an attack as well as communication between laboratories in response to an attack. This infrastructure must serve to facilitate and coordinate information exchanges and warning between surveillance entities, epidemiologists, and laboratories.

Because of the lack of highly robust security and power outages, this layer requires development of a dedicated, secure infrastructure. One locality is planning on establishing an area network between hospitals and the local public health department using a dedicated secure, microwave transmission system. Another locality is considering the use of virtual private networks, a relatively new technology combining the wiring of the Internet with vastly improved software to create highly secure wide area networks. The final layer of the infrastructure must provide reliable and robust emergency communications in order to coordinate and implement responses to incidents of bioterrorism. This means providing various local response entities with a single integrated emergency communication system that will reliably continue to operate despite the surge created during an actual incident and deliberate attempts to disable all or part of the communication infrastructure.

Due to the size of certain types of responses, the demand placed on radio bandwidth and the telephone system, and the possibility that a bioterrorism incident may be coordinated with cyber attacks on the communication infrastructure, it is vitally important that both the national and local emergency communication infrastructure is secure and highly redundant. Thus, this layer also requires a secure, dedicated communication system. Normal wireless communication such as radio pagers, radios, and cell phones could be overwhelmed and prove inadequate for use in a large-scale disaster. This could be overcome by having independent local reserve communication capacity in place before an event occurs. An emergency cellular system or reserve radio system could provide such redundancy. *Satellite communication* systems could also provide a useful reserve function because they are independent from the local communication infrastructure. Satellite systems also provide a means of long distance medical communication and consultation. Emergency response procedures could be developed with communication providers like AT&T to rapidly provide dedicated communication capabilities when normal systems are not available.

Consultations between infrastructure providers and the public health community should also focus on the development of standards for infrastructure, to include hardware and software standards and standards for information protocols. In order to ensure interoperability of their communication systems, health departments, hospitals and other primary care givers, and public safety agencies need to be contacted and consulted throughout the process of developing such standards. Consultations between government and the private sector might also prove useful in developing these standards. Achieving common standards can serve to remove barriers to information movement between communities and enable public health to mine and exploit information gathered by hospitals, clinics, and other care providers. Logical Observations Identifiers Names and Codes (LOINC) and Systemized Nomenclature of Medicine (SNOMED) are two types of code standards.

LOINC is an extensive database of synonyms and cross-mappings covering a wide range of laboratory and clinical subject areas (i.e. blood bank, microbiology, vital signs, etc). Private industry could help government understand the current state of information technology and the design systems necessary to meet requirements and work with government to put these systems into place.

Finally, federal departments and agencies must coordinate their various information infrastructure-building initiatives. Such coordination should involve the Office of Justice Programs at the Department of Justice, the National Domestic Preparedness Office at the FBI, the Bioterrorism Preparedness and Response Office and the Public Health Practice Program Office at CDC, the Office of Emergency Preparedness at the Department of Health and Human Services, the National Laboratories, and the Advanced Systems and Concepts Office at the Defense Threat Reduction Agency.

Building and sustaining capacity for communication and information sharing requires an active partnership between the federal government and its partners at the state and local level. The federal agencies, specifically Health and Human Services and the Centers for Disease Control, can provide leadership in a number of key areas.

The first important area is to ensure sustained funding and assistance to their state and local partners for the explicit purpose of bolstering information infrastructures. During the initial years of CDC's bioterrorism preparedness effort, special emphasis should be given to the HAN program to include increased funding allocations for building upon information infrastructure. During discussions with Congress, federal level public health agencies like HHS and the CDC should stress the key role played by communication and information in enabling and integrating an effective public health and medical response to bioterrorism, as well as and the current lack of information infrastructure within the nation's public health system.

CDC, in partnership with HHS, DoJ, and DoD should develop a strategy for identifying the various organizations involved with bioterrorism preparedness and response, determining their communication and information requirements, developing social constructs to facilitate communication between them, and then using various instruments of leverage to implement these structures. With such a strategy, a national communication infrastructure can be developed that supports both preparedness and response to bioterrorism. This national infrastructure should serve as the communication hardware backbone for communication and information dissemination in support of a number of areas. This strategy should be based on the current infrastructure needs of the public health and medical system. The federal government should work with state and local entities to assess their information infrastructure requirements.

CDC's urban strategy for bioterrorism preparedness must include coordination and building of communication and information processes and capabilities at the local level. Local municipalities working on bioterrorism response plans should be asked to answer the following questions in the affirmative:

1. Is the local public health agency a primary author of the bioterrorism response plan?
2. Are local public health officials trained in the incident command system?
3. Can local public health officials and representatives of local medical care givers communicate in real time with local public safety agencies, including fire, police, and emergency management? Has that capability been exercised?
4. Can the local public health department and area primary care provider communicate in a bidirectional fashion during a bioterrorism event?

CDC's Bioterrorism Preparedness and Response Office should also take the lead role in ensuring that local public health agencies and medical care providers are able to communicate and exchange information in the period preceding an event. Through the CDC's bioterrorism grant process, local level health departments need to be provided with the resources to establish real-time electronic linkages with area hospitals and other care providers. Such linkages would be established for a number of purposes including *surveillance*, *epidemiology*, *training*, *response coordination*, asset and materials tracking, and consultation. BPRP should also leverage the grants to ensure local level response entities are not only developing response plans, but also have adequate communication capabilities.

Finally, the *Bioterrorism Preparedness* and *Response Program Office* should continue to strengthen the office's information sharing and outreach activities. BPRP has undertaken several improvements to enhance the office's information sharing and outreach capabilities. These include hiring a full-time Congressional and Executive liaison, hiring a full-time constituencies liaison, and improving the amount and quality of information. While these actions represent significant improvements, the creation of a small office focused on information dissemination and outreach (including liaison personnel and the Bioterrorism webmaster) would relieve the burden placed on the staff by focusing on developing and maintaining mechanisms for answering commonly asked questions and facilitating information exchanges between BPRP and the various partners.

The purpose of this office would be two fold. First, it would provide a day-to-day point of contact within BPRP for government officials and representatives from non-governmental partners involved in bioterrorism preparedness. Second, this office would exploit telecommunications technologies—specifically the world wide web, *listservs*, newsgroups, and internet chat groups. In serving these functions, this office would facilitate BPRP's role as a information clearinghouse for bioterrorism preparedness within the nation's public health system. This would include improving and maintaining the CDC bioterrorism website to provide information on bioterrorism preparedness events—including training opportunities, workshops, and conferences—exchange ideas on developing local response systems, and even provide regular updates on the nation's health status based on incoming data from various surveillance systems.

6

ORGANIZATION AND CO-ORDINATION

Many federal departments and agencies have been mandated to work with local entities to bolster the nation's preparedness to respond to a *WMD terrorist attack*. As federal, state, and local interaction has evolved over time, it has become apparent that the initial approach to building WMD preparedness needed mid-course adjustment. Central to these adjustments has been the increased integration of the public health and medical communities into preparedness activities, largely because of the growing realization that a response to bioterrorism will largely depend on their expertise with disease outbreaks. While progress has been made, some problems in the process of building public health and medical capacity to respond to bioterrorism, as well as integrating these communities into the response system, have occurred. This is partly due to differing federal, state, and local perspectives on the issue, but is also a function of how programs were initially designed. Momentum was created at the start of this process, but it is possible to slow this momentum down and redirect it.

TOP DOWN APPROACH

The way the counterterrorism agenda has evolved has resulted in perceptions of a "*top down*" approach that in some cases causes friction among federal, state, and local entities. With respect to the health and medical dimensions of bioterrorism preparedness, the perception exists at the state and local level that federal authorities often dictate rather than facilitate bioterrorism preparedness planning. Such a view may be a function of how the CDC grants process is structured for building public health capacity. When a state health department applies for a federal bioterrorism grant thought the CDC, for example, it can apply in any or all of five focus areas established by the *Bioterrorism Preparedness* and *Response Program*, the CDC office that administers the grants. In most cases, however, states have not received funding for projects in all five focus areas. State health departments have complained, therefore, that federal authorities do not always have a good understanding of the best way to allocate this money within a particular locale. For example, often a locality will receive money for one or more focus areas, such as laboratories or improved detection and surveillance, but will not receive any money for planning. This means that they have to find their own planning money because some planning is essential to utilize the federal grant. One local health official complained that, "Effectively utilizing federal grant money for improving surveillance and IT infrastructure is impossible without planning staff who can implement these initiatives. How are we supposed to implement a surveillance system if someone from the Department of Health doesn't go out into the community and establish reporting agreements with hospital staff, doctors, pharmacies, and other providers of surveillance data?"

Although funds can sometimes be shifted from one focus area to another after the money has been awarded, this process is difficult and time consuming at both the federal and the local levels. In many cases funding specified for a single focus area would be better utilized if some flexibility existed to spread the money across multiple focus areas, should the need or opportunity arise. Some locales have suggested that increased flexibility be provided to local officials. Rather than have federal authorities decide how local entities should use grant money, local officials argue that these grants should be given in block sums and used in ways that best suit their particular situation.

Issues of Coordination

A biological agent release presents potential coordination challenges that will be difficult to address according to current planning guidelines. A major problem with response planning as it is being implemented is the bifurcation of overall command into two phases. According to current counterterrorism policy, the FBI has the "*lead agency*" responsibility for crisis management, while FEMA will be responsible for the consequence management phase of the response. Clearly, this bifurcation complicates unity of command, as half of the response will be dominated by the federal government, while the other half, although overseen by

FEMA, will rest mainly in the hands of state and local authorities. Moreover, there is no definitive point at which the response to a terrorist incident moves from the crisis to consequence management stage; in some cases, these phases may occur simultaneously, or consequence management may precede crisis management. As a result, confusion exists over which agencies will take the lead if federal assistance is requested. This determination will likely have to be made on a case-by-case basis, taking into consideration the nature of the incident, the source, the actual or potential consequences, and the capabilities available. The main concern will be to coordinate crisis management and consequence management activities in such a manner that command issues do not compromise patient care.

Local responders also harbor fears of having their authority assumed by federal officials. Many local responders have expressed concern that federal agents will try to assume command following an attack without any knowledge of or attention to local dynamics. They point out that local response agencies have a better grasp of the synergies of their city or region, know where excess supplies exist, how to get around, and whom to contact if something is needed. As the Emergency Management Coordinator of a major metropolitan area commented, "this is a local problem that will be dealt with by locals under local organization." Consequently, most responders see the proper role of federal agencies as one of assistance to and augmentation of local resources. The Federal Response Plan insists that final authority to make decisions regarding consequence management rests with the local Incident Commander. However, this view of command and control has not been clearly conveyed to local authorities, and does not address the problems inherent in the coordination of responsibilities among local responders and a federally mandated "*lead*" agency. Fear of a federal "*takeover*" may lead those in charge at the state and local levels to delay seeking federal help.

Federal agencies are currently working to clarify command and control issues through interactive exercises that test and validate policies and procedures, probe the effectiveness of response capabilities, and increase the skill level of the personnel involved. Most important, exercises allow various agencies' personnel to become familiar with each other and learn to coordinate their operating procedures. Through these exercises, response organizations have attempted to establish the mechanisms needed for coordination before federal assets arrive, as well as to educate local responders about how to use federal assets properly to augment the existing response structure. However, a GAO report underlined that domestic crisis response exercises led by federal law enforcement agencies did not include many of the state and local authorities that would be needed to respond. From the perspective of this study, there has been minimal inclusion of public health or medical personnel in many command exercises. The continued focus by federal agencies on the public safety community has only enhanced the confusion that many health personnel feel about coordination between local and federal responders.

The FBI has begun taking steps to include local and state agencies in federal drills, although staffing and budget considerations sometimes hinder their participation. Most programs have not practiced crisis and consequence management simultaneously. For a true improvement in overall response coordination, training programs and interactive exercises must be reorganized to include a broader range of responders, including public health and medical officials, and scenarios that to do not depend on a separation of crisis and consequence management.

Emergency Preparedness

Through the U.S. Public Health Service (PHS), the Department of Health and Human Services has developed four specialized National Medical Response Teams for Weapons of Mass Destruction (NMRTWMD), three of which are deployable in the event of a *biological terrorist attack*. The deployable teams are based in North Carolina, Colorado, and California, and are designed to provide medical services and assist federal or local agencies in the event of an incident involving biological or chemical agent release. Each team consists of 50 members, the majority of whom are physicians, nurses, paramedics, or other allied health care professionals. The NMRTs supplement the 24 deployable Disaster Medical Assistance Teams (DMAT) composed of professional and paraprofessional medical personnel that can provide medical support in any type of disaster. DMATs can deploy with at least 35 team members to disaster sites for a period of 72 hours to triage and provide medical care to patients. Any of these teams may help augment local public health and medical resources in the event of a bioterrorist incident, although they cannot provide the manpower that will be required in larger attacks.

The *Office of Emergency Preparedness* (OEP), located in the PHS, coordinates the federal medical management response and recovery activities for HHS in the event of catastrophe, natural or man-made. Initially, OEP developed the Metropolitan Medical Strike Teams

(MMST) because of the rapid response times required for responding to terrorist acts. MMSTs were designed to be highly trained, readily deployable, and fully equipped local response teams organized to address the effects of biological and chemical weapons on humans and to aid hospitals and other health centers with medical response issues. Each MMST would operate within a system that provides an initial, on-site response, safe patient transport to hospital emergency rooms, definitive medical and mental health care, and movement of patients to other regions, should local health care resources be insufficient to meet demand.

Today OEP's strategic plan takes a system-wide approach by developing partnerships with local jurisdictions to develop enhanced Metropolitan Medical Response Systems (MMRS) as the primary local resource for dealing with the medical consequences of a CBRN terrorist incident. The MMRS plan serves to coordinate the response of public safety, public health, and the health services sector to a CBRN terrorist incident by enhancing local capabilities, particularly in the public safety community, and by developing medical management plans that utilize the unique characteristics of each city's existing system. The goal is to develop MMRS for the 120 most populous metropolitan areas in the United States within five years.

OEP has made significant strides toward these goals since expanding the Metropolitan Medical Strike Teams (MMST) to a systems level approach in late 1995 and pilot testing the MMRS programs in Washington, D.C. and Atlanta the following year. In fiscal year 1997 the MMRS program expanded to include an additional 25 cities which began systems level planning and coordination activities, and to date MMRS programs have been initiated in over 90 cities. In addition, cities that develop certified MMRS plans are then awarded a contract to develop a bioterrorism Response Plan. A number of cities have completed their MMRS plans and begun their Bioterrorism Response Plan contracts.

One of the most important achievements of the MMRS program has been its ability to bring together response entities that in many cases had formerly been unfamiliar with one another. For example, in most cities the public health community was not accustomed to working closely with the public safety, law enforcement, or national security communities.

Although today many of these gaps have been bridged as a result of the MMRS program, significant challenges still remain. The structure of the MMRS program has some inherent shortfalls that have raised concerns among local responders. First, the MMRS targets the same 120 cities as DoD's Domestic Preparedness Program, an approach that builds response capacities in these cities but leaves many of the next largest urban centers unprepared (although DoD's Center for Domestic Preparedness has trained some smaller city and rural responders in residence). Furthermore, the MMRS program is specifically focused on activities in areas deemed "*metropolitan proper.*" For example, metropolitan Chicago, as it is officially defined, is a relatively small geographic area compared to the sprawling suburbia that is usually associated with "*Chicago.*" The MMRS system for Chicago only integrates this small area into the system, and excludes response entities located in the surrounding suburbs. This approach is problematic, especially in a bioterrorism attack when people do not present for treatment for several days or even weeks after a release. Because of the delayed onset of symptoms, many of these victims will have returned to suburbs and municipalities outside of the immediate metropolitan area, which will require some coordinated response across city boundaries.

Second, funding for the development of a Bioterrorism Response Plan normally takes the form of an appendix to the general MMRS plan and is contingent on completion of MMRS planning. By not including the Bioterrorism Response Plan as part of the MMRS planning process from the beginning, some of the health and medical requirements for bioterrorism response preparedness are not taken into consideration. As a result, locales run the risk of developing response plans and procedures that do not adequately meet the requirements of responding to a bioterrorism event. This approach has an inherent bias toward emergency response with a public safety framework and assumes that even in a bioterrorism event there is a "*crisis scene*" to which responders go. It has become increasingly apparent that there is no crisis scene in a covert bioterrorism event, and that the "*incident*" will emerge at hospital and care facilities in the area and depend on public health and medical entities as "*first responders.*"

Third, the MMRS program is largely focused on organizing medical management response capacity at the local level, but not surveillance, detection, and assessment (epidemiology and laboratory capacity) preparedness. These tasks are the responsibility of CDC's Bioterrorism Preparedness and Response Program (BPRP) Office. This may be an understandable division of responsibilities, but it does create some problems. Each office, for example, worries about the "*mission creep*" of the other into its defined domain, a worry that is somewhat justified. One example is OEP's inclusion of guidance for the MMRS Bioterrorism Annex regarding surveillance and monitoring, tasks that CDC's BPRP rightly considers its responsibility. Clearly, it is critical that the medical management response system being promoted by OEP is compatible with the awareness and assessment functions being built by BPRP. It is also important that OEP and BPRP support one another and ensure that their efforts do not work at cross purposes. Currently, there is considerable interaction between the two offices, but the working relationship does not always appear to be an easy one. It is critical that their roles and responsibilities be clearly defined and understood and that their activities remain within the boundaries of those defined functions. Senior HHS officials should ensure the integrity of each set of activities if necessary.

Finally, officials in many locales are concerned that state and local budgets will not be able to sustain planning and coordination that have been initiated by the MMRS program once the contract period is over. Questions have arisen about funding for training of new members of the response community in local MMRS plans as well as maintaining the relationships and level of cooperation that have developed between response entities. Some people fear that the results of years of hard work will begin to degrade if federal funds are not made available to sustain what has been achieved to date.

In sum, the MMRS program has made significant strides in better preparing local communities to respond to bioterrorism attacks as well as a range of medical emergencies, yet concerns remain that many gaps still exist in that system which will begin to widen if progress is not sustained.

Clash of Cultures

Bringing together response entities who previously had little interaction has improved relationships among them, but tension continues to be generated by culture clashes between communities, as well as turf wars and differing perspectives on the importance of the issues at hand. This may be most evident between the public safety and public health communities. Public safety officials often see themselves as "*action oriented*" while describing public health personnel as "*analytically oriented*". Public health sees the public safety community as performing largely a support role—security, transport, and possibly staffing—in a bioterrorism event, given that their expertise is not dealing with disease outbreaks or medical management. In some instances public health resents that the fire department has been given the lead for bioterrorism response planning. Meanwhile, fire departments see bioterrorism responsibilities as a logical extension of their HAZMAT responsibilities.

In addition to the cultural disconnect, part of the clash is a momentum problem. DoD's Domestic Preparedness Program, while incorporating biological aspects, has been largely designed around a HAZMAT template. This is in part because chemical weapons attacks resembled HAZMAT incidents, in part because the target audience of the DPP was initially the public safety community, in particular, fire departments. The DP training initiatives built on the fire departments' operational experience in responding to HAZMAT incidents. As a result, especially in the early years, some training seminars had a heavy bias toward chemical attacks, and bioterrorism tended to be underplayed. The comment of one trainer during a program that, "If you can do radiological, you can do bio" is an example of the kind of mindset to which the public health community points in arguing that biological events have not been given enough attention in light of their differences from chemical or radiological incidents.

As policy makers became increasingly concerned about bioterrorism, it became apparent that bioterrorism events—especially covert attacks—would not have scenes to which public safety personnel would rush off. The realization also grew that a public safety response to bioterrorism would not be sufficient and that the public health and medical communities had to play a key part in medical management of casualties, surveillance, detection, assessment, and response.

Today it is more widely—although not universally—understood that the public health and medical communities will have a central role to play in responding to bioterrorism. Although relationships between the public health and public safety communities continue to improve as they become more familiar with each other, some competition still exists between the two over resources and incident command and control. In many locales, the public health community feels that they were overlooked as key players in early planning efforts despite the central role they would obviously play. They resented the lion's share of federal funding going to build response capacity in fire departments and other "*first responders*" whose role in a bioterrorism event would likely be limited. Today, the public health community receives more money to build capacity, and some resistance is apparent on the part of fire departments who feel that they have to defend their stake in the issue, sustain funding levels, and maintain their importance as a player.

In other cases, certain entities that are logically part of the bioterrorism response system, particularly hospitals and private practitioners, do not see the bioterrorism issue as a significant problem. As one hospital administrator put it, "The probability of a catastrophic bioterrorist attack occurring that overwhelms the medical system is extremely low, but the probability of such an attack in this state, in this city, that overwhelms my hospital, is rapidly approaching zero. Given this probability, what am I going to concern myself with, heart disease, cancer, gunshot wounds, common infectious disease outbreaks that we see all the time, or bioterrorism which I will probably never witness?" This attitude stems partly from the constraints under which hospital administrators must operate. Both public and private hospitals are struggling to adapt to a managed care system and declining budgets which have forced them to reduce operating costs. Under these circumstances, hospital administrators have few resources to dedicate to bioterrorism issues. Furthermore, resistance stems from the for-profit oriented culture of private hospitals who see little profit incentive in the bioterrorism business.

Incident Command System

Coordination of response activities after an act of domestic terrorism is organized under the *Incident Command System* (ICS), the most widely accepted command and control model for emergency response. ICS is a management system that promotes coordination and communication between responding agencies and attempts to minimize duplication of effort. In essence, ICS creates a unified command to oversee the actions and interactions of the various organizations involved in response, and sets forth standardized procedures for managing personnel, communications, facilities, and resources. The Incident Commander is usually the senior responder of the organization with the preponderance of responsibility for the event (i.e., the police chief, fire chief, emergency medical coordinator) at the local level. However, if local assets are insufficient to respond effectively to an attack, state or federal organizations may assume the overall command role.

To date, the ICS system has served as the primary response model for weapons of mass destruction attacks; developing a unified command structure has been essential because of the number of local, state, and federal agencies involved. Responding to a bioterrorism incident requires clearly defined roles and relationships, as well as effective operating procedures for local, state, and federal public safety and public health officials and medical care providers. Most of the current programmatic efforts to build a response capacity at the local and state levels have focused on the public safety community and have been based on military or HAZMAT models. Consequently, fire, police, and emergency management agencies have taken the lead responsibility for implementing response plans. Depending on the region or city, a top official from one of these organizations has usually been designated as Incident Commander.

Because a bioterrorist event may occur covertly and unfold over an extended period of time in numerous locations, the applicability of the ICS to biological attacks is potentially problematic. A covert bioterrorist attack rarely has a "*scene*." By the time a covert attack is recognized, it is possible that victims may be dispersed throughout a city or region. With no one "*incident*" to oversee, it is unclear what role the Incident Commander would serve. To deal with this kind of BT event, it may be more appropriate to create response "*managers*" or "*coordinators*" who can assess and adjust response activities on a continuous basis, rather than asserting command of a specific, ambiguous "*scene*." The coordinator would require an exchange of information among local, state, and federal agencies involved to assess the degree of effectiveness of certain response initiatives and would make changes in the response activities as needed.

Few bioterrorism response plans have incorporated public health and medical personnel into command roles, despite their frequent description as the "*first line of defense*." To some extent, this is a result of funding decisions—because response funding was initially channeled through the public safety community, police and fire departments developed systems based on existing approaches with which they were familiar and in which they would play a lead role. According to the Chief of Communicable Disease Control at an urban public health department, "public health was really an afterthought."

While creating a command and control infrastructure will depend in large part on the individual dynamics of each community, it is important that public health and medical personnel be more fully included in the command structure. Medical personnel will play a key role in determining what resources are needed, where they will come from, and how they will be disseminated. Given that most medical personnel will be heavily involved with treatment and triage, it is unlikely they will be able to play a large role in overall coordination. Public health officials could serve as incident coordinators, at least until federal assistance arrives on scene, but only a few public health entities have been trained in the system.

Public health personnel need greater experience in working with disaster management systems, and specifically with the incident command system. This experience can be generated in two ways: first, through active education and participation in training exercises, and second, through stronger partnerships and communication with other agencies involved in bioterrorism response. Those organizations involved with disaster management, however, must seek out health personnel as partners and work to foster greater communication between the two communities. Many cities are beginning to incorporate public health officers and hospital administrators into the ICS response system, with varied levels of success. In one major metropolitan area visited during this study, a comprehensive effort was underway to include public health in developing response protocols and to brief them in the particulars of command and control.

The effort centered on monthly planning meetings attended by representatives of the public health community, hospital emergency management coordinators, fire department leaders, public safety personnel, and the head of the local emergency management agency. At the meetings, members of these different communities took part in developing the city response plan while negotiating the roles each would play in the overall response structure. As a result of the meetings, a strong dialogue was fostered between the public health community and other response entitites, and both the public health and public safety communities felt more comfortable with each other and with their respective response roles.

However, a complaint of those overseeing incident command, namely the public safety community, has been that public health and medical personnel have trouble understanding how the system works once they are brought in. In many ways, this is a result of the clash of cultures discussed previously. Most public safety communities use the ICS system on a day-to-day basis; it serves as the key response model for both fire and police departments. Public health and medical personnel, on the other hand, work in more collaborative environments where strict hierarchies and task designations are not as pervasive.

Although relationships between public health and public safety continue to improve, some competition and confusion between the two communities over incident command and control still exists. In many regions and cities, the public health community still chafes at the supporting roles it has been handed in the command structure. One official at a metropolitan public health department complained that the public safety entity charged with overseeing BT response had unwisely used funds "*to buy new trucks*" instead of shoring up medical capabilities, a comment that underlines the public health sector's frustration at its lack of authority within the response system. In most locales, the two communities are working together to resolve these issues. However, before an ICS can be truly effective, public health and medical personnel must both understand the system and be incorporated into it in a meaningful way.

Integration of the Public Health and Medical Communities

Even when significant efforts are made at the local level to integrate elements of the health and medical communities into the response system, the result is sometimes less than satisfactory. The most glaring example is the lack of involvement of the hospitals, both public and private, and primary care physicians in the bioterrorism response planning and coordinating processes. While hospital representatives often participate in planning meetings, hospital administrators and staff generally are largely ignorant of bioterrorism response issues, and administrators have been less than cooperative about considering serious engagement or integration of hospitals into the MMRS plan. For them, bioterrorism response planning is at the bottom of a long list of priorities.

A lack of consideration of the public health and medical community's roles in responding to bioterrorism is also evident at the federal level. A glaring example occurred last year when the original construction of the DoJ needs assessment survey was solely aimed at the public safety and law enforcement communities and did not contain any questions related to public health infrastructure. It was only after the public health community exerted pressure on DoJ that the survey was appended to include a section on public health and medical assets. Today, bureaucratic biases still inhibit a full integration of the public health community. Many federal departments and agencies, however, have begun to understand that the health and medical communities are partners in fighting bioterrorism. This acceptance is probably most strongly indicated by the growth of the DHHS counterterrorism budget which has made the department a significant counterterrorism player.

An often noted problem plaguing federal counterterrorism activities is the large number of departments and agencies involved. The bureaucratic maze is dizzying, and in many cases significant overlaps exist. A number of GAO reports have raised this concern, as did the Gilmore Commission Report to the President and Congress. The creation of an integrating body at the level of the Executive Office of the President that possesses executive and budgetary authority is being called for more often in recent months. An Executive Office could be extremely useful for

1. Devising a national strategy;
2. Ensuring that the various departments and agencies work together towards a strategic objective;
3. Conducting a comprehensive review of all current federal counterterrorism programs; and
4. Determining where unnecessary overlap exists and beginning the process of streamlining the bureaucracy, especially if they are granted budgetary authority.

While a national coordinator in the Executive Office of the President would greatly benefit the nation's overall counterterrorism initiative, it could also be a catalyst for integrating the public health and medical communities more thoroughly into bioterrorism response activities. The political atmosphere surrounding counterterrorism activities has traditionally been driven by the national security community, a community that is, generally speaking, not sensitive to the role that public health and medical personnel would play in responding to bioterrorism attacks. An executive body that is sensitive to the nontraditional entities that contribute to WMD preparedness could ensure the integration of the public health and medical communities in counterterrorism planning, both at the federal and local levels. Such an entity could also more clearly define the public health and medical requirements for responding to bioterrorism and more clearly distinguish between chemical, biological, radiological, nuclear, and conventional terrorism and the tools needed to address each.

Integration of State and Federal Assets

State-level Response Teams

To date, most state level response assistance has been organized through the National Guard and coordinated through the state Office of Emergency Services. In the event of a bioterrorist attack, National Guard units may be called upon by governors or federalized by the president to assist states in need. The Guard's rapid response capabilities, manpower, and ability to provide security assets may prove to be an asset in managing the response to a biological incident. Guard units are to be capable of mobilizing at their armories within 12 hours of being activated, and deployed within 24 hours of activation.

Some states' National Guard units have WMD Civil Support Teams (CST), formerly known as Rapid Assistance and Initial Detection (RAID) teams. The role of the Civil Support Team is to "assist local first responders in determining the precise nature of an attack, provide medical and technical advice, and to help pave the way for the identification of and arrival of follow-on federal military response assets." The teams are supposed to be able to deploy anywhere in their region of responsibility within four hours of notification. Each team is staffed with 22 full-time National Guard members organized into 6 functions: command, operations, administration and logistics, communication, medical, and survey. The medical unit primarily provides medical support to other CST personnel, not to victims of an attack, but can "*provide guidance*" to the incident commander on the medical implications of a WMD event and coordinate with health care facilities for follow-on support requirements. Originally, 10 teams were created—one for each of FEMA's designated geographical regions of the United States. In January 2000, Secretary of Defense William Cohen announced the creation of an additional 17 teams. DoD aims eventually to raise the number to 54, one for each state and territory, and the District of Columbia.

In designing the CST teams, Army officials stated that they tried to create a capability that would detect and identify WMD, an element missing from most local and state response units. According to these same officials, having a CST team in the National Guard gives a state governor "an asset that can be rapidly deployed in the event of an attack". However, while CST teams may prove useful in responding to a chemical attack, it is unclear whether they would be so effective in responding to a covert biological attack. One of the most useful elements the National Guard has to offer—a triage component—would take 72 hours to deploy to a site. If reacting to the clandestine release of a fast acting agent such as tularemia, the triage element of the team will be of little use, as most of the patients will already have presented themselves to hospitals or other facilities. The teams themselves have limited medical capabilities, and those they do possess are advisory, not operational. In fact, the majority of the Civil Support

Team's functions are based on on-site agent identification and decontamination, both of which have little applicability to a covert BW event.

Officials from both the FBI and FEMA have expressed concern about how the teams would fit into the federal response structure, and have further underlined the potential for conflicts between CSTs and other federal assets. Given their HAZMAT focus, it is questionable whether Civil Support Teams will provide resources different from those already available through local HAZMAT teams or other federal teams like the Chemical Biological Incident Response Force.

This does not mean that these teams do not have a role to play in consequence management. Because of their rapid mobilization abilities, National Guard units and Civil Support Teams will prove effective in a tiered response structure, working to aid first responders between the initial call for federal help and the arrival of that help. While it is unlikely that the teams will be qualified to participate in direct patient treatment or dispense medical advice, they may be critical in enforcing security or transporting supplies and equipment, and may serve as liaisons between local authorities and the Department of Defense. According to the DoD Plan for Integrating National Guard and Reserve Component Support for Response to Attacks Using *Weapons of Mass Destruction*, published in January, 1998, officials are working with partners in both the public and private sector to develop a more detailed medical response mission and task base. However, in order for these teams to truly provide the assistance they were designed to offer, they must be incorporated early on into a local community's response plan. Issues of coordination and integration must be worked out ahead of time, and exercises must be held to determine how these teams will interact with additional response entities.

Federal Response Teams

The Department of Defense's official role in consequence management is to support FEMA, the lead federal agency. The Secretary of the Army directs DoD efforts to provide a wide variety of support services, ranging from laboratory assessments to specialized teams trained and equipped to detect, neutralize, and respond to incidents involving biological agents. These specialized teams include the *Army's Technical Escort Units* (TEU) and the Navy's Defense Technical Response Group (DTRG). For biological incidents, response teams and laboratories at the U.S. Army Medical Research Institute of Infectious Diseases (USAMRIID) and the U.S. Naval Medical

Research Institute can help identify biological agents and administer appropriate antidotes and vaccines. USAMRIID can also deploy Aeromedical Isolation Teams consisting of physicians, nurses, medical assistants, and laboratory technicians who are specially trained to provide care for and transport of patients with diseases caused either by biological agents or infectious diseases requiring high containment. The Mobile Analytical Response System, a part of the Edgewood Research Development and Engineering Center, is further capable of providing assessments of biological contamination at incident sites.

The Marine Corps also established the Chemical Biological Incident Response Force (CBIRF) in July 1996 as a consequence management tool capable of rapid response to chemical and biological attacks. CBIRF consists of a 350-man self-sustaining force that can assemble within four hours to respond to an incident involving biological or chemical weapons. CBIRF's response elements include reconnaissance, detection, decontamination, medical, security, and service support. Specifically, CBIRF has the ability to provide command and control support to a civilian incident site commander, conduct detection in a contaminated environment, and insert Navy doctors into an infected zone for triage and decontamination. The force is supported by an "*electronic reachback*" group of scientific and medical consultants. With these myriad assets contained in one deployable unit, CBIRF may have the extended support structure capable of helping local communities respond to a crisis situation.

However, CBIRF has a number of inherent problems that will diminish its ability to aid local responders effectively during the critical period before federal resources arrive. Like the Civil Support teams, CBIRF has focused its activities on "*incident*" response. In fact, a majority of its capabilities, including environmental detection and decontamination, depend on an overt agent release. CBIRF has also relied primarily on HAZMAT training, and has emphasized response to a chemical or radiological disaster over a biological one. Of its 350 members, only 23 are slated for medical management, including 17 corpsmen, three physicians, one Environmental Health Officer, one physician's assistant, and one nurse. Furthermore, CBIRF does not currently have its own stock of prophylaxis for biological agents. Consequently, it is doubtful that it will be able to play a large role in aiding a community response to a biological outbreak during a period when treatment and triage will be paramount. As with the Civil Support Teams, it is possible that CBIRF can contribute in other ways to local and federal response efforts. Because it can be mobilized fairly rapidly and is independently equipped, CBIRF may be useful in enforcing security or transporting supplies and equipment. CBIRF may further serve as a communication pathway between local authorities and the Department of Defense. Although still limited, CBIRF's medical capability is more extensive than that of the Civil Support Teams, and in the event of an attack with a particularly high number of casualties, it is possible that CBIRF could be called upon to aid in patient triage and treatment.

Without careful coordination and pre-planning, the numerous state and federal teams that may arrive to respond to an event will exacerbate the confusion and friction of an already complicated response network. For the most part, federal agencies developed their assistance teams without first coordinating them with existing state and local emergency management structures. While HHS has built its response teams into already-existing local networks, DoD has built its teams at the federal level. Consequently, the majority of the teams are unfamiliar with the response mechanisms of any given locality. Moreover, many of these teams have been trained independently of other response organizations and do not know how they will coordinate or communicate their actions with these disparate agencies and groups. For example, FBI officials have expressed concerns about conflicts between Department of Defense response teams and their own units. Without a clear understanding of how these teams will operate within a multi-tiered response system, their utility is greatly diminished.

It is also important to assess the applicability of these teams in the event of a simultaneous attack on multiple cities, or the dispersion of casualties over a wide geographic area. While such scenarios admittedly are of low probability, they are nevertheless a contingency for which some planning must be done. Both CBIRF and the National Guard teams operate as small, self-contained response cells; Civil Support Teams have only 22 members, while CBIRF's medical unit is made up of just 23 marines. Because of their size, it is unlikely that they will have the manpower to respond to attacks that occur in more than one region or city. Similarly, if casualties are dispersed over a wide region, particularly across state boundaries, it is unclear how these teams would distribute their resources while remaining operational. Members of the National Guard and CBIRF have been trained to work interdependently with other members of their teams; as a result, breaking down the teams into smaller operational groups is not feasible.

In the event of a two-state outbreak, it is possible that more than one Civil Support Team could respond, especially if both states have indigenous teams. However, integrating two separate teams raises difficult coordination challenges given the already confusing nature of a geographically dispersed attack. Finally, as previously underlined, both CBIRF and the Civil Support Teams have at most three or four physicians and nurses—not enough to make a large difference in triage or treatment capabilities if they are dispersed among several different sites. It is thus doubtful that either team will be able to play a large role in aiding a community response to such an outbreak.

Key Issues and Recommendations

The initial WMD preparedness programs largely targeted the public safety community and the capabilities and experience that they acquired from responding to HAZMAT incidents. While the HAZMAT template applies in many ways to chemical and radiological incidents, bioterrorism has unique response requirements. Current and future WMD preparedness initiatives should make a conscientious effort to distinguish more clearly between biological, chemical, radiological, and nuclear terrorism, with particular attention to how the response requirements for bioterrorism differ from the others.

Federal agencies are often perceived by local officials as taking a "*top down*" approach to bioterrorism preparedness planning. The most salient examples include a lack of flexibility in how federal grants are distributed on the local level, and current federal response plans that call for command and control of a bioterrorism incident to be passed from local authorities to the FBI, and FEMA's consequence management mandate. Given their familiarity with the local geography, resources, and personnel, local authorities should play a significant role in response management. Command and control of a bioterrorism incident should be shared between federal and local entities, and capabilities should be built by recognizing the differing but complementary strengths of the two levels.

The MMRS program has targeted the most populous cities of the country but has largely neglected additional cities that may be targets as well as suburban areas which will likely be involved in bioterrorism response. Bioterrorism Response Plan contracts are awarded after a city is certified as having a MMRS plan. This approach does not allow for sufficient input of bioterrorism-related response entities from the outset. Sustaining MMRS and bioterrorism response planning after the federal contracts expire will be difficult for locales operating with small budgets. While the MMRS program is a good first step, these activities should be administered at the state level to ensure that not only "*metropolitan proper*", but the surrounding municipalities and suburbs are included in planning activities. The Bioterrorism Preparedness Plan contracts currently included as an annex to the MMRS emergency response plans should be developed at the outset. Some level of federal follow-on funding is required to sustain bioterrorism planning activities to ensure that the current level of communication and interaction between the local health and medical and public safety communities continues.

The OEP and CDC's federal preparedness initiatives operate simultaneously, but target different aspects of bioterrorism preparedness. OEP concentrates on medical management response planning and coordination; the CDC builds incident awareness and assessment tools in the public health and medical communities. Although distinct streams, they need to be integrated to ensure an effective system. HHS must develop an overall strategy at the department level that integrates these functions and ensures that they work together rather than dilute each office's respective effort through bureaucratic competition.

To date hospitals represent a significant challenge in creating a robust bioterrorism public health and medical response system, largely because of tight budgets and other health care priorities. Planning and coordination activities at all levels need to pay special attention to the challenge of integrating hospitals into the bioterrorism response system. A Task Force or Working Group should be established at both federal and state levels to identify the challenges that hospitals face in becoming integrated in the bioterrorism response system, and to devise some realistic solutions for overcoming those challenges. Federal grants for building public health and medical capacity for responding to bioterrorism should be extended to a sixth focus area aimed at hospitals.

Few bioterrorism response plans have incorporated public health and medical personnel into command roles, despite their frequent designation as the "*first line of defense*." Moreover, some competition and confusion still exists between the public safety and public health communities over incident command and control. Before an ICS can be truly effective, public health and medical personnel must both understand the system and be incorporated into it in a meaningful way. Public health representatives must be more fully integrated into the command and control infrastructure at the local level.

Finally, a major problem with response planning is the bifurcation of overall command into crisis management and consequence management phases, which both complicates unity of command and causes confusion over which agencies will take the lead if federal assistance is requested. This confusion has been exacerbated by the number of agencies and teams with potential roles in a response effort. Roles of the federal government versus the state and local government need to be examined and clarified to prevent confusion. Responders at all levels must continue to resolve intergovernmental issues, including minimizing redundancy among federal, state and local efforts and eliminating confusion at the recipient level.

7

PUBLIC-PRIVATE PARTNERSHIP

Building a strong partnership between the government and the private sector will be a vitally important element of the national bioterrorism preparedness and response effort. The private sector holds a number of unique resources and capabilities directly pertinent to bioterrorism preparedness and response. Private entities play key roles in detecting, assessing, and responding to incidents of bioterrorism, including medical treatment, provision of medicines, supplies, and vaccines, public outreach, and information technologies. The importance of the private sector in any biological terrorism response system requires the U.S. government to complete two key tasks: First, the government itself must recognize the need for a partnership with the private sector in *bioterrorism preparedness*. Without private sector involvement, the nation's ability to respond will be less than adequate. Second, the government should work actively to encourage and facilitate the private sector's involvement in the *national preparedness* effort. This begins by demonstrating to the private sector that bioterrorism is a national priority and requires its participation.

GENERAL ISSUES

Effectively building the relationship between the private and public sector in bioterrorism health and medical response efforts has several dimensions. In particular, the government must do more in the following areas to incorporate the private sector as a full partner:

Public and Private Dialogue on Common Concern

A public-private sector dialogue could take place with the private sector as a whole or on a sector-by-sector basis. Through such a dialogue, both sides can exchange ideas and recommendations, criticisms, and concerns regarding their perceived roles and responsibilities, differences in perspectives and respective motivations, and issues related to burden sharing.

To date, most discussions have been lower-level exchanges between private sector and government officials relating to implementation of specific preparedness programs. In a way, these discussions have been premature because they did not have the context of previous senior level exchanges among government and private business leaders. In one example provided by the health care industry, hospital representatives indicated they are being asked by government officials at both the federal and local levels to develop certain biological response capabilities when administrators and industry officials remain dismissive of the need for such preparedness. Today's challenge is working to develop mechanisms at which senior-level discussions can occur to foster the interest and cooperation among senior industry officials needed to facilitate progress in preparedness implementation.

Motivations and Perspectives

A natural tension is created by differences in *motivations* between the private and public sector. For most private sector entities, the driving motivation is increasing revenues. Even for non-profit entities like certain health care facilities or public radio and television, their motivation is not profit but a desire to seek new sources of financial support and secure those sources already in place. On the other hand, the government's driving motivation in bioterrorism preparedness is its mandate to promote national security.

The government, however, must also accomplish its goal in the context of increased fiscal responsibility, balanced budgets, cuts in *Medicaid* and *Medicare* and other entitlement programs, and cuts in discretionary spending. The trend has been toward shaping the government to be smaller, less intrusive, and less burdensome. This makes developing and implementing solutions based on direct government support or leveraging the government's regulatory authority especially difficult.

Cooperatively Roles and Responsibilities

An important feature of public-private dialogue must be development of a *cooperative process* to define respective roles and *responsibilities* clearly. The government's most challenging step in opening a dialogue with the private sector is the first one: convincing them that they play an important role in preparedness. Government and industry can develop sound approaches to overcoming some of the current obstacles, but before that can occur, both sides must begin using available communication mechanisms to begin an active dialogue.

Burden Sharing Issues

Cost has served as the main deterrent preventing greater involvement of the private sector in preparedness activities, especially the health care industry. This cost question and the resulting reticence have fostered tension between government and industry. At one level, government entities perceive the private sector as not willing to forgo revenues for the sake of national security. On the other hand, private sector entities perceive parts of the government as lacking understanding of the economic and market realities of their industry. They fear, in particular, a series of cascading costs that result in the loss of competitive advantage and of their ability to shape market perceptions of their particular goods or services.

Government and the private sector must develop cooperative approaches for equitably distributing the cost of preparedness and response. Some approaches that have been suggested include shifting the burden of *bioterrorism preparedness* and response to government, having the government subsidize the private sector's activity, and encouraging dual-use programs and identifying secondary benefits for bioterrorism preparedness. For example, working with the media on current bioterrorism programs provides them with information in which the general public is becoming increasing interested; selling more papers or increasing viewers could be the result.

KEY INDUSTRY SECTORS

A number of specific private industries play key roles in bioterrorism preparedness and response. Hospitals and other medical care providers must serve as the central data source for health surveillance systems and provide the core element of the national capability to provide care to victims. The print and electronic media will serve as the main interface between the government and the general public before, during, and after bioterrorism incidents. Pharmaceutical and medical supply companies will support both preparedness and response by providing the necessary medicines, vaccines, medical supplies, and technologies to provide prophylaxis and medical care. The information technology sector will provide the hardware, software, and expertise needed for a national information and communication infrastructure. If these sectors are to become full partners in the bioterrorism effort, however, government and private industry require an improved understanding of the major difficulties of increasing their involvement and new, cooperative approaches to overcoming these challenges must be identified.

Hospitals and Medical Care Providers

As has been mentioned on several occasions in this report, hospitals, clinics, physician offices, and even individual physicians have a two-part role in bioterrorism preparedness and response. First, they provide a sentinel in the nation's *bioterrorism surveillance* systems. Since they are likely to be the first professionals to examine *bioterrorism victims*, they are a key source of information that must be integrated into infectious disease reporting and syndromic surveillance systems. Second, hospitals, clinics, and private practices form the core of the nation's medical treatment capacity.

On a nation-wide basis, hospitals have been only partially involved in *bioterrorism planning* and preparedness and must be better integrated into the national *bioterrorism preparedness* effort. To date their involvement can best be described as marginal but improving. Some cities have developed bioterrorism response plans with little or no input from hospital representatives. When hospitals have been involved with planning at the local level, they usually have been represented by less-than-senior officials from the hospital or the local hospital industry association. With some exceptions, few senior executives from local hospitals or the local hospital association have engaged in bioterrorism planning. In general, they have paid little attention to bioterrorism issues.

Some hospitals have begun to develop CBRN, and more specifically bioterrorism annexes to their individual disaster response plans. Some localities have also been able to integrate hospitals successfully into local response planning efforts, mainly through the municipality's individual bioterrorism planning contracts with the Office of Emergency Preparedness at HHS. The degree of integration has depended on local dynamics and personalities.

Little if any progress has been made in building hospital capacity to detect, assess, or provide treatment related to bioterrorism events. Training provided through the Nunn-Lugar-Domenici program was designed to improve the ability of physicians to recognize and treat the victims of *biological attack*. The program, however, has been plagued by poor hospital and physician participation, mainly due to a combination of tight schedules and the absence of marketing by the training providers. A small number of hospitals have been involved with some of the various syndromic surveillance projects currently underway. But even those systems have ceased operations once external financial support was removed. For example, the syndromic surveillance system installed for last year's meeting of the World Trade Organization in Seattle was completely dismantled when CDC discontinued support following conclusion of the meeting. Many of the hospitals who have participated in these experiments, such as the University of New Mexico Medical Center, are either university medical centers or large not-for-profit institutions. Not surprisingly, these institutions emphasize research and the public good. Finally, there has been no progress in improving hospital capacity to treat high numbers of bioterrorism victims. In fact, that capacity continues to shrink as the number of available hospital beds and the associated staffing and infrastructure declines in most major U.S. cities.

Why has integrating hospitals and care providers been so difficult? The answer is cost. Most of what the hospitals have accomplished in bioterrorism preparedness, namely, the development of hospital-specific and local area response plans, have cost hospitals little in the way of financial resources or time. To make meaningful progress from this point forward, serious differences between the hospital industry and the government on respective roles and responsibilities and the financial burdens related to them will have to be addressed.

Hospital representatives argue that hospitals and medical systems operate within a completely different economic structure than existed as little as 5 or 10 years ago. This new situation has been produced by such factors as growth in managed care and health maintenance organizations created by the desire among consumers for reduced health care costs. This reduced economic margin has been further squeezed by the political drive for balanced budgets, which has been achieved in part through cuts in Medicaid and Medicare payments to hospitals and private physicians. In response to these shifts, hospitals have sought improved efficiencies. They have reduced the frequency of hospital stays and increased outpatient care. Within urban centers, smaller hospitals have either closed or joined with bigger hospitals to create large hospital networks. In addition, HMOs and managed care organizations have encouraged hospitals and doctors to reduce the frequency of expensive tests and procedures, including laboratory tests.

This desire for improved economic efficiencies has worked synergistically with an increase in the level of competitiveness between

HMOs and insurance companies, between hospitals and care providers, and between physicians. In part, cost saving measures foster competitive advantages that are used to attract new patients. This includes not only reducing costs incurred by patients, but also reinvesting savings derived through cost reduction measures to provide for improvements in the facility's quality of care. In this way, a hospital can invest in a new piece of state-of-the-art technology or build a new treatment center and then use it to attract new patients.

How does this dual dynamic of increased efficiencies within the health care industry and increased competition affect hospital preparedness for bioterrorism? Quite simply, eliminating excess capacity within the health care system directly counters the perceived need to maintain some "*surge*" capacity within the health care system in the event of a bioterrorism incident. The basic objective for which most health systems are striving is to create as closely as possible a one-to-one relationship between the available health care services and the normal demand for those services. The closer the industry comes to achieving that objective, both the excess treatment capacity existing within the nation's health care system and any surplus financial resources available for bioterrorism preparedness diminish.

Increased competition between medical care providers further reduces the involvement in bioterrorism preparedness. In some cases, increased competition between care providers makes it more difficult for them to work cooperatively. In one major metropolitan area, for example, the two major hospital networks have waged an intense, often bitter, and personal competition that has not only spilled over into the city's media but has been pursued in the corridors of political power in the state capital. While these barriers might be lowered during the response to an actual incident of bioterrorism, cooperation in planning, capacity building, training, and surveillance activities is hampered.

Hospitals have also expressed some trepidation regarding bioterrorism-related systems that will provide increased information about hospital operations, for example improved surveillance systems. They argue that competitors might use information from these systems to critique their operations. It might also reduce the appeal of their institution to potential customers. In addition, any excess resources are probably going to be used to improve their standard of care rather than to prepare for an event that is unlikely, has little bearing on their daily business, and generates few revenues. Finally, competition makes it difficult for government officials, at either the federal or local level, to approach hospitals as a single entity with which they could deal more effectively than with many smaller ones.

How can this impasse between government, hospitals, and medical care providers be resolved? First, the government must do much better in communicating to the hospital industry that bioterrorism preparedness is a national priority and that hospitals play a central role. This is not simply a matter of providing the hospitals with additional information. Some senior leaders within the hospital industry already know bioterrorism is a priority. What is needed is an expenditure of political capital to help gain increased cooperation from these and other leaders of the medical care industry. One idea for a first step, both as a means of demonstrating political commitment and fostering an improved dialogue, is a national summit on the medical dimensions of bioterrorism preparedness. In order to demonstrate the importance of this issue, such a summit should include senior representatives from the executive branch, including the Secretary of Health and Human Services and the Attorney General, representatives from Congress, and senior representatives from the health care industry. This last group of participants should include the President of the American Hospital Association, CEOs from local hospital associations and major medical centers, and CEOs of the leading national medical insurance companies. Such a meeting would be an opportunity for senior leaders from both the executive and legislative branches and senior representatives from the hospital and medical care industries to discuss their objectives, exchange their perspectives and concerns, and begin developing agreed approaches.

One of the key objectives of such a meeting must be agreement on what is expected of hospitals and other local medical care providers in both detecting and responding to a bioterrorism event. Agreeing to their appropriate role and responsibilities is an important step in defining necessary capabilities and developing programs to achieve objectives.

At a minimum hospitals and local care providers should provide a level and amount of care agreed with government authorities responsible for bioterrorism response. A tiered approach to medical treatment might be best. Such an approach would require local hospitals and treatment facilities to treat a certain level of casualties, above which state or federal assistance will be necessary. Reflecting previous sections of the paper, the hospital systems of most major metropolitan areas are capable of quickly absorbing approximately 100-200 additional patients at any single time. A *bioterrorism attack* producing 300 to 500 casualties is quite possible. Based on these two figures, a key question that must be addressed by the government and the hospitals is to what degree *can* and *should* the figure specifying the number of patients to be treated be increased. Clearly additional state and federal resources will be needed to treat casualty numbers higher than 500. But how should the range between 200 and 500 be handled, especially given the time required for additional resources to arrive on scene?

A number of solutions have been suggested to bolster the current shortcomings in hospital response capabilities. One is for the federal government to subsidize, perhaps through some type of grant program, bioterrorism preparedness activities of hospitals and care facilities. But such a program would be very expensive and could quickly "*break the bank*". A closely related solution is for the government to support *bioterrorism preparedness* in a more indirect fashion. One suggestion is linking Medicaid and Medicare payments to progress in building detection and response capacity. Such a program might provide an incentive to hospitals if the additional payments associated with preparedness are above current levels. If not, hospitals are likely to see such a strategy as another unfunded mandate.

Another approach is to exploit the government's regulatory and oversight responsibilities to "*encourage*" preparedness for bioterrorism. A frequently mentioned possibility is to change the hospital accreditation process to include requirements for developing certain capabilities or conducting certain preparedness activities before accreditation is approved. This approach might force hospitals and care providers to undertake preparedness activities or develop certain capabilities, but they would do so in a very reluctant and resentful fashion if there is no funding to support these requirements. Because the costs of meeting these additional requirements are likely to be passed on to the consumer, this approach is unlikely to receive support either from the general public or from Congress, let alone from the hospitals themselves.

A third approach is for the government to reduce as much of the cost incurred by hospitals as possible. This means the government spends its available resources to provide hospitals with preparedness tools without directly providing the hospitals with additional financial resources. For example, hospitals would be given the equipment and software to incorporate their hospital into a local surveillance system.

Hospitals could also be provided with additional beds, medicines, and equipment that could be kept in reserve for bioterrorism or other disasters. This approach is a two-edged sword. A key argument in favour is that it relies upon the hospital as little as possible to undertake certain actions. On the other hand, some argue that directly providing hospitals with the additional resources needed for these activities, like installing the telecommunications equipment or purchasing additional medicines and equipment, allows them to do so more efficiently and with better results than if they were executed by government agencies.

The last solution, paraphrasing a senior representative from the national hospital industry association, is doing nothing, especially in attempting to bolster hospitals' capacity to respond to mass casualty situations. Their argument is that because current economic forces are strongly allied against preparedness, any increase in excess treatment capacity would be expensive and provide only marginal improvements. Hospitals have dealt with disaster situations and have protocols and procedures already in place. They will do their best to creatively utilize available resources until assistance arrives.

In the end, no single approach will provide an adequate solution to developing a true partnership between the government and the medical care industry. It must be some combination of all of them. But, it must be a combination that is cost effective, agreeable to both sides, and based upon a common vision.

Print and Electronic Media

A second key sector with which the government should build a partnership is the print and *electronic media*. Communication with the public has been a cornerstone of the practice of public health. It must also be a cornerstone of bioterrorism preparedness and response.

Media outlets are likely to play an important role by acting as the main interlocutor between the government and the general public. Both during and before an incident, these outlets serve as the main channel by which the general public receives most of its information regarding terrorism.

During a bioterrorism event, the public will be clamoring for information. The media will fulfill that demand, regardless of the quality or the accuracy of the information provided. The government, therefore, must work with the media to provide critical information to the public. This material should be designed to provide timely and accurate information regarding the nature of the incident and the response. Public communication can also serve not only to calm the public's fears and concerns, but to enable incident response by providing information on which measures should be taken by people to protect themselves, where they can find prophylaxis or medical treatment, etc. Government officials have recognized communication's role in response and have made considerable progress in developing media relations strategies, creating protocols and formal procedures detailing who has responsibility for public information during a bioterrorism incident, and formulating the types of messages and information that should be provided.

In addition to crisis communications, the media provides the main source of information for the public on two issues. First, how much of a problem does the government perceive bioterrorism to be? Second, if this is such a problem or threat, what is the government doing to prevent it and prepare for such an attack? These are important questions because the general public's reaction to a bioterrorism incident will be determined as much by information and perceptions formed before the event as by the information provided to them during an event. The government must develop strategies for working with the media to help shape pre-incident public perceptions.

Creating a partnership with the media is challenging for a number of reasons. One is the sheer number and variety of media entities. There are a number of different media outlets, each with different perspectives, designed for different types of audiences, and possessing a different degree of proficiency and professionalism. Attempting to predict how information might be reported to the public in an environment of such diversity is virtually impossible.

Also, the media is motivated by profit. But unlike the other sectors, the supply and demand relationship between the media and the government is reversed. The government is not a consumer. Buying more of the media's services does not fulfill the government's objective. On the contrary, the media relies on the government as a source of much of its information, especially on defense and national security issues. It is because government is such an important source of information that government can find means of leveraging the media.

Another difficulty, but one in which the government can make some headway through a stronger partnership, is the general lack of understanding of bioterrorism issues within the journalism community. Most journalists are not well versed in matters pertaining to biological weapons. Few are knowledgeable in the areas of public health or medical care. If journalists are not well informed about these issues, it will be harder for them to ask the right questions; the more difficult it will be to evaluate the quality and sources of information; the risk of omitting key dimensions of issues that provide needed balance will be created; and the possibility of fostering panic in the event of a bioterrorism crisis will be higher. Journalists do not just need information they can report to the public, they also need a firm grounding in the more technical aspects of both the problem and the response.

What are some of the next steps government entities should take to bolster this partnership? First, both the content and the process of crisis communications in the event of a *bioterrorism attack* must be refined. While there has been progress in preparing the communication dimension of the response to bioterrorism, further work needs to be completed in a few areas. First, public health officers should be better incorporated into procedures for conducting public information activities during an incident. While the FBI and FEMA have been designated to lead the formation of joint information centers at the local scene and in Washington, representatives from the local public health department, the CDC, and HHS must be active participants within these centers. Second, these procedures need to be exercised on a regular basis to ensure their effectiveness. These exercises or simulations should include actual members of the press when possible. Third, the national media strategy for CBRN terrorism incidents and other disasters needs to be better integrated into the federal response plan. This will ensure effective dissemination of the media strategy and allow state and local officials to develop their own approaches for media relations.

An additional step is improving cooperation with the media for pre-incident communications. Recognizing the bureaucratic and political hurdles that will have to be overcome, HHS and CDC should strive to become the recognized governmental "authority" regarding medical and health issues associated with bioterrorism preparedness and response. They must take a more active role in developing strong relationships with the media to better inform them on the technical aspects of public health practice and biological terrorism. This begins with recognition of the media's role in communicating with the public before incidents. It entails providing reliable streams of information to the media on both the nature of the bioterrorism problem and the work to prevent, prepare, and respond. It means establishing reliable mechanisms for communicating with the media. Some examples include:

1. Providing improved information on the HHS and CDC webpages to both the media, but also the general public, keeping in mind the role of the internet in communicating directly with the public;
2. Making senior HHS and CDC officials available for interviews and news programs; and
3. Establishing programs to educate journalists and other media on issues relating to bioterrorism, public health practice, current preparedness programs. This might be accomplished through more formal mechanisms like seminars or workshops. This also might be accomplished through special sections of webpages.

Pharmaceutical and Medical Supply Industry

Another key private sector partner is the pharmaceutical and medical supply industry. These companies are being asked to provide pharmaceuticals, vaccines, medical supplies, and medical technologies.

Both pharmaceutical and medical supply companies will be involved with supplying the standing stockpiles and in establishing the vendor managed inventories. Given the number and size of the push packages, it will take time to produce sufficient quantities to compile the packages while also meeting regular demand for these drugs and materials. In certain cases, the CDC has purchased the entire available quantity of certain drugs in order to compile the first packages as rapidly as possible.

CDC and HHS will have to work closely with industry to develop a sound, efficient, and economical approach to developing the vendor managed inventories. One approach is to have a company, either the pharmaceutical company supplying the specific material or a third party, rotate a certain amount of excess medicines or equipment into a cache of supplies available for bioterrorism and then rotate it back into regular circulation after a certain period of time. The other approach is to pay the producing company to produce excess goods to ensure they are available for bioterrorism response.

The relationship between the government and the drug and supply companies appears to be reasonably cooperative. Pharmaceutical manufacturers are actively working with the government to develop both the standing stockpiles and the vendor managed inventories because it is in their interest—they are being compensated for the goods and services. Pharmaceutical manufacturers and medical supply companies are not being asked to donate their materials to supply the standing stockpiles. They are not being mandated to produce excess capacity even though there is no demand for that additional material. The government is directly paying those companies for their goods and services. Because of this, the government's relationship with these companies will remain more cooperative than its relationship with the medical care industry.

As has been discussed elsewhere in the paper, consideration is being given to the use of normal pharmaceutical distribution systems to provide medicines and prophylaxis in response to a bioterrorism event. This includes national drug stores chains, for example CVS and Walgreens, and increasingly discount department store chains like Wal-Mart. It is not clear that the stores themselves, their parent companies, or the pharmacists and technicians manning them have been consulted about the concept. Their input and reaction to these plans could prove useful in providing some evaluation and means of refinement.

Another area in which improvements are needed in the relationship between government and the pharmaceutical and medical supply industry is in research and development. One specific piece of this problem is a need for greater cooperation in working through the regulatory and approval process, for both new and existing drugs and equipment.

Many existing antibiotics have not been approved for use in treating many of the diseases produced by biological weapons. One example was Bayer's recent application with the *Food and Drug Administration* (FDA) to add treating inhalational anthrax to the list of indicated uses for an antibiotic it produces. That application was the first time a company had applied for FDA approval for a medicine to be specifically approved for treating biological casualties.

Another specific area for improvement is working with and supporting industry research and development projects in improved laboratory diagnostic technologies. Government needs to actively scan the environment to identify promising technologies being developed in the private sector and then nurture those most promising technologies.

A dual challenge is the number of governmental and private sector entities involved in this area, both directly and in a supporting capacity. The list includes the Department of Energy through the national laboratories, the DoD, including the Defense Threat Reduction Agency, HHS, and DoJ. While it would be impossible to provide a single department or agency with the oversight authority for diagnostic research and development, it is possible and important to develop methods for government agencies to share information and ideas.

Information Technology and Telecommunication

This report has argued strongly that building improved information and communication infrastructure is a key to a number of functional capabilities including detection, assessment, and response. The private sector's role should not only be providing the hardware and software necessary to build the national public health information infrastructure, but also sharing their expertise and advice. This includes information on what technologies are available and advice on how to meet the requirements and challenges of assembling this national infrastructure.

Currently, there is no formal mechanism or process for developing a strong partnership between government officials charged with building bioterrorism preparedness and response capacity and representatives from the IT and telecommunications industries. Interaction between these entities has taken place on an ad hoc basis. Most of what has occurred at both the federal and local levels is a process in which the government actor develops a set of IT or telecommunication requirements, identifies a range of companies who could help meet that need, and then chooses a company to provide that good or service. This includes a local public health department using grant money to purchase a set of desktop computers from Dell or leasing high-speed internet access from AT&T. It also includes CDC grants to support the work of various university research centers in surveillance technologies and improved information security projects.

A good example of the ad hoc nature of the relationship between information technologists and public health officials is the recent conference sponsored by the CDC and others on the public health informatics and improvements in the practice of public health. Almost every one of the scheduled panelists and keynote speakers were members of the public health community. It is surprising that a national conference whose objective was a discussion of how information technology can be used to improve the practice of public health did not include input from the information technology sector. While one must not draw conclusions or generalizations from a single conference agenda, it does provide a demonstration of the need for a better partnership between these two communities.

There are a number of factors contributing to this disconnect. One is a lack of mutual understanding among members of the two communities. Given the lack of support and resources available to the public health community until the bioterrorism grant program began, most public health practitioners have little professional exposure to recent improvements in computers, software applications, and telecommunications. On the other side, because the nation's public health system spent so little on information infrastructure improvements, it did not provide the industry with a potential market and the industry paid it little attention.

This situation is changing with the bioterrorism grants, but the need to strengthen dialogue between these communities remains. Government is fearful of directly approaching industry for fear of appearing biased toward a small subset of companies or segments of the industry. This is complicated by the many government entities and offices involved with bioterrorism preparedness and the myriad of companies and subsectors within the IT/telecommunication industry.

One way to circumvent this problem is to establish a single point of contact within HHS and CDC to work with industry to build the necessary infrastructure. The best office to serve this liaison function is the Public Health Practice Program Office at CDC given its program management responsibilities for the Health Alert Network (HAN) program. Once provided with this authority, this office should work with the various national IT and telecom industry organizations on a regular basis. Through these organizations, this office can obtain information on the latest technology development, advice on its strategy for information infrastructure building, and solutions for unforeseen challenges.

8

Conclusions and Recommendations

This part offers conclusions and recommendations based on the assessment of the bioterrorism threat and its relationship to the function and organization of preparedness and response efforts. In addition to the specific recommendations related to each of the functional areas, this discussion formulates a series of general recommendations on the HHS's and CDC's bioterrorism preparedness program based on how the nature of the threat shapes each function in an integrated bioterrorism detection, assessment, and response system.

For a number of reasons, including technical difficulties and motivational issues, a catastrophic bioterrorism event is not the most likely contingency U.S. officials and the American people will confront. The number of technical pathways available for achieving a catastrophic bioterrorism incident is limited.

The technical pathways for producing a low to mid-range bioterrorism incident, however, are more numerous, less technically challenging, and fit better within the motivations and constraints of more traditional concepts of terrorism. At the top of the pyramid rests the narrow set of high-consequence, low-probability bioterrorism attacks. Moving down the pyramid, the likelihood of attack increases, the severity of consequences decreases, and the number of technical pathways increases.

This threat analysis shapes the nature of the public health and medical response at a number of key points. The first issue is which segment of the pyramid is the basis for HHS and CDC planning and

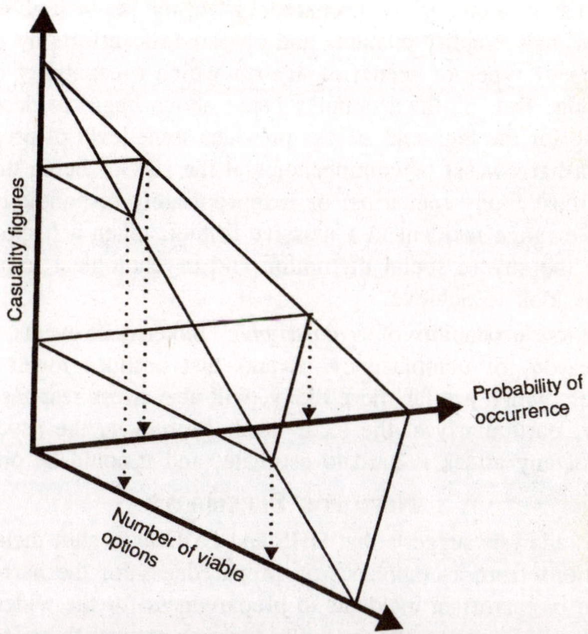

Fig. 8.1. Graphic representation of the bioterrorism threat.

preparedness. Today, the answer seems to be the top section in which the driving factor is the potential of some agents to create catastrophic casualties even though such scenarios are less probable than other types of incidents. It is assumed that preparing for the high-end attacks provides a capability to respond to the middle and low range attacks. But in certain areas, this assumption does not necessarily hold true. Examples include:

1. Providing doctors and nurses with only the training to recognize and treat the list of top three or four agents defined by their casualty potential;
2. Conducting training, and providing protocols and reagents for a limited set of threat agents to laboratories;
3. Developing the National Pharmaceutical Stockpile based on the treatment and prophylaxis requirements for a large-scale attack using the most lethal agents, including large expenditures of resources on stockpiling large quantities of smallpox vaccine; and
4. Drafting local-area response plans with a focus on massive response capability with little attention provided to responding to low or middle range attacks.

Focusing planning and preparedness on the set of high-end attack scenarios may simplify planning and preparedness efforts by narrowing the range of types of scenarios against which a capability should be developing. But, as the examples listed above begin to demonstrate, preparing for the high-end attacks provides some level of preparedness against a narrow set of contingencies at the risk of being unprepared for the most likely scenarios, or inappropriately responding to a low or middle range incident in a massive fashion. Such a response could produce the severe social disruption and psychological impact many terrorists look to achieve.

The low probability of "*catastrophic*" bioterrorist events, however, is no reason for complacency. Events that produce lower levels of casualties, which are far more likely, will also stress response systems severely, particularly at the local level. Moreover, the psychological impact of any attack is hard to estimate, and it could be profound.

Need for Flexibility

This analysis suggests that HHS and CDC must shift their planning assumptions from an emphasis on preparedness for the narrow set of high-end bioterrorism incidents to preparedness for the wider array of low and middle-range attacks while hedging against the possibility of a high-end attack. This shift in emphasis entails improving the nation's public health and medical system in such a way as to promote robust awareness and assessment tools as well as flexibility within the response system. *Robust awareness* capabilities will increase the likelihood of early detection; effective assessment tools allow for proper characterization of the event; and flexibility gives the system the ability to react to incidents according to their actual nature.

Emphasizing flexibility imposes the need to alter planning and programmatic activities in a number of areas. Greater emphasis, for example, should be placed on developing response systems that are flexible and scalable according to the nature of the agent utilized and the number of people affected. Scalable response capability provides the ability to tailor the type and size of response to the type and size of attack. Importantly, increased flexibility and scalability allows the response to change over time as the event unfolds.

Improving flexibility and scalability requires execution of a number of specific planning and preparedness initiatives. Local and federal response plans should take a tiered approach that links a range of casualty figures with certain actions. Specific response capabilities should also be constructed along the basis of this tiered approach.

Local response capabilities should be bolstered to be capable of responding to a certain level of casualties with a combination of regular treatment capabilities and the establishment of secondary treatment mechanisms when regular capabilities become overwhelmed. Flexibility and scalability should also be built into state and federal assistance capabilities for those incidents that overwhelm local capacity require additional assistance.

Increasing flexibility increases the demand for effective detection and assessment tools. Such robust tools facilitate early and effective intervention. Early detection and intervention decreases the burden placed on response capabilities by increasing the effectiveness of prophylaxis while simultaneously decreasing treatment requirements. Robust assessment tools provide the ability to tailor the response to the incident by identifying the agent utilized and the group of people who are likely to have been affected by the incident. Without these tools, it is impossible to assess the nature of a bioterrorism incident and impossible to calibrate the response to the attack. In situations in which detection and assessment capabilities are weak, all bioterrorism incidents are likely to be treated as high consequence incidents if they are detected at all to eliminate the possibility of some potential victims having not been provided with appropriate care.

Promoting flexibility and scalability will enhance the ability to deal with tensions inherent in the current system between the need to initiate treatment and prophylaxis as quickly as possible and the need to know the nature and extent of an attack before mobilizing a massive response. Thresholds need to be built into the bioterrorism response system to avoid a massive response to a limited, localized incident, especially given that the most likely bioterrorist contingencies are likely to produce casualty levels that do not require mass prophylaxis or treatment. Because a smaller-scale bioterrorism attack may be indistinguishable from a large-scale attack early on, however, giving priority to assessment tools is essential to determining the scope of a bioterrorism attack to guide a response that is proportional. Without these tools, officials will be prone in an atmosphere of uncertainty to initiate mass prophylaxis just to be on safe side.

A three-part response system might be contemplated to achieve flexibility and scalability. The first inclination of a suspicious outbreak should trigger an *initial response phase* and should alert hospitals and physicians and other response personnel, require doctors to take culture samples, seek laboratory diagnosis, and notify the appropriate federal, state, and local authorities. It should also mobilize all available assessment tools, including federal assessment assets, to characterize the nature of the attack and identify available medical resources. A *mobilization response* may be needed when larger numbers (approaching 100 or more) of patients present, or when awareness and assessment tools indicate that an attack was fairly substantial. At this point, medical resources may need to be transported to care facilities that are receiving the bulk of patients and limited prophylaxis and treatment options may be exercised in localized areas where the attack is suspected. A *large-scale response* should be initiated when it becomes apparent that the attack is widespread. Considering the current nature of the bioterrorism threat, staggered response thresholds are necessary to ensure that the system does not overreact to what is most likely to be a lower-impact attack.

Another example of improving flexibility and scalability is the design of the National Pharmaceutical Stockpile. The eight push packages are uniform in size, contents, and design. In lower-consequence, higher-probability incidents, the whole push package will be deployed, but it is unlikely that everything, or even most things in it will be needed. The resulting waste is not only expensive but could leave the country open to additional attacks. One approach would be to make the individual packages more modular, allowing them to be tailored to the type of incident, but this may increase deployment times to unacceptable levels. The other approach is to maintain uniformity among the packages, but further subdivide them into a larger number of smaller packages. This approach could increase the scalability of the amount of medicines and equipment deployed to an incident while decreasing transit time.

Importance of Information and Communication

Flexibility depends in large measure upon providing the right people with the right information at the right time. A *robust information* infrastructure underpins all of the components of an effective response system. Surveillance, epidemiology, and laboratory capacity depend on information infrastructure both in terms of capacity building—training, networking, sharing ideas and lessons learned, and development and exchange of procedural guidelines—and day-to-day execution. Coordinating the providers, materials, and recipients during the response to a bioterrorism incident requires robust information and communication infrastructure. Importantly, integrating detection, assessment, and response components into a system depends on developing the necessary social and technological information infrastructure to provide accurate information in a timely manner. Tightening the integration between the detection, assessment, and response will increase the system's capability to detect and assess bioterrorism incidents and then calibrate the response according the assessment.

Value of Public-Private Partnerships

Accomplishing many of these objectives will require cooperation between the public and private sectors. There are key preparedness activities in which the private sector should play a role, but other preparedness activities should not burden the private sector, especially those that are only relevant in the event of a massive response to a large-scale attack. At present, the threat of a large-scale attack is low, and asking the private sector to assist in preparing massive distribution plans for medications or to maintain unnecessary surge capacities for this contingency is unreasonable.

On the other hand, there are key preparedness activities from which the participation of the private sector would greatly benefit. Surveillance is one area in which the private sector should become more involved. Health Maintenance Organizations should be encouraged to permit physicians to request laboratory culture analyses on a more routine basis, but HMO's cannot be expected to pay for hospitals to maintain surge capacities to absorb casualties from a large-scale *bioterrorist attack*. Likewise, private laboratories and hospitals, work places, pharmacies, etc. have a wealth of data to provide a surveillance system, and the more data sources that are integrated into the surveillance system, the better public health awareness will be. Given that surveillance is critical for providing the overarching response system with awareness, private sector participation in surveilling should be encouraged over participation in response measures that will only apply in a mass casualty attack.

It is these types of measures, the kinds that are flexible and relevant for dealing with the range of bioterrorist contingencies as well as natural outbreaks, that must be emphasized when building preparedness, at least initially. Having a massive capability to respond to a *bioterrorist attack* is not as useful at the present time as having a less robust response capability but good awareness and assessment tools that can detect an outbreak early, characterize it, and guide the response system effectively.

The time frame over which preparedness efforts are made is important to keep in mind. Not everything can be done immediately.

The key question is what is given priority today and, as improvements in key sectors are made, what shifts in priorities can be contemplated. In essence, emphasis must be placed at the outset on building the "*front-end*" of the bioterrorism response system. As those capabilities are enhanced, efforts can then begin to focus more intensively on other capabilities, such as treatment requirements.

Achieving a robust health and medical response capability will require the successful exploitation of all available information and tools. One item in this regard is the DoJ needs assessment. The data provided by the assessment is extremely comprehensive and could be very valuable as a tool for state public health departments to identify gaps in public health and medical preparedness and direct resources to their most efficient possible use. In addition, the data should be used as the basis for establishing more concrete cooperative agreements between public and private sector entities to aid one another in responding to a bioterrorist attack.

At the federal level, data from the assessments should be a used not only as a tool for determining the best allocation of resources to build bioterrorism preparedness, but also to raise awareness about the degree to which the nation's public health system has been degraded. Given a growing interest in public health on Capitol Hill, in particular the Frist-Kennedy sponsored Public Health Threats and Emergencies Act of 2000, the DoJ survey may give lawmakers some ammunition to reinvigorate public health capacity across the board. Therefore, it is important that the public health community, primarily HHS or CDC, have a central role in analyzing the public health and medical data compiled by the survey to ensure its accurate and credible interpretation.

Having identified the public health and medical requirements for responding to bioterrorism, HHS and CDC must elaborate a viable strategy - especially an "*urban strategy*"—for building public health and medical capacities for meeting the bioterrorism challenge. Given the nature of today's threat, a bioterrorist attack is likely to be a limited event for which local authorities will have primary operational responsibilities. Therefore, a strategy should take a "*bottom up*" approach that recognizes that the federal role in responding to a bioterrorist attack will depend on the severity of the attack, and for this reason the delineation between local, state, and federal responsibilities should be clear. The strategy should, above all, articulate how priorities and programs will be integrated into a holistic system in support of public health and tie capacity building to a timeline for achieving these objectives.

Recommendation

Surveillance

1. The first step toward the creation of a national system would be the development of a national strategy for building such a system. The strategy would examine the feasibility, determine the requirements, and design a multi-year program for creating the system.
2. Surveillance systems should establish and integrate automated disease reporting systems, syndromic surveillance systems, and automated data reporting systems from non-traditional partners.
3. CDC must devise a program for developing a national health surveillance system to provide early warning of bioterrorism incidents. A national system would integrate federal, state, and local public health departments, health care providers, and non-traditional surveillance partners such as local pharmacies, emergency medical services, and the veterinary community.
4. Mechanisms should be established to provide the necessary surveillance information without compromising proprietary or confidential patient information. An important element of the solution is enforcement of federal regulations for patient data confidentiality. Another is development of technological solutions for parsing data to compile general and statistical information without association with specific patients, customers, or businesses.
5. Local providers of surveillance information, including health care providers, should not be expected to use their own resources to develop the required communication infrastructure.
6. Developing a national health surveillance system to detect bioterrorism incidents requires the establishment of electronic data networks between local public health departments and local area health care providers.
7. CDC should establish a separate surveillance grant program and work with Congress to ensure adequate funds are available to build the necessary information infrastructure.
8. A national research and development program focused on improving surveillance technologies should be initiated.

Epidemiology

1. Thresholds for triggering particular responses should be defined to avoid unnecessary "hair trigger" responses. The first inclination of a suspicious outbreak should trigger an *initial response phase—*

alert hospitals and physicians, require doctors to take culture samples, seek laboratory diagnosis, and notify the appropriate federal, state, and local authorities. *Large-scale mobilization* of the response system should require that a second threshold be crossed, for example, laboratory identification of the etiologic agent representing an imminent public health threat or the accumulation of surveillance data that indicates such measures are necessary.

2. Local departments of health need funds to make use of, and integrate, information technologies that can be used to collect, deposit, analyze, and share surveillance and epidemiological data from a central location in the department of health.
3. The labour-intensive nature of epidemiology requires that more funding be provided to state departments of health to hire additional epidemiological staff. This should be a priority focus area for building assessment tools that can make the response more focused and efficient. In rural states, this capacity should be built at the state level. In mixed urban and rural states, urban centers should maintain a robust epidemiological capacity to deal with incidents in that city, but efforts must be balanced with state efforts to develop a state-wide capability.
4. Developing better disease surveillance systems bolstering epidemiological staff in state health departments to manage surveillance functions are critical.
5. The CDC should emphasize a wider range of bioterrorism agents than those that currently receive most of the attention. Greater awareness of the range of bioterrorism agents should be better conveyed to epidemiologists.

Laboratory Requirements

1. Physicians must be encouraged to take cultures and request laboratory analyses on a more routine basis to ensure that something unusual is not underway, especially if patients are presenting in large numbers or with flu-like symptoms out of flu season.
2. State laboratories should also bolster their ability to test for microbial sensitivity and determine whether a particular medication will be effective against the given agent.
3. The LRN must expand its network of Level A laboratories and better integrate food, water, and veterinary laboratories to ensure that diagnostic capabilities for the range of bioterrorism agents are available.

4. Funding is needed to renovate or redesign laboratory floor plans to ensure the best use of space and to accommodate additional equipment and personnel.
5. The CDC should continue to provide funding through the federal grants process to build advanced laboratory capacity at the state level.
6. Training for laboratory technicians is needed to expand their awareness of the range of potential bioterrorism agents.
7. Level B and C laboratories need to continue to upgrade their capabilities, including increasing the range of potential bioterrorism agents that they are capable of positively identifying, so as to reduce their dependence on the CDC laboratories.
8. Laboratory communication and information infrastructure should be bolstered.
9. The CDC's Rapid Response and Advanced Technology laboratory (RRAT) should continue to expand its technical capacity for rapidly diagnosing critical agents as well as a broad range of potential bioterrorism agents that may be used in an attack.
10. Laboratory technicians at all levels, particularly in Level A laboratories, should receive awareness training and proficiency screening for issues related to bioterrorism.
11. Technology-based training is continuously needed.

Medical Management

1. Localities should be provided with the resources needed to develop an independent first-tier prophylaxis capacity within local medical care providers, either through mutual aid agreements or regional buy-ins, to allow for a comprehensive response in the 48 hours before federal aid arrives.
2. Improved evaluation methods, including the development of computer simulations, must be developed to assess the adequacy of local prophylaxis and treatment plans.
3. Localities should develop prophylaxis and treatment plans that are phased or broken into escalatory segments.
4. Local plans for prophylaxis should recognize and account for additional state and federal assets that will be made available by planning for how these assets will be utilized.
5. A pre-incident plan for where triage will take place needs to be in place before an event. A public information strategy should be devised in advance of an attack that will provide clear and accurate

information about when treatment is required and where it should be received.

6. To ensure efficient use of local resources, a tracking system should be set up to track the movement and use of medical supplies during a bioterrorism response.
7. Arrangements for counseling patients should be made to reduce panic and confusion at triage points and to ensure order.
8. Some thought might be given to providing certain segments of the population with pre-event prophylaxis.
9. Additional planning is needed to determine how the state and federal government can provide additional manpower in support of prophylaxis and treatment as a hedge against large-scale bioterrorism incidents. Given the size of its available manpower base and its logistical capabilities, the Department of Defense should lead this effort.
10. Agreement must be reached in advance about who can make triage decisions in the event of a bioterrorist attack, and the medical and legal ramifications of these decisions need to be considered.
11. As a hedge against a possible smallpox incident, the current supplies of vaccine should be readied for a rapid, mass prophylaxis program and a surge vaccine production capability should be established.

Training and Education

1. Efforts must be made to attract medical personnel to training sessions. Greater emphasis should be placed on flexible training sessions and the exploitation of electronic and multimedia training techniques to accommodate the schedules of health care practitioners. A good first step is making DP training materials available through the internet.
2. Medical personnel should be involved with the planning of local, state, and federal government response efforts.
3. Properly training medical, public health, and emergency personnel is essential to a comprehensive detection, assessment, and response framework.
4. The Domestic Preparedness Program should place a greater focus on health and medical response issues, and training should be adapted from HAZMAT criteria to focus more closely on procedures dealing specifically with biological weapons response, including agent and outbreak recognition and treatment measures. Training should focus on "*big picture*" response, incorporating

integrated response issues, communication, surveillance, and reporting.

Information and Communication

1. During the initial years of CDC's bioterrorism preparedness effort, special emphasis should be provided to the HAN program to include increased funding allocations for building upon information infrastructure.
2. The keys to developing a national BT preparedness and response information infrastructure are making sure the individual components and initiatives already in train are able to meet key requirements, defining and implementing new initiatives where gaps exist, and then working to integrate the various technical communication systems into an effective network.
3. The Bioterrorism Preparedness and Response Program Office should establish an information sharing and outreach branch within the office.
4. CDC and other federal agencies should further emphasize the need for improved information infrastructure and actively work to provide state and local partners with both the necessary financial resources and the consultative expertise to build a truly national public health information network that includes traditional local public health agencies, as well as other key bioterrorism preparedness and response partners like federal and local law enforcement entities.
5. Federal departments and agencies must coordinate their various information infrastructure-building initiatives to ensure the communication systems they are supporting are integrated and interoperable.
6. In order to ensure interoperability of their communication systems, health departments, hospitals and other primary care givers, and public safety agencies need to be contacted and consulted throughout the process of developing such standards.

Federal, State and Local Preparedness and Response

1. Given their familiarity with the local geography, resources, and personnel, local authorities should play a significant role in response management. Command and control of a bioterrorism incident should be shared between federal and local entities, and capabilities should be built by recognizing the differing strengths of the two levels.
2. Roles of the federal government versus the state and local government need to be examined and clarified to prevent confusion.

Responders at all levels must continue to resolve intergovernmental issues, including minimizing redundancy among federal, state and local efforts and eliminating confusion at the recipient level.

3. Planning and coordination activities at all levels need to pay special attention to the challenge of integrating hospitals into the bioterrorism response system. A federal Task Force or Working Group should be established to identify the challenges that hospitals face in becoming integrated in the bioterrorism response system, and to devise some realistic solutions for overcoming those challenges. Federal grants for building public health and medical capacity for responding to bioterrorism should be extended to a sixth focus area aimed at hospitals.
4. Current and future WMD preparedness initiatives should make a conscientious effort to distinguish more clearly between chemical, biological, radiological, and nuclear terrorism, with particular attention to how the response requirements for bioterrorism differ from the others.
5. Public health must be more fully integrated into the command and control infrastructure at the local level.
6. Bioterrorism planning related activities should be administered at the state level to ensure that not only "*metropolitan proper*", but the surrounding municipalities and suburbs are included in planning activities. The Bioterorism Preparedness Plan contracts currently included as an annex to the MMRS emergency response plans should be developed at the outset. Some level of federal follow-on funding is required to sustain bioterrorism planning activities to ensure that the current level of communication and interaction between the local health and medical and public safety communities continues.

Public-Private Partnership

1. Through the Health Alert Network Program, CDC should work more closely with the information technology sector to build public health information infrastructure and exploit information technology to improve bioterrorism preparedness and the practice of public health more broadly.
2. Because the media will serve as the main interface between the government and the public before, during, and after bioterrorism incidents, a media strategy for bioterrorism and other disasters must be integrated into counterterrorism efforts.

3. The health care industry is an especially important private sector partner in bioterrorism preparedness. As such, federal government officials need to focus on integrating the health care sector into bioterrorism efforts. One idea for a first step, both as a means of demonstrating political commitment and fostering an improved dialogue, is a national summit on the medical dimensions of bioterrorism preparedness.
4. Government must work with the private sector to ensure they become a full partner in the bioterrorism preparedness activities. The sectors of greatest importance are the health care industry, the print and electronic media, the pharmaceutical industry, and the information technology sector.
5. HHS and CDC should strive to become the recognized governmental "authority" regarding medical and health issues associated with BT, preparedness, and response. They must take a more active role in developing strong relationships with the media to better inform them on the technical aspects of public health practice and biological terrorism.

Centers for Disease Control and Prevention

1. Senior leadership at Health and Human Services needs to better coordinate CDC's Bioterrorism Preparedness and Response Initiative with the Office of Emergency Preparedness' disaster preparedness initiatives.
2. CDC planning assumptions should shift from the narrow set of low probability, high consequence events to the array of more likely middle and low consequence incidents while maintaining a hedge against high-consequence incidents.
3. BPRP should develop and implement a strategic plan to educate lawmakers about the importance of both BT issues and public health more broadly to ensure that efforts that are currently underway will be sustained financially into the future.
4. For each component of the bioterrorism detection, assessment and response system, CDC must clearly define the operational capability requirements the respective component should be able to meet.
5. The Bioterrorism Preparedness and Response program Office should be elevated to the level of the Office of the Director at CDC and be provided with budgetary authority over CDC's bioterrorism preparedness initiative. This move will provide BPRP with the necessary leverage to manage the direction, integrate, and, when

necessary, adjust public health and medical bioterrorism programs at the CDC.

6. BPRP should be serving an information "*clearinghouse*" function and embark on a concerted outreach and education program that is aimed at building critical constituencies for BT preparedness.
7. In its programs, BPRP must place greater emphasis on developing the "*front-end*" of the system—surveillance, epidemiology, and laboratory response—to ensure the creation of a robust ability to both detect and assess suspected bioterrorism incidents.
8. CDC must develop an "*urban strategy*" for supporting the organization of local-level partners—public health departments, public safety organizations, medical care providers, and non-traditional partners—into county and municipal systems for bioterrorism detection, assessment, and response.

9

BIOTERRORISM EDUCATION

Biological agents were used as weapons in North America as early as the 18th century, when British forces distributed smallpox-tainted blankets to indigenous people during the French and Indian War. The potential for modern-day use of biological agents as weapons was made evident during the fall of 2001, when letters containing anthrax were disseminated by use of the automated distribution system of the U.S. Postal Service. As a consequence of these events and the World Trade Center disaster, billions of dollars have been spent to reduce the threat of terrorism in the United States.

The U.S. public health workforce is ill prepared to meet the challenges posed by bioterrorism, as Senator Joseph Lieberman pointed out in a letter to Health and Human Services Secretary Tommy Thompson cited by NewsMax.com. The bioterrorism preparedness knowledge gap is partly due to a general lack of availability of scientifically and medically relevant curriculum material developed for practicing public health and medical professionals, groups that are in greatest need of this information. Since 1998, federal initiatives have resulted in the establishment of Public Health Training Centers across the country, as well as Academic Centers for Public Health Preparedness (A-CPHP), as partnerships among academic institutions, public health agencies, and community organizations. There is no longer any doubt that the public health workforce and infrastructure are among the most important components of the earliest phases of response to bioterrorism.

Prior to the events of September 2001, only a few graduate programs had introduced courses to teach medical, public health, and government professionals about the comprehensive defense required against biological weapons and bioterrorism. These included full-semester courses offered by the F. Edward Hebert School of Medicine of the Uniformed Services University of the Health Sciences (since 1996); the University of California, Los Angeles, School of Public Health (since 2000); and the University of Connecticut Graduate Program in Public Health (UConn MPH Program), located at the University of Connecticut Health Center (UCHC) (since 2001).

UConn's Bioterrorism Prepardness Course

Since 2001, the UConn MPH Program, which is structured as an evening program for working professionals, has offered a comprehensive semester course in bioterrorism preparedness to the Connecticut public health workforce. The course uses curriculum and teaching methods that have been highly popular with students, and have stimulated a high degree of scholarship on their part. The overall course goal is to train future public health leaders to cope with the multiple crises likely in a bioterrorism event. A range of instructors, including representatives of the Centers for *Disease Control and Prevention* (CDC) and the U.S. Army Medical Research Institute of Infectious Diseases (USAMRIID), present basic concepts of bioterrorism preparedness.

Distance Learning

Use of distance learning methods has been a hallmark of this course since its inception. Class size at the primary class location at UCHC has ranged from 20 to 30 students, supplemented by live telecasts to as many as three additional class locations throughout Connecticut. Total graduate student enrollment for the first three years consisted of 20 students in 2001, 40 in 2002, and 25 in 2003. Guest lectures are regularly videotaped, with the videotapes placed in the main campus library for viewing and additional copies available for borrowing by students. The ability to telecast guest speakers has proved invaluable due to the prominence of some of the speakers and the uncertainty of New England weather during the winter months, which can interfere with travel to this evening class. Class lecture materials are made available through a UCHC website that students enrolled in the course can access.

Interdisciplinary Learning

An elective course in the UConn MPH curriculum, the course is open to others as well, and class size is not limited. Attendees have included municipal health directors and their staff members, epidemiologists, physicians, sanitarians, hospital and public health nurses, pharmacists, medical residency program directors, laboratory directors, and military Reserve and National Guard personnel. Full-time medical, public health, and other biomedical science graduate students have enrolled as well. This diverse student group promotes interdisciplinary learning. Individual lectures, especially those by visiting lecturers, are publicized in advance, and are attended by university faculty and staff and members of the local community. Local municipal and district health directors and their staff have been encouraged to attend, and some have done so. The UConn MPH Program currently offers no other bioterrorism-specific courses, but pertinent seminars and lectures are presented frequently at UCHC and announced to the university and public health communities.

Local Resources

Locally available resources are heavily utilized in the curriculum of this course. Personnel from the regional office of the Federal Bureau of Investigation and the Connecticut State Police lecture about law enforcement and public health interactions, including the similarities and differences between law enforcement and epidemiologic investigations. *Infectious disease*, *toxicology*, and *emergency medicine* experts from nearby Hartford and Stamford hospitals teach infectious disease, toxin and chemical agent detection, patient diagnosis and treatment, and triage methods. Experts from the Connecticut Department of Public Health (CDPH) and CDC's pharmaceutical Strategic National Stockpile (SNS) have presented up-to-date information on pharmaceutical stockpile deployment and use.

The knowledge and experiences gained in the Connecticut anthrax case and the subsequent discovery and mitigation of anthrax spores in a Connecticut postal facility in 2001–2002 were described by an occupational physician working for the U.S. Postal Service and the State Epidemiologist. Representatives of the state public health laboratory and the nearby federal Plum Island Animal Disease Center have discussed their roles in bioterrorism preparedness and detection. Personnel from the local Metropolitan Medical Response System, the U.S. Public Health Service (USPHS), the state's Disaster Medical Assistance Team, and the Connecticut and Massachusetts National Guard Weapons of Mass Destruction Civil Support teams have presented the responsibilities and functions of their organizations.

Guest Speakers

We have been able to attract national subject-matter experts as course contributors, including Ken Alibek, former deputy director of the Soviet Union's biological weapons program and co-author of *Biohazard*; Giandomenico Picco, former Under Secretary General of the United Nations, international hostage negotiator, and author of *A Man Without a Gun*; U.S. Representative Christopher Shays; John Marr of the Virginia Department of Health, author of *The Eleventh Plague*; Laurie Garrett, author of *The Coming Plague* and *Betrayal of Trust* ; David Huxsoll, then Director of the Plum Island Animal Disease Center; Ronald Berger, Arnold Kaufmann, Martin Meltzer, Stephen Reissman, Timothy Uyeki, and Mitchell Wolfe from CDC; David Jarrett (now Director of the U.S. Armed Forces Radiobiological Research Institute), Mark Kortepeter, and Ross Pastel from USAMRIID; and Mohamed Mughal from the U.S. Army Soldier and Biological Chemical Command (SBCCOM).

Enhanced Learning Modules

This course was designed two years prior to the development of bioterrorism core competencies for the A-CPHP. However, our course anticipated most of the A-CPHP core competencies. Our lecture modules may also suggest some potential future additions to the core competency list, such as health economics, distribution of the SNS, agricultural and zoonotic pathogens, and interactions between law enforcement and public health workers.

As subject matter experts, guest lecturers have been asked by the course instructors to assist in determining course content and related learning objectives. Many innovative lectures have subsequently been delivered in this course. For example, the lecture on principles of medical management of biological casualties is one designed for military clinicians by USAMRIID physicians. Students were introduced to concepts of treatment for nonspecific initial symptoms resulting from exposure to Class A biological agents by the infectious disease division chair of the Department of Medicine at Hartford Hospital. This was then reinforced by a lecture presenting the algorithm for empirical patient care in the absence of a definitive diagnosis developed by USAMRIID physicians.

The lecture on the epidemiology of diseases of bioterrorism was made pertinent to Connecticut clinicians and public health officials through the use of Connecticut examples, including the human inhalational anthrax case of 2001 and the tularemia index case of the Martha's Vineyard outbreak of 2000. Similarly, occupational health perspectives on processing and distribution of the U.S. mail were discussed in connection with the Connecticut anthrax mailing case by occupational health and postal service officials involved in the protection of U.S. postal workers in Connecticut.

The health risks and economics of preparing for a bioterrorism event were introduced by a CDC health economist and then reinforced through the students' use of CDC software and mathematical models for influenza and smallpox outbreak simulations, available on the Internet. Lectures on the development and use of biological weapons have been updated with new information, e.g., recent research on the spread of smallpox in colonial America and information on various state-sponsored biological weapons programs, including the extensive Japanese effort during World War II. Lectures by former bioweapons scientist Ken Alibek brought these topics to life.

An example of emerging crosscutting challenges now facing public health officials and clinicians is the composition and deployment of the SNS. This was explored and demonstrated in our course by federal and state participants who have actually utilized this resource. New research areas related to bioterrorism have been regularly folded into the course curriculum. One example is the potential psychological impact of the use of biological weapons and bioterrorism, as examined by a research psychologist, Ross Pastel, convener of an international conference on this topic. Finally, greatly adding to the students' enthusiasm for this course are book signings at the conclusion of classes offered by authors (e.g., Ken Alibek, Laurie Garrett, John Marr, and Giandomenico Picco). These classes have proved to be especially popular, and have often been standing room only.

Tabletop Modeling as an Instructional Tool

Students learn to integrate the new material in a real-world context midway through the course with an assignment using a tabletop exercise. A tabletop bioterrorism response scenario was conducted at the Connecticut Fire Academy in Windsor Locks, CT, in 2001 and 2003. This facility includes a ping-pong table-size model of a hypothetical city, "Peterboro," with 1:87 scale-size model buildings, vehicles, and associated equipment.

In the hypothetical scenario, Peterboro's population of 14,593 is spread over 43 square miles, with two fire stations (three fire engines and ladder, command, utility, rescue, and ambulance vehicles, all staffed by fire and EMS personnel); a police department (three cars available per shift, with off-duty officers subject to call); and a small community hospital with a 10-bed emergency department. Altogether, 40 buildings are represented on the tabletop, located on six main highways. A railroad spur is located in the northern section of the town.

Students with appropriate experience participated in the tabletop exercise, while others acted as observers. Participants included first responders at the federal level (representatives of the USPHS, the FBI, the Federal Emergency Management Agency, Connecticut and Massachusetts National Guard Weapons of Mass Destruction Civil Support Teams, and the U.S. Army SBCCOM); the state level (the State Police bomb squad, the Department of Environmental Protection hazardous materials [hazmat] team, and staff of the Office of Emergency Management); and the local level (police, fire, and EMS personnel; local health officers; physicians; nurses). Players participating in the tabletop exercise at the Fire Academy were identified by reflective vests clearly marking their role, e.g., Fire Department, Police Department, EMS. The exercise assessed the participants' ability to create and adhere to an Incident Command System (ICS) or Hospital Emergency Incident Command System (HEICS) disaster response model within the context of a fire or hazmat incident combined with a bioterrorism event involving a level A biological agent.

The exercise commenced with the participants introducing themselves, followed by a general situation briefing to set the groundwork for the scenario. This briefing explained the layout and logistics of the community of Peterboro and the resources available to fire, police, EMS, hospital, and associated personnel. During the course of the exercise, participants were handed timed situation cards, which were read aloud. Each participant then decided upon an appropriate response to the situation, and whether other participants needed to be included in the decision-making process. The exercise lasted about 60 to 90 minutes, and was followed by at least 60 minutes of group discussion and analysis of the response by participants. The tabletop exercise served as a training tool to promote a coordinated community and state response to a bioterrorism event. The students wrote a brief synopsis of their interpretation of the tabletop exercise's events, aiding integration of knowledge gained in the course.

Redesign of Examinations and Term Papers

Additional course requirements have included in-class and take-home comprehensive examinations, as well as a term paper on a subject dealing with biodefense. Guest lecturers are asked to contribute to examinations by providing essay questions. The term paper requirement has proved to be a popular tool for enhancing students' writing skills, with the offer that superior papers are forwarded to the appropriate course lecturer for review. One term paper requirement has been to design a bioterrorism attack or defense scenario. These theoretical exercises have contributed to the development of novel bioterrorism security planning. For example, one student with knowledge of the building maintenance industry described how a terrorist attack could be carried out by someone culturing a category A biological agent and then placing it in automatic deodorant sprayers commonly found in restrooms in public buildings. Another student described how certain events present opportune targets when appropriate security precautions are lacking, e.g., the annual maritime Fleet Week held in New York City, San Diego, and San Francisco. Convincing term papers addressing novel threats, scenarios, or biodefense measures are forwarded with the permission of the student to interested parties at universities or federal or state biodefense agencies.

Another term paper requirement has been for students to work with a local health agency to assist in developing a framework for a comprehensive local bioterrorism plan based on four core elements: surveillance, disease control, communication, and coordination. This requirement forces the students to confront many of the real-world issues involved in such planning, including scale of response, local vs. regional control over resources, inter-agency rivalries, and all-hazards vs. biological agent-specific planning. This requires multiple interactions between students and local health directors or their representatives and various stakeholder agencies involved in a community disaster plan. Several of the plans thus developed have become models for bioterrorism planning for local communities throughout the state.

Student Evaluations

The course instructors review the end-of-semester student evaluations provided by the UConn MPH Program as a tool to improve the course curriculum and teaching methods. The course evaluation form uses a five-point scale ("*very high*," "*high*," "*average*," "*low*," and "*very low*"). Ninety-two percent of the raters checked "*very high*" or "*high*" for course topics, as did 94% of the raters for the educational content of the lectures. Class discussions (69%) and exercises (68%) did not fare as well, but during those two years in which a tabletop exercise was included (2001 and 2003), the latter score rose appreciably (to 84%). Examinations were less well rated (54%), but take-home finals in 2001 and 2003 were rated higher (70%) than the in-class final in 2002 (33%). The course term paper appeared to be well received; 80% of the ratings were "*very high*" or "*high.*" The level of scholarship of instruction (87%) and level of interest/stimulation (84%) were also rated favourably.

Students also provide written course comments to the UConn MPH Program. These comments have been highly favourable, praising the instructors and guest lecturers as well as the nature and amount of material learned in this course and requesting that the UConn MPH Program continue to offer this course. Comments on the class tabletop exercise have been very favourable. On the other hand, since this course has a final examination (either in-class or take-home) and the term paper is due at the end of the semester, students have complained about the timing of these requirements. Suggestions to alleviate this problem have included the use of a mid-semester examination or earlier graded assignments. The tabletop exercise offered in 2001 and 2003 was held midway through the semester, and students were graded on a two-page written description of their interpretation of the events.

There have also been complaints about technical problems with the quality of two-way video links between the main site at UCHC and the satellite campus sites. Students have stated that they would prefer to have the instructor and lecturer with them at the main campus site whenever possible. The presence of a teaching assistant at all sites greatly assisted with student participation and with technical difficulties during telecasts. Student comments have also pointed to the need to avoid repetitive information as much as possible. This unavoidably occurred during 2002, in the aftermath of the intense focus on anthrax cases during the fall of 2001, including a Connecticut case, and the subsequent discovery of anthrax spore contamination of a Connecticut postal facility. We have also learned from student comments that it is especially useful when course instructors elucidate the connections between aspects of the public health response to bioterrorism, such as the SNS, public health laboratories, the psychology and epidemiology of bioterrorism, and law enforcement initiatives. The use of tabletop modeling has proved invaluable in this regard, as have lectures by the course instructors integrating these aspects of bioterrorism preparedness.

Development of Enhanced Public Health Competencies

The A-CPHP is a network of 21 accredited schools of public health partnering with state and local health departments. The key bioterrorism core content areas initially developed for training public health professionals by A-CPHP in 2002 included characteristics of biological agents classes A, B, and C associated with bioterrorism; clinical manifestations; surveillance and epidemiology; laboratory systems; health risk communication and media relations; the psychosocial impact of bioterrorism; worker safety issues; information technology; and public health law.

The Institute of Medicine (IOM) has recently delineated needed improvements in academia to meet the requirements of educating public health professionals. This IOM report also recommends that academic institutions increase integrated learning opportunities for students in public health and other related health science professions, including multidisciplinary and interdisciplinary education. Many of the education and training needs for the public health workforce identified in the IOM report from an earlier study funded by the Health Resources and Services Administration (HRSA) are also addressed in our course curriculum. The IOM/HRSA core public health training needs, as identified in the report, are information systems and computer skills, technical writing and presentation skills, research and policy development skills, management and administrative skills, grantsmanship, public relations, transition skills, and leadership skills. The UConn MPH Program course has also met many of the curriculum goals of the HRSA requirements for funding Public Health Training Centers, including: (*i*) use distance learning technology and other new educational approaches to provide basic and specialized public health education; (*ii*) improve public health providers' ability to make improved and informed public health decisions based on relevant data and information; (*iii*) develop field-based educational opportunities for students in traditional on-campus graduate public health programs; (*iv*) develop new curricula for public health practitioners on emerging public health issues; and (*v*) train lay workers from local boards of health and community health offices.

Students have been taught by example the successful methods used for planning and management of state and national bioterrorism programs. Students have been able to develop their competencies through case studies presented in class and through written assignments and exams. The ability to interact with state and national policy makers has helped to raise the level of the students' comprehension and utilization of the material presented in lectures. Promotion of creative problem-solving by students through work in interdisciplinary teams has occurred during the tabletop exercise. The overall course goal to advance the ability of future public health leaders to deal with the multiple crises involved in a bioterrorism event has been met in a manner that has helped the students become enthusiastic about their place in the public health partnership for defense against bioterrorism.

Conclusion

We have developed a comprehensive curriculum using innovative materials and methods designed to engage public health professionals in a didactic experience. This approach has proven itself. It involves the successful integration of academic contributions from local leaders who will be potential responders in the emerging preparedness community with the experiences of national policy makers. Training the public health workforce to standards of competency for bioterrorism preparedness requires extensive and constantly changing efforts to reflect the evolving responsibilities of public health practice.

10

Bioterrorism Education for Medical Students

The events of September 11, 2001, the following month's anthrax outbreaks, and the reinstitution of *smallpox vaccinations* have called dramatic attention to the need for physicians to be prepared for the health consequences of the use of weapons of mass destruction (WMD). WMD include biologic, chemical, physical (i.e., explosive), and radiological agents. Polls have shown that the general public prefers to turn to their doctors for guidance on how to protect themselves and their families in case of public health emergencies, such as a bioterrorism attack. In order to meet the expectations of their patients and of their communities, physicians must not only become familiar with rare clinical syndromes and exotic offending agents but must also develop an understanding of their roles in the public health systems' preparedness and response to the use of WMD.

Since the autumn of 2001, considerable effort has been given to assess the capacities of the systems and individuals that are expected to prevent, detect, and respond to terror incidents involving WMD. Public health agencies academic health centers, public health workers, and specific physician specialists in practice have been the focus of activities to identify competencies that help to assure their readiness. Medical schools have also responded by integrating WMD-related topics into their curricula; but no guidance has existed regarding the content and the teaching methods that would be most appropriate for medical students. The Association of American Medical Colleges (AAMC) convened a multi-disciplinary group of experts to share their insights about the learning objectives and educational experiences that they would recommend. The group included representatives with expertise in medical, nursing, and public health education, as well as experts in WMD preparedness, from schools of medicine, nursing, and public health, the Centers for Disease Control and Prevention (CDC), and the Uniformed Services University of the Health Sciences (USUHS). They were specifically tasked to respond to two questions:

1. What should medical students learn about bioterrorism (learning objectives)?
2. What kind of educational experiences would allow students to achieve those learning objectives?

The expert panel broadened the scope of their discussion beyond bioterrorism to include other potential WMD. Their deliberations identified medical student competencies that should prepare students to identify and to respond specifically to WMD incidents. The panel agreed that an integral component of the curriculum should focus on physicians' interactions with the public health system in order to help facilitate effective and coordinated medical and public health responses to WMD, as well as to more common threats to health, including chronic and infectious diseases, injuries, and substance abuse. Panelists acknowledged that better coordination between medicine and public health would improve the management of public health challenges ranging from food-borne illnesses to natural disasters to emerging infectious diseases such as Severe Acute Respiratory Syndrome and West Nile Virus. They recognized that in the absence of WMD incidents, conventional public health threats help "drill" the coordinated systems that are central to an effective medical and public health response in the event of a WMD incident. Panelists also concluded that because the science associated with WMD-related topics is evolving, medical students should adopt a life-long learning perspective with regard to this subject.

Background

Many of the subjects in a WMD curriculum are part of traditional medical school teaching. Pathophysiology, toxicology, infectious diseases, emergency preparedness/disaster response, biostatistics, and epidemiology introduce concepts and topics that are the foundation for information more specific to WMD preparedness and response. Building upon these familiar concepts should help to assure that medical school graduates are armed with the necessary knowledge and skills to become competent and prepared physicians who will practice effectively in a transformed societal and clinical environment, where the theoretical potential of a WMD event has become a real possibility. Depending on the characteristics of a WMD event, physicians may play critical roles in identifying, responding to, and recovering from the WMD.

Physicians may be the first to recognize the use of a WMD, particularly in the case of a covert (unannounced) release of a biologic agent. Unusual clinical presentations or clusters of cases, particularly in vulnerable populations such as the very young, very old, and the immunocompromised, should raise suspicion. Physicians will also need to routinely consider the possibility of WMD in their differential diagnoses of more typical clinical presentations because many of the early signs and symptoms of exposure to biologic WMD mimic common viral syndromes. Clinicians' abilities to efficiently analyze signs, symptoms, and basic diagnostic tests that lessen or rule out the possibility of a WMD will also be critical. Once the possibility of a WMD event is raised, physicians must know how to elicit critical data from patients, how to record these data, and how to report their suspicions to their public health agency. After contacting public health authorities, physicians should be prepared to proceed clinically in consultation with their public health colleagues.

During the response to a WMD event, physicians' responsibilities will vary by their practices and their institutional affiliations. Some physicians may not care for any patients who are directly affected by the WMD but should understand the rationale behind the public health and medical interventions that may be implemented to treat and contain the morbidity and mortality associated with the WMD event. Public health interventions can include epidemiologic investigations, environmental testing, public health education campaigns, immunization programs, and quarantines.

Physicians may find that they are identified as the experts in their community and may be asked to help explain and clarify these response activities, regardless of their level of involvement, usual practice, or specialty. Physicians may also find that their patients who did not suffer physical exposure or injury are nevertheless concerned about their health and welfare. In addition to understanding when and how to withhold inappropriate diagnostic tests and treatments, clinical practitioners must know how to recognize and care for those suffering from psychological trauma following a WMD event. Physicians who are directly involved with physically injured or exposed populations must have a more intimate knowledge of treatment protocols and their roles in any public health or emergency management interventions that may be implemented. While the details of response plans will vary with regard to physician roles, medical students must be aware that they may have both explicit and implied roles in these plans as practicing physicians, including leadership roles in interdisciplinary teams. As students, they should also be aware of any responsibilities they may have within their medical school and/or teaching hospital's response plans.

Unique to the WMD context is the illicit and purposeful exposure of individuals and communities to harmful agents. Because of the unlawful nature of the exposures and the potential population-wide impact, physicians may be interacting with law enforcement, emergency personnel, public health agencies, the media, and their communities in a manner that is qualitatively different from their typical day-to-day practice. In addition to clinical knowledge and skills, medical schools will need to equip their students with the skills to interact within multi-disciplinary teams in the context of WMD preparedness and response, including the collection and preservation of forensic evidence.

Curriculum Contents

General Principles

Although the meeting of the expert panel was entitled "*Bioterrorism Education for Medical Students*", the group determined that focusing only on biologic agents of terrorism was inappropriately limiting. Because physicians in practice should be prepared to respond to any event that may result in mass casualties, the expert panel agreed to adopt an "*all-agents*" approach by considering biologic, chemical, physical, and radiological agents.

1. *In the medical school curriculum, WMD education should be considered in the context of any threats that may result in mass casualties, including the use of biologic, chemical, physical, and radiological agents.*

   The expert panel acknowledged that with this broader perspective, the list of potential agents of terrorism, particularly when considering chemical agents, is extensive. Requiring medical students to memorize the characteristics of all possible agents was not thought to be a productive activity. Focusing on general concepts that distinguish particular classes of agents, their mechanisms of injury, and their containment/treatment options was recommended.

2. *General concepts should be emphasized rather than details regarding every potential agent.*

   The expert panel stressed that in addition to becoming familiar with potential WMD agents, medical students needed to augment their clinical knowledge with an understanding of their roles in the implementation of WMD preparedness and response interventions. The panel identified working in multidisciplinary teams and working in coordination with public health systems as critical aspects of a physician's responsibility.

3. *The roles and responsibilities of physicians during a WMD event should be presented, including the need to work in multidisciplinary teams and in coordination with the public health system.*

Learning Objectives

The expert panel identified learning objectives that could be integrated into the traditional basic science and clinical curricula, as well as learning objectives that focus on the public health system, the emergency management system, the physicians' roles in the public health and emergency management response to a WMD event, and professional ethics, topics that may not be included in existing coursework at all schools.

Basic sciences

The basic science curriculum includes natural opportunities to discuss WMD examples in the presentation of core concepts of biochemistry, microbiology, pathology, pathophysiology, physiology, pharmacology, and radiation physiology.

For its part the medical school must ensure that before graduation a student will have demonstrated, to the satisfaction of the faculty, the following:

1. Knowledge of specific Category A and B biologic agents and general classes of chemicals identified as potential WMD
2. An understanding of the multiple routes of potential exposure to WMD and the associated pathophysiology of injuries and illnesses
3. Knowledge of the biochemical, infectious, physical, and radiological mechanisms and properties that characterize potential WMD
4. An understanding of the epidemiology of classes of WMD
5. Knowledge of the pharmaceutics and pharmaceuticals used to combat WMD (e.g., burn therapies, biochemical antidotes, antibiotics)
6. Knowledge of prevention strategies associated with WMD

Clinical sciences

During clinical training, medical students should learn how to recognize and treat patients who have been exposed to WMD, along with the precautions they should take to protect the safety and health of other patients, staff, and themselves.

For its part the medical school must ensure that before graduation a student will have demonstrated, to the satisfaction of the faculty, the following:

1. The ability to interpret results of the medical history, physical exam, and diagnostic workup to determine an accurate diagnosis of WMD exposure
2. The ability to use appropriate precautions to prevent WMD exposure to other patients, care providers, and themselves (e.g., isolation, decontamination, personal protective equipment, appropriate waste disposal)
3. The ability to take medical histories that:
   - Determine the absence or presence of symptoms that are characteristic of exposure to WMD
   - Identify patients who may have psychological trauma following a WMD event
   - Identify occupational and psychosocial risks for exposure to potential WMD
   - Characterize exposures to potential WMD, including type of agent, timing, and length of exposure
4. The ability to conduct physical exams that:
   - Are guided by exposure or potential exposure to WMD
   - Determine the absence or presence of physical signs that are characteristic of exposure to WMD
5. The ability to identify patterns of signs and symptoms likely to be associated with occult exposure to WMD
6. The ability to consider critical aspects of treatment plans for patients who may have been affected physically and/or psychologically by WMD, including:
   - Acute care management
   - Long-term management
   - Secondary and tertiary prevention
   - Attention to mental health concerns
   - Referrals

- Awareness of concomitant psychosocial issues
- Consultation with public health authorities

7. The ability to consider WMD exposure when establishing differential diagnoses and developing problem lists
8. The ability to incorporate evidence-based diagnostic procedures and laboratory studies to confirm the diagnoses and/or causative agents
9. The ability to interpret results of the medical history, physical exam, and diagnostic workup to rule out, when possible, the likelihood of WMD exposure
10. The ability to recognize the need for, and to collect and preserve, forensic evidence from patients who may be victims of a WMD event
11. The ability to utilize risk communication skills when informing patients and their families about WMD

Public health system

Information regarding public health is not yet a standard part of medical school curricula. Nevertheless, medical students should understand the structure and function of their public health system, including the linkages between the medical care and public health systems during public health emergencies, such as one involving a WMD. As physicians, they may be asked to explain and to clarify public health policies and programs to their patients and to their communities.

For its part the medical school must ensure that before graduation a student will have demonstrated, to the satisfaction of the faculty, the following:

1. An understanding of public health interventions that are part of the response to public health emergencies such as the use of WMD (e.g., mass vaccination, quarantine, epidemiologic investigations, environmental decontamination, public health laws)
2. An understanding of public health system interventions that prepare for public health emergencies, such as the use of WMD (e.g., public health education, disease and syndromic surveillance, vaccination programs and their rationale, risk communication, public health laws)

Emergency management system

Information regarding emergency management systems is also not a standard part of medical school curricula. Medical students should understand the structure and function of emergency management systems, including the rationale for incident command systems.

For its part the medical school must ensure that before graduation a student will have demonstrated, to the satisfaction of the faculty, the following:

1. An understanding of state and federal resources that contribute to emergency management and response at the local level
2. An understanding of the incident command system
3. An understanding of community and hospital all hazards planning
4. An understanding of community emergency response systems

Public health and emergency management roles and responsibilities

Medical students should also be aware of the spectrum of roles and responsibilities of physicians within the public health and emergency management systems to prepare for and respond to emergencies.

For its part the medical school must ensure that before graduation a student will have demonstrated, to the satisfaction of the faculty, the following:

1. Knowledge of unusual clinical scenarios that may represent sentinel cases of victims of an unannounced use of WMD
2. Knowledge of local and national resources that provide information about WMD
3. An understanding of the importance of risk communication skills when informing communities or the media about WMD
4. An understanding of their community's public health and medical response system and its interactions with law enforcement, National Guard, emergency medical system, etc.
5. An understanding of procedures used to collect patient data for surveillance or tracking
6. An understanding of the methods and rationale for environmental decontamination
7. An understanding of their assignment, if any, within the community response plan, the incident command system, and their school or hospital's emergency response plan
8. An understanding of procedures for reporting cases that are suspicious for WMD

Professional ethics

Physicians may confront a variety of moral and ethical issues regarding their professional obligations to treat and protect their patients and themselves in the face of a WMD event. Medical students should understand the framework and limitations of the professional ethics that guide their actions. For its part the medical school must ensure that before graduation a student will have demonstrated, to the satisfaction of the faculty, the following:

1. An understanding of professional liability issues in the context of WMD events
2. An understanding of their professional obligations to treat
3. An understanding of their responsibilities and rights as a volunteer
4. An understanding of their rights to protect their personal safety

Learning Opportunities

General Principles

The existing medical school curriculum includes opportunities to introduce WMD topics throughout the four-year curriculum, building upon and augmenting the students' growing knowledge and skill base. The panel agreed that WMD related learning objectives should be integrated into the existing curriculum across all four years.

1. *WMD-related learning objectives should span all four years of medical school.*

   WMD-related topics cut across a variety of subjects that are part of the standard medical school curriculum. The expert panel agreed that WMD-related topics should be integrated across subjects such as microbiology, pathology, and toxicology. Horizontal integration may also be achieved in the clinical sciences across specialties such as emergency medicine, primary care specialties, and infectious diseases.

2. *WMD-related learning objectives should be integrated horizontally through the curriculum.*

   The panel agreed that the most effective methods of teaching should be used to teach the WMD-related topics. For early, basic knowledge acquisition, didactic methods could be utilized; however, for later learning objectives that require the integration of knowledge and skills, experiential learning is preferred.

3. *A combination of didactic sessions and experiential learning exercises should be used.*

Educational Strategies

The panel described a spectrum of teaching strategies that correspond to the varying levels of knowledge and skill desired of students. Many medical students may achieve WMD-associated competencies through a combination of didactic and experiential learning exercises that are folded into existing curricula. The integration of WMD examples in their basic science and clinical experiences, the inclusion of information regarding the public health system, and the use of WMD case scenarios for discussions regarding professional ethics may provide a minimum level of competency for medical students. Alternatively, schools with a special interest or obligation to train physicians for the military and the U.S. Public Health Service, such as the Uniformed Services University of the Health Sciences, can require large-scale disaster drills in their curriculum. Other schools could also consider fourth-year capstone activities to help consolidate the information from all four years, such as a tabletop exercises or case study discussions.

Educational strategies to help students achieve the necessary competencies in the area of WMD preparedness and response include:

1. Use of existing distance-learning courses, including those developed by the Centers for Disease Control and Prevention
2. Participation in community emergency planning activities
3. Research in WMD and WMD-related health care delivery
4. Lectures
5. Objective structured clinical examinations
6. Participation in public health emergency planning activities
7. Directed reading
8. Disaster drills
9. Use of standardized patients
10. Tabletop exercises
11. Review and discussion of case studies
12. Seminars to address student anxiety and fears regarding their responsibilities

Implementation Strategies

In addition to the development of curricular resources, the expert panel agreed that increasing the cadre of faculty prepared to teach WMD topics, and including WMD topics in student and institutional evaluation activities will be critical to the successful integration of this subject into the medical school curriculum.

Development of Curricular Resources

The panel identified a need to develop curricular resources, such as standardized patients, on-line study modules, and elective opportunities that could be shared by institutions and departments.

Faculty Development

Although a paucity of medical school faculty currently identify themselves as "WMD experts", a desire to quickly impart this information to medical students exists. The expert panel identified a variety of opportunities in which their faculty could be trained in WMD competencies. These range from distance-based, self-study experiences to fellowship experiences at institutions with expertise in WMD.

Activities that would facilitate faculty development in the topic of WMD preparedness and response include:

1. Establishing year-long fellowship programs in WMD preparedness and response for faculty
2. Establishing partnerships with Veterans Administration Centers, Department of Defense medical facilities, and Centers for Public Health Preparedness to facilitate faculty development
3. Establishing distance-based self-study modules for medical school faculty
4. Establishing month-long "faculty-in-residence" programs that allow faculty to observe and learn at institutions with a robust WMD curriculum
5. Requiring faculty to participate in medical school/teaching hospital disaster drills
6. Establishing "train the trainer" symposia for medical school faculty

Evaluation Activities

The panel agreed that students' competency in WMD topics and medical schools' teaching of WMD topics should be assured through the existing evaluation systems. Written examinations as well as the evaluation of students' clinical skills should include cases of WMD use. WMD content should also be considered for inclusion in national examinations and in reviews and evaluations of medical school curricula.

Examples of Innovation

Almost immediately after the events of September 11, medical schools across the country began to include or enhance information regarding mass casualty events, including the use of WMD, in their curriculum. Many schools sponsored grand rounds lectures or other special presentations on the identification and treatment of potential biologic agents of terrorism. While not a comprehensive listing, the following schools have developed educational opportunities beyond the insertion of isolated lectures on WMD, and may serve as models for other schools:

Medical College of Ohio

The Medical College of Ohio offers an eighthour mandatory course, "Basic Anti-Terrorism Emergency Lifesaving Skills", to their students. The course includes an overview of disaster management and focuses on preparedness. Medical students cover topics such as triage, treatment of blast and crush injuries, hazardous materials situations, biological and chemical agents, and mass casualty management. The multi-disciplinary faculty also presents information regarding epidemiology, surveillance, and public health. A case scenario of a smallpox outbreak in their area is featured. This course is a cooperative effort between the Medical College of Ohio and the University of Findlay Center for Terrorism Preparedness.

Uniformed Services University of the Health Sciences

The Uniformed Services University of the Health Sciences (USUHS) was established in 1972 with a mission to educate health professionals dedicated to career service in the Department of Defense and the United States Public Health Service. Because topics that are unique to military medicine have been woven into typical medical school courses, students at USUHS are provided with more than 28 hours of training in WMD-related subjects throughout the four years of the curriculum. These experiences range from the inclusion of WMD information in pharmacology, biochemistry, and microbiology curricula to extensive field operations. Topics in the curriculum include the medical effects of nuclear, biological, and chemical agents on the human body; the response to suspected exposure, including detection, decontamination, and medical countermeasures; and the psychological stresses of combat and trauma.

University of Arizona College of Medicine

The University of Arizona College of Medicine, in collaboration with the other colleges within the University of Arizona Health Sciences Center, developed and presented an "interprofessional" seminar, *Bioterorrism and Consequence Management*, in the spring of 2002. The Colleges of Medicine, Nursing, Pharmacy, and Public Health developed a fourhour program that highlighted the clinical, environmental, public health, and emergency response issues associated with the use of WMD. Faculty from all four colleges, along with members of the local emergency response and public health communities, contributed to the development of the program and participated as speakers. The audience consisted of third-year medical students, graduate students in public health and epidemiology, fifth-semester and graduate nursing students, and third-year pharmacy students and residents. The format of the seminar included didactic sessions as well as a case-based, interprofessional small-group discussion. The University of Arizona Health Sciences Center plans to repeat the seminar in an intercollegiate setting as a method of fostering the interprofessional teamwork necessary to respond to public health emergencies.

University of Pittsburgh School of Medicine

The University of Pittsburgh School of Medicine originally introduced a small-group case-based workshop, "The Medical Management of Biological and Chemical Exposures", into the required third-year clinical curriculum in the summer of 2000. Emergency Medicine faculty taught the workshops during the students' integrated clerkship in Internal Medicine/Emergency Medicine/Critical Care Medicine. The workshops focused on mechanisms of toxicity, common agents used as weapons, differential diagnoses, syndrome recognition, decontamination, and treatment. Although student feedback was positive regarding the relevance of the topics and the teaching method prior to September 11, 2001, their perception regarding the relevance of WMD subjects increased after the identification of the Florida anthrax cases in October 2001. In 2003, WMD topics have been integrated throughout the curriculum as a four-year longitudinal theme, titled "Biologic Threats to Society". WMD issues are presented in a variety of courses ranging from neuroscience to ethics.

University of Tennessee College of Medicine

At the University of Tennessee College of Medicine, a group of first-year medical students established the "University of Tennessee Community Disaster Response Unit" as their Longitudinal Community Program project, a requirement in their first and second years. The goal of the project was to identify and train student volunteers to participate in disaster response activities, should any WMD or general disaster events occur in their community. Since its establishment in spring 2002, students have prepared and delivered two two-hour training modules on biological agents and chemical agents to medical students at their university. Future plans include the development of modules on general disaster response and radiological agents, as well as participation in a disaster drill. Students interacted with their local Emergency Management Agency, the Tennessee Emergency Management Agency, and hospital administrators in the development of this program, and hope to sustain this effort beyond their participation in the Longitudinal Community Program course.

University of Utah School of Medicine

The University of Utah School of Medicine addresses bioterrorism through activities that span the four-year curriculum. The topic of bioterrorism is introduced to first-year students by the inclusion of potential agents of bioterrorism in their medical microbiology course. After potential agents have been presented individually, a one-hour summary lecture is offered on bioterrorism. During students' third-year clerkships, bioterrorism cases are included in their "Topics in Medicine" discussions. Bioterrorism cases are also in development for their fourth-year required public health rotation.

Conclusion

Although integrating WMD subjects into the already-full curriculum of medical students is a challenge, the insertion of WMD-based examples and cases into the existing basic science and clinical curriculum may be an effective and relatively uncomplicated first step. The current focus on WMD preparedness and response also highlights what has been a deficit in the education of many medical students—an understanding of their role in their public health system. An effective response to a public health emergency, such as the use of a WMD, requires a physician workforce that is familiar with the resources and interventions of their local and state health agencies. The learning objectives and learning activities for medical students should reflect the need for a greater familiarity with potential WMD agents, as well as an understanding of their roles and responsibilities as physicians within the public health system. Because the science, scope, and context of WMD-related topics will continue to evolve, medical students must be encouraged to stay abreast of new developments as they continue their training and begin their practices.

11

PREVENTION OF TERRORISM

The al-Qaida attacks of 11 September 2001 and the delivery of *Bacillus anthracis* (anthrax) via the US Postal Service triggered a significant increase in initiatives to improve defense against biological attacks. They also reinvigorated a decades-old debate about the contributions that openly published scientific research might make to the efforts of bioterrorists and others who may be developing a biological warfare (BW) or other weapons of mass destruction (WMD) capability. Resolution of this debate could be made easier by input from knowledgeable intelligence and other national security professionals. Collaboration involving the national security and bioscience research communities could be key to minimizing the challenges posed by proliferation of research findings that have bioterror and BW applications.

Unfortunately, while there have been recent discussions involving these communities, the relationship between them has been nearly nonexistent. Accordingly, initial approaches and interactions must be planned and carefully carried out to ensure that the bridges built between the two communities are solid and long lasting. A necessary first step is to make sure that national security professionals who enter this collaboration are thoroughly familiar with the current and past debates among scientists about the potential openly published research findings have to enable BW or bioterrorism. This article is an overview of this debate, and it summarizes the most recent discussions among bioscience researchers. In addition, it offers some options the Intelligence Community (IC) can consider to help the life science community continue its work effectively, while safeguarding national security.

National Security and Science

Since the 1940s the US national security community has worked with scientific organizations and research communities to develop a policy for identifying areas of basic and applied research requiring control of information. Such research, historically related either to weapons development or sensitive nuclear technologies, has been designated as classified and is subject to strict dissemination controls. For example, before the United States entered World War II, physicists in the private sector researching nuclear fission voluntarily stopped publishing results in scientific journals for fear of contributing to Germany's nuclear bomb project. In early 1940 the joint *National Academy of Sciences* (NAS)-*National Research Council* (NRC) Advisory Committee on Scientific Publications was established to explore options for restricting publication of information about nuclear fission. After US entry into the war, this committee secured the cooperation of scientific journals in the United States.

Control of information concerning research into nuclear power has also been instituted. Private industry was permitted to explore limited applications of nuclear power under the Atomic Energy Act of 1954. Before then, the federal government protected nuclear energy activities with security and secrecy programs. The Atomic Energy Act prohibited dissemination of nuclear research information from its creation regardless of who controls it. Such information, even if developed privately and without federal government aid, is regarded as "*born classified*." Importantly, when fundamental research is not classified, no other information controls are placed on it. However, the federal government retains authority over results that relate to *atomic weapons*, production of special nuclear material (SNM), and use of SNM in the production of energy.

Federal government controls have been relatively successful in mitigating security concerns related to the proliferation of specific nuclear technologies. In large measure this is because federal regulations regarding nuclear research were implemented at a time when the research field was relatively young and expertise was consolidated within a handful of talented minds. This made it possible to, in effect, capture fission research by creating mutually beneficial relationships between key scientists and the federal government, in which Washington supported research and development in a secure environment under classification control. The same circumstances do not exist in the life sciences, making the challenge of providing protection against threats enabled by the life sciences much greater. With the exception of specific work pertaining to the former US bioweapons program—halted in 1969 under executive order by Richard Nixon—and a handful of biodefense projects funded by the Department of Defense (DOD), the vast majority of life science research projects over the past 50 years have advanced without any restrictions or controls. Expertise exists in an international network containing tens of thousands of researchers working to address fundamental questions across a broad spectrum of life science fields. Federally mandated containment is not the effective option it was 60 years ago.

Not only is generalized federal restriction of life science research impractical, it could be disastrous. Life science research builds upon multiple findings across a variety of seemingly unrelated fields in a manner not unlike a spider's web. Removing one strand of that web through federal restriction likely would have negative implications for the other fields that are difficult to estimate. Even generalized restriction within fields with greatest application towards bioterrorism or BW could greatly hinder biodefense research efforts to develop medical countermeasures, including new vaccines and therapeutics. Before national security professionals can productively engage the scientific community regarding threats presented by the open publication of some research findings, there must be mutual agreement that the generalized, federally-mandated restrictions used to contain nuclear research are not a viable option.

National Security Debate

Discussions about the impact on national security of discoveries in life science first received major attention in the US research community after major advances were made in recombinant DNA research—specifically the development of reliable techniques to manipulate an organism's genetic material and elicit a novel effect. *Genetic engineering* and the creation of recombinant species thus became topics of great contention in the 1970s and led to calls for regulation of methods for manipulating DNA and control of experiments containing genetically engineered species. To find ways to resolve these concerns, a number of leading scientists gathered in 1975 at the Asilomar Conference in Pacific Grove, California, to discuss mechanisms for assessing and managing the risks of such research.

Conference participants drafted a consensus statement that called for a voluntary moratorium on certain aspects of recombinant research and an increase in personal security and containment requirements for related research areas. This consensus statement was the starting point for rules later developed by the *National Institutes of Health's* (NIH) *Recombinant DNA Advisory Committee* (RAC), which was formed to oversee such research. The RAC and its decentralized Institutional Biosafety Committees have remained the basis for oversight of the safe conduct of recombinant DNA research in the United States and have served as models used by other countries to regulate the creation of genetically modified organisms.

In the early 1980s, concern that potentially hostile foreign students and scientists had too easy access to fundamental information across a wide range of scientific disciplines, including information that might be considered to fall under export control regulations, led to an effort by the DOD to restrict information presented in classrooms and conferences. To better understand the risk to national security, DOD helped fund a study through the NAS, which convened a panel of leading researchers to evaluate the situation in which "recent trends, including apparent increases in acquisition efforts by our adversaries, have raised serious concerns that openness may harm US security by providing adversaries with militarily relevant technologies that can be directed against us."

The panel's extensive report offered a set of principles to "*resolve the current dilemma.*" The panel, with the Soviet Union as its prime focus, concluded that potential security benefits derived from restrictive controls were outweighed by the potential that such controls would weaken US security by hampering scientific advancement. The panel identified three categories of information for consideration of security controls:

1. Activities and findings in which the benefits of total openness overshadow their possible near-term military benefits to the Soviet Union.
2. A small "*gray*" area that lies between the first two and for which limited restrictions short of classification are appropriate.
3. Areas of research for which classification is clearly indicated.

Furthermore, the panel provided guidelines to assist the federal government in categorizing research activities.

According to the panel, "no restriction of any kind limiting access or communication should be applied to any area of university research, be it basic or applied, unless it involves a technology meeting all the following criteria:"

1. The US is the only source of information about the technology, or other friendly nations that could also be a source have control systems;
2. The technology is developing rapidly and the time from basic science to application is short;
3. Transfer of the technology would give the USSR a significant near-term military benefit;
4. The technology has identifiable direct military applications, or it is dual-use and involves process- or production-related techniques.

The panel suggested that in dealing with gray technologies and federally-funded research, the government could achieve sufficient security by restricting the access of foreign students and researchers to the laboratory undertaking the research and stipulating a policy of federal review of research manuscripts and other products before their publication or open dissemination. The panel's findings appeared to provide sufficient guidance for the federal government at the time to adequately address the issue of Soviet acquisition of dual use technologies. The panel recommended that the federal government take the lead in implementing the suggestions, but it stressed the critical need for partnership between the scientific and national security communities to ensure effective and appropriate implementation.

Following the release of the NAS panel report, President Ronald Reagan issued National Security Decision Directive (NSDD) 189, which reaffirmed US policy regarding the flow of scientific information:

It is the policy of this administration that, to the maximum extent possible, the products of fundamental research remain unrestricted. It is also the policy of this administration that, where the national security requires control, the mechanism for control of information generated during federally-funded fundamental research in science, engineering, technology and engineering at colleges, universities and laboratories is classification. Each federal government agency is responsible for: (a) determining whether classification is appropriate prior to the award of a research grant, contract, or cooperative agreement and, if so, controlling the research results through standard classification procedures; (b) periodically reviewing all research grants, contracts, or cooperative agreements for potential classification. No restrictions may be placed upon the conduct or reporting of federally-funded fundamental research that has not received national security classification, except as provided in applicable US statutes.

NSDD 189 has not been superseded and remains federal policy concerning the control of federally-funded research. However, throughout the late 1980s and early 1990s, a handful of individuals raised the possibility of increasing security by compartmentalizing research of concern. According to Raymond Zilinskas, "compartmentalization, a less restrictive form of secrecy, allows scientists to exchange data only if they can establish that their colleagues need the data to proceed with their research." The idea did not develop legs at the time, possibly because so few were concerned about the issue.

Ultimately, although the Asilomar Conference, NAS panel, and later, but infrequent, discussions into the 1990s provided helpful insights, the efficacy of their proposed resolutions must be considered in a broader political and historical context. In general, the recommendations and findings of these groups have largely been superseded by the fall of the Soviet Union, the emergence of international terrorism, and the advancement of science. For example:

Although researchers at Asilomar were able to assuage public concerns at the time through their consensus statement and subsequent work within NIH, the central tenet of the conference's recommendations was that personal integrity and accountability were sufficient to prevent the misuse of genetic engineering technology acquired through scientific exchange. Such principles will not deter the nefarious researcher, and information regarding the former Soviet bioweapons program reveals a concerted effort to incorporate genetic engineering technology to enhance biowarfare threat agents had been occurring.

Close analysis of the subtext of the 1982 NAS panel report on Scientific Communication and National Security reveals that the panel was principally concerned with sciences and technologies other than the life sciences. Discoveries in the life sciences are likely to decrease the amount of time, effort, and expertise needed to develop a *biological weapons* capability at a rate that will outpace the monitoring ability of the national security community. Thus, people doing security assessments of life science findings need to consider that the applicability of life science findings to BW or terrorism is not as clearly defined as in many of the physical sciences.

The NAS panel report focused exclusively on risks relative to Soviet militarization. The panel itself acknowledged the limitations of their recommendations even as they looked ahead to new challenges: "there are clear problems in scientific communication and national security involving Third World countries. These problems in time might overshadow the Soviet dimension." Clearly, a reevaluation of the findings of the 1982 panel would be prudent.

SECURITY DEBATE

In the post-9/11 and *post-anthrax* attack environment of heightened security awareness the public, legislators, and government leaders have increased their scrutiny of potential sources of support for terrorists. The openness of the life science research community is again a subject of discussion. For example, in an effort to curb the flow of potentially valuable information to bioterrorists, the DOD drafted a report "Mandatory Procedures for Research and Technology Protection within the DOD," which outlined plans to provide DOD program managers greater oversight of whether DOD-funded laboratories could publish some of their findings. The proposal drew harsh criticism from the scientific community and was eventually discarded.

In addition, NIH and Congress implemented new restrictions on federally-funded life science research laboratories to try to reduce the potential that bioterrorists would gain access to dual-use technologies. The *Public Health Security and Bioterrorism Preparedness and Response Act* required tighter laboratory security, government registration, and background checks for scientists and others handling any of more than three dozen potential bioterror agents identified on the Center for Disease Control's (CDC) "*Select Agent List.*" In addition, agencies such as NIH for the first time considered supporting classified research. Following implementation of these regulations, scientists began to express concern that some biologists with government funding were being encouraged to rein in full publication of their own work. Following similar developments in the United Kingdom, some scientists became concerned that the defensive response was disproportionate to the actual threat.

Growing tension between some leading researchers and the federal government continued to escalate throughout the spring and summer of 2002, largely due to media reports that highlighted the dual-use potential of a number of recent scientific publications.

1. In July 2002, researchers at the State University of New York at Stony Brook revealed that they had successfully created infectious poliovirus from artificially engineered DNA sequences. Some observers saw open publication of their achievement in the journal *Science* as enabling the proliferation of a methodology with high BW potential.

2. Researchers in Germany reported the creation of a DNA-based system for performing reverse genetics studies on the *ebola* virus. This system introduced the possibility of reconstituting live *ebola* virus from DNA in the absence of a viral sample. Other researchers expressed concern that this information could lead to the artificial synthesis of the virus, increasing the potential for agent proliferation, as DNA can be more safely transferred than viral samples.
3. In 2000, Australian researchers genetically engineered a strain of mousepox virus in a way that inadvertently increased its virulence. At the time, publication of their findings was met with harsh criticism. This mousepox research and associated criticism were raised again in 2002 during additional debates on science and security.
4. Researchers at the University of Pennsylvania successfully developed a hybrid virus composed of an HIV core surrounded by the surface proteins of *ebola*. This new virus was capable of infecting lung tissue, potentially enabling aerosol delivery, and could facilitate the expression of foreign genes in infected cells. The published findings arguably provided a roadmap to engineering of a viral vector capable of efficiently delivering bioregulatory agents.
5. Researchers at the University of Pittsburgh identified key proteins in *variola* (smallpox) that contribute to the virus' virulence and demonstrated how to synthesize the virulence gene via genetic modification of smallpox's less deadly cousin *vaccinia*. The published report was the subject of a highly publicized news article that questioned the value of publishing discoveries that might aid bioterrorists.

Dana Shea at the Library of Congress has nicely assessed the overall response: "these articles have led some to question the wisdom of openly publishing information that could be used to threaten national security." An editorial in *New Scientist* stated: That this mind-boggling quantity of information is going to transform medicine and biology is beyond doubt. But could some of it, in the wrong hands, be a recipe for terror and mayhem?

Maybe so. Bioethicist Arthur Kaplan from the University of Pennsylvania was reported as saying: We have to get away from the ethos that knowledge is good, knowledge should be publicly available, that information will liberate us. Information will kill us in the techno-terrorist age, and I think it's nuts to put that stuff on websites."

Apparently, a number of members of Congress agreed with Kaplan. After a series of news reports about the prevalence of dual use in scientific journals, a handful of members of Congress filed a resolution that criticized *Science's* publication of the synthetic creation of a poliovirus and called on journals, scientists, and funding agencies to exercise greater caution before releasing such information. Representative Dave Weldon (R-FL) and seven other congressmen introduced a resolution criticizing Science's publisher, the American Association for the Advancement of Science (AAAS), for publishing "a blueprint that could conceivably enable terrorists to inexpensively create human pathogens." Weldon's resolution called on the executive branch to review current policies and ensure that information that could be useful in the development of WMD is not made accessible to terrorists or countries of proliferation concern.

In addition to congressional interest, the Office for Homeland Security (OHS) announced that it would be considering initiatives to create a category of information that would be "*sensitive*, but unclassified" for application to a variety of dual-use topics, possibly including life science research of concern. This naturally raised the suspicion and concerns of researchers who feared OHS might seek to make decisions that in their opinion would be more appropriately made by NIH. Separately, the American Society for Microbiology (ASM) sent a letter to NAS requesting a meeting of biomedical publishers to discuss whether and how editors of leading research journals should publish research that might be coopted by terrorists. By fall 2002, the debate on scientific openness and national security had officially been reopened.

Current Debate

As the federal government initiated informal efforts to develop a strategy for addressing the issue of science and security in late 2002, insights were coming from a variety of highly knowledgeable sources. Mitchel Wallerstein, former deputy assistant secretary of defense for counterproliferation policy (1993-97) offered guiding principles:

- First, open access to scientific knowledge on university campuses remains as important as it was 20 years ago;
- Second, the areas of scientific knowledge and/or technological application that are immediately applicable to the development of WMD are already known;
- Third, carefully conceived restrictions on scientific and technical communications remain necessary but should be applied to

substantially fewer areas of scientific inquiry and technology development than during the Cold War;

- Fourth, university faculties have a responsibility for imparting values that emphasize the positive role of S&T in addressing human needs and the immorality of their use to cause mass casualties and human suffering.

Wallerstein's first, third, and fourth recommendations provide a good roadmap to address many underlying concerns. However, it may be presumptuous to assert that all "areas of scientific knowledge and/or technological application that are immediately applicable to the development of WMD are already known." The central issue of the exponential increase in discoveries in the life sciences and the potential implications of those discoveries for a revolution in BW fundamentally requires a continuing reevaluation and identification of research disciplines with application to BW and biodefense. Ideally, such evaluations should include insights from leading life science researchers actively engaged in "*cutting edge*" science, as they will have the clearest insights on the technical capabilities and limitations of biotechnologies for malevolent purposes.

Partially in response to media frenzy surrounding the Weldon resolution, on 18 October 2002, NAS outlined its recommendations for addressing the issue in its "Background Paper on Science and Security in an Age of Terrorism." It contained a list of action items for the life science research community and the federal government, citing the success of recent collaborations between government and scientists:

The nation must balance two needs for achieving a safe and secure society: (i) the need to restrict access to certain information, and (ii) the need for a strong research enterprise that improves both our general welfare and our security. Clearly, policy-makers must seek mechanisms by which both interests can be served.

To this end, we call for a renewed dialogue among scientists, engineers, health researchers, and policy-makers. To stimulate such a dialogue, we present two "*action points*": one focused on scientists, engineers, and health researchers and the other focused on policy-makers.

Scientists quickly voiced support for the highlighted principles, including their distaste for the concept of creating a category for "*sensitive but unclassified*" research. Ron Atlas, the president of ASM, and others testified before the House Science Committee that the government needs to clarify what constitutes a threat before it can implement protective guidelines, such as screening foreign graduate students for entry to U.S. laboratories. Moreover, scientists argued that clear distinctions need to be made between classified and unclassified research since "poorly defined third categories of sensitive but unclassified research that do not provide precise guidance on what information should be restricted from public access ...generate deep uncertainties among both scientists and the officials responsible for enforcing regulations."

Editorials in leading scientific journals expressed concern that many scientists would either deal with the issue of classification by determining that it should be rejected from university laboratories as unsuitable (as was the case at the Massachusetts Institute of Technology) or deem the "*sensitive*" label as prone to too many interpretations to be accommodated in an academic setting. Despite these views, however, NAS demonstrated its willingness to withhold certain information from general release without a demonstrated "*need to know*." This option came into play when the academies agreed to remove an entire chapter of the 2002 NAS study on agricultural bioterrorism that the authors and the Department of Agriculture agreed would be of high-dual use value to individuals with bad intentions. Also, with some scientists, the concern over research classification was secondary to the potential consequences of misuse of their research. As one such researcher wrote, "scientists need to be aware of the regulatory and ethical implications of bioweapon proliferation."

In addition to lobbying Congress and federal agencies, biologists began to independently discuss new voluntary guidelines on publishing potentially dangerous information, in part to head off possible government rules. On 9 and 10 January 2003 NAS and the Center for Strategic and International Studies (CSIS) hosted a workshop for life science researchers and national security experts to discuss the issue of assessing and mitigating potential threats presented by biological research. Although many of the 200 senior scientists and researchers argued that scientists should be free to publish all unclassified work, some academicians acknowledged that the community needs to reassure the public and the government that it is acting responsibly.

Moreover, statements by senior policymakers reassured scientists but challenged them to take the initiative. According to Dr. Parney Albright, then associate director of homeland security for the president's Office of Homeland Security, "it is the policy of this administration that, to the maximum extent possible, the products of fundamental research remain unrestricted" and that as per NSDD 189, "no restrictions will be placed upon the conduct or reporting of federally-funded fundamental research that has not received national security classification." However, Dr. Albright did not give the research community a free pass, making it clear that "the science community ought to come up with a process before the public demands the government do it for them...that will be driven by the rate at which controversial papers hit the street."

Ultimately, scientists at the NAS/CSIS meeting agreed that there may be some research that should not be published, although clear guidelines would be helpful in identifying future papers of concern. To help craft a better definition of such "taboo" science, the academies and CSIS announced a plan to convene such meetings in the future. Gerald Epstein, a security expert with the Institute for Defense Analyses, proposed a simple question to aid scientists in deciding whether a paper should be more closely reviewed: "Would you like it to be found in a cave in Afghanistan with sections highlighted in yellow?"

During the second day of the workshop, a group of editors from leading scientific journals crafted a statement on the publication of research with potential for aiding bioterrorism. An editorial that ran alongside the statement in Science highlighted the need for researchers, editors, and national security professionals to reach a consensus on guidelines for scientific information that should not be published. The editorial did not represent a radical departure from standing policy, but concisely stated the opinions of the editors present at the workshop. It made four points:

- First, the scientific information published in peer-reviewed journals carries special status, and confers unique responsibilities on editors and authors.
- Second, the editors recognize that the prospect of bioterrorism has raised legitimate concerns about the potential misuse of published information, but also recognize that research in the very same fields will be critical to society in meeting the challenges of defense.
- Third, scientists and their journals should consider the appropriate level and design of processes to accomplish effective review of papers that raise such security issues.
- Fourth, on occasion an editor may conclude that the potential harm of publication outweighs the potential societal benefits.

The response of researchers and security experts to the statement was mixed. Some researchers complained that they were not consulted. For example, Steven Block, a biophysicist at Stanford University, was quoted as saying the statement is "more equivocal and less definitive" than he would like to see. Others believe that scientists should go much further to address security concerns about life science research. David Heyman, a science and security expert at CSIS, said that the statement was "*only a step*" and that scientists should make changes earlier in the research process to reduce the risk of biological research being misused.

By far the sharpest public critic of the statement, respected microbiologist Stanley Falkow, has taken issue with the failure of its authors to elicit more discussion before its publication. Falkow faults the authors for failing "to provide guidelines regarding who exactly would make decisions about publication and what constitutes a potential contribution to the activities of bioterrorists." Falkow's statement suggests that he supports the formation of a committee to provide insight and oversight regarding research of concern. However, it is his opinion that the issue should be "earnestly discussed by the broad community of scientists, together with those whose mission it is to guard national security."

In a further effort to characterize the challenges posed by misuse of biotechnology, the NAS created the Committee on Research Standards and Practices to Prevent the Destructive Application of Biotechnology. It directed the committee to consider ways to minimize threats from BW and bioterrorism without hindering the progress of biotechnology. The committee's report, *Biotechnology Research in an Age of Terrorism*, released in October 2003, proposed a new system for mitigating the potential for the misuse of life science knowledge by establishing "a number of stages at which experiments and eventually their results would be reviewed to provide reassurance that advances in biotechnology with potential applications for BW or bioterrorism receive responsible oversight."

The Fink Report included seven recommendations for the mitigation of the potential for misuse of dual-use knowledge and seven guidelines for identifying "research of concern." The report clearly identified the absence of an "established culture of working with the national security community among life scientists as currently exists in the fields of nuclear physics and cryptography" as a challenge to achieving consensus on the identification of dual use information and mitigation of its potential misuse. In one of its seven recommendations, the NAS committee called for a role for the life sciences in efforts to prevent bioterrorism and biowarfare, recommending that "the national security and law enforcement communities develop new channels of sustained communication with the life sciences community about how to mitigate the risks of bioterrorism." The report suggested that leading scientists believe some guidance from intelligence professionals would assist the scientific community as it seeks to identify information that may be of use to terrorists and to support comparative assessments regarding the cost-benefit ratio of limiting the availability of such information.

In response to the recommendations of the report, the Department of Health and Human Services (DHHS) recently announced the creation of a National Scientific Advisory Board for Biosecurity (NSABB). According to the DHHS press statement, the NSABB will "advise the Secretary of HHS, the director of the NIH, and the heads of all federal departments and agencies that conduct or support life sciences research" by "recommending specific strategies for the efficient and effective oversight of federally conducted or supported potential dual-use biological research taking into consideration both national security concerns and the needs of the research community." According to the NSABB Web site, the group will be charged specifically with guiding the development of guidelines for the identification and conduct of research that may require special attention and security surveillance.

Although NSABB members have not yet been publicly identified, the board will consist of voting and *ex-officio* members from the national security and intelligence communities as well as an abundance of leading life scientists. Thus, the NSABB may serve as one vehicle for consistent and productive interaction between the intelligence and life science communities. Maximum benefit of this relationship could best be realized by ensuring that intelligence and national security professionals assigned to support NSABB efforts possess a strong background in the life sciences; it will do little good for intelligence professionals who do not adequately understand the underlying principles to engage life scientists in discussions on the potential security implications of highly technical research findings.

Intelligence Support

The life science research community clearly would benefit from insights of the IC and other national security professionals if it is to progress beyond the current state of discussion and develop a coordinated strategy for assessing and mitigating threats enabled by research of concern. Engagement of the scientific community should be of paramount importance to biological warfare and CBRN terrorism analysts in the IC.

In addition to obvious areas in which security experts could contribute, such as providing insights and methodologies for deriving threat assessments and offering national security information to cleared life science experts, there are many less obvious opportunities for IC input. For example, the IC is well positioned to see that life science experts are educated about the activities terrorist groups and foreign states allegedly undertake to support their BW efforts. Also, IC personnel possess access to a wealth of information pertinent to the physical properties and characteristics of biothreat agents. Much of this information, at least that which is unclassified or for official use only (FOUO), would be useful to researchers struggling with the development of novel countermeasures and systems for civilian biodefense.

A deeper relationship between the IC and life science communities has the potential to benefit the IC, which has long struggled to maintain an internal core of bioscience expertise. In addition, formulation of a positive view among life science professionals about the IC could lead to an increase in the number of top graduate students and young life science researchers who seek employment in intelligence or national security agencies. Most importantly, closer and continuing contact with life science investigators could yield greater insight regarding suspicious attempts of foreign researchers to acquire from legitimate scientists information, reagents, or technology of high dual-use value. Such insights could enable further targeting of IC resources. In order to develop the potential synergy between the two communities; the national security community will need to take the first steps. Ultimately, none of the potential benefits will be realized until long after IC professionals have sown seeds of goodwill within the life science research community and engaged influential scientists as partners on BW counterproliferation initiatives.

12

Natural Disasters, Major Accidents and Terrorism

Planning for Natural Disasters and Major Accidents

Planning for Emergency Response

It is essential that plans be made to manage emergencies that involve our families and ourselves. Emergency situations may range from natural events, including earthquakes or high winds, to major accidents impacting utilities and other resources, to terrorism events, including bioterrorism, chemical exposures, and explosions. Planning before an emergency event can help overcome the very natural tendency to panic. In a panic situation, people may carry out actions that are not only ineffective but also may actually make the situation worse, with resultant injuries or life-threatening situations that might otherwise have been avoided. Having a plan, and reviewing it with family members at least every 6 months, will help everyone involved respond in a coordinated and effective way, helping to assure their safety.

Planning Emergency Escape Routes

It is important to plan escape routes from all rooms in the house. There should be at least two ways to exit each room in the event that one way is blocked by fire or by falling objects. If the home is two stories, this requirement may necessitate providing a means, such as a rope ladder, to escape through an upper story window. If a home office or work area is located in a room with only one door, the windows should be large enough to permit exit. If bars are over windows, these should be affixed so that they can be readily detached from the inside. If outside doors have locks that require a key to be opened from the inside, it is important to place extra keys at locations where they can be readily located in case of an emergency.

It is absolutely essential that an assembly point be chosen that is away from the house and the possibility of any falling debris. All family members should immediately proceed to the assembly point in the case of fire, earthquake, or similar major event. Such assembly will confirm that everyone is out of the house, or, if not, who is missing. Emergency responders can then be advised of the situation. If all are accounted for, the responders will avoid placing themselves at risk by attempting to rescue someone who, in actuality, has escaped. All family members should know the number of an out-of-state contact who can be contacted to "*check in*" if family members are separated, e.g. at work or at school. The contact person can then let other family members know of each person's location and status.

It is also important to plan evacuation routes if events require evacuation from a disaster area. Planning should include possible alternate routes since primary roads and highways will likely be very crowded. Both Katrina and the 2004 Florida hurricanes demonstrated the importance of having a full tank of gas should it be necessary to evacuate an area. Since an earthquake or other disaster may occur without warning, it is a good practice to "keep the top half of the tank full". Conversely, it may be necessary to "*Shelter in Place*", where doors and widows can be locked; air conditioning and heating systems turned off; windows; and vents and fireplace dampers can be closed. You will be advised via the radio and television emergency communication systems if you do need to shelter in place.

Emergency Communications

A fire, explosion, chemical or biological contamination, earthquake, flood, or severe storm may affect power-generating facilities with a resultant loss of electrical power. Many phones now rely on external power for such items as recording messages, caller ID, and similar services. Loss of power may mean the phones cannot be used. Those at home should consider having a charged cellular phone available for such situations. It is also advisable to have a portable radio or television with fresh batteries readily available. This will provide access to status reports and guidance from authorities if an emergency occurs.

Smoke and Carbon Monoxide Detectors

Smoke and carbon monoxide detectors should be placed in each floor of the house. Batteries for these devices must be checked annually.

Tragically, deaths still occur each year because the smoke detectors in a home struck by fire did not have working batteries. Changing batteries when changing to standard time in the fall is an excellent memory aid for this process.

Carbon monoxide cannot be detected by smell and is not visible. In the United States, approximately 1,800 people die each year from carbon monoxide poisoning. Depending on circumstances, it can be produced by any flame in the house. To reduce risk, never use a fire place or other combustion device indoors that is not properly vented to the outside.

A person exposed to carbon monoxide is not aware of the problem until symptoms, including headache, fatigue, and dizziness, occur. Unfortunately, the symptoms are often considered to be Aflu@ or a Acold,@ are treated with aspirin or similar medicine, and the person continues to be exposed to the gas. By the time the person recognizes that something is seriously wrong, he or she is often so incapacitated that it is not possible to get out of the house, and death ensues. If the exposure occurs while the person is sleeping, the individual is not aware of any problems and dies without waking.

Central monitoring of detectors by an alarm company could be particularly valuable if some occupants were away from the home at the time a fire occurred.

Earthquake or Explosion Preparation

During earth tremors, or if an explosion occurs nearby, it may be wise to leave the home if it can be done immediately. Plan alternate exits from the home ahead of time in the event that the normal exits become blocked. If debris is falling, moving under a desk, a sturdy table, or within a doorframe may be the best alternative, although some question the safety of doorframes. If possible, take a cellular phone. This will permit contact with rescuers for anyone who is unable to get out of the building. Once outside the building, family members who were home should meet in the previously designated assembly area. After-shocks from an earthquake or explosion should be expected, and they may be severe. Do not attempt to re-enter the home until advised to do so by authorities. Homes that look sound after an earthquake may be hazardous due to structural weakening that is not readily apparent.

Since the Wasatch Front is an area with significant risks of earthquakes, it is important to take steps to prepare your home. Some recommended steps include the following:

1. Anchor water heaters with a strap affixed to a sturdy wall. Straps are available in hardware stores for self-installation or can be installed by commercial home service personnel.
2. Anchor any bookcases, file cabinets, or other furniture over 42" tall.
3. Do not stack furniture or heavy boxes.
4. Move tall furniture, file cabinets, or other objects away from exits. They should be moved a sufficient distance so that they will not block the exit if they topple over.
5. Do not use tall furniture as room or work area dividers.
6. Secure computers, equipment, and display or bookcases.
7. Store heavy items at floor level.
8. Back-up important work data and store away from the home workplace.
9. Develop an Emergency Survival Kit.

Fire Response

Fire remains a major hazard for any home. Good housekeeping, avoidance of overloading electrical outlets, use of Underwriters-Approved appliances and cords, and Ground Fault Interrupters will help reduce the risk of fire. Any use of candles or burning of incense must be carefully monitored and the materials properly extinguished.

In view of the heavy concentrations of electrical and electronic computer equipment in home work areas, such areas should be equipped with an ABC (meaning it can be used on paper and wood, grease, or electrical fires) fire extinguisher. ABC fire extinguishers are also recommended for the kitchen, garage, and any floor of the home that does not otherwise have an extinguisher.

It must be recognized that fire extinguishers have limited capabilities. Even if it appears that the extinguisher will stop the fire, the responder should immediately call the fire department by using 911. If calling from the standard house phone, most monitoring agencies will be able to tell the location to the responding fire fighters. At the present time, if using a cell phone, it will be necessary to tell the person receiving your call the location of the home.

In addition to calling the fire department, it is important to notify everyone in the home to evacuate the home immediately. Wait in the assembly area for fire fighters to respond.

Solvents may be used in homes to clean equipment or for other purposes. Never use solvents near an open flame, such as the pilot light of a stove, water heater, or furnace. Assure solvents are stored only in properly labeled and tightly capped containers. If a person smokes in the home, it is imperative that the smoker be alert when smoking. A significant number of home fires occur each year from smokers who fall asleep watching television or are otherwise distracted. Use ashtrays that will not tip and be certain that each cigarette is completely extinguished before leaving the room or disposing of the cigarette.

Power Failure

Loss of power may be due to a simple malfunction in the electrical distribution system or due to a disaster such as an earthquake, tornado, or explosion. Abrupt loss of power can pose serious problems for the home worker as well as other family members. If a power outage happens at night, there is the potential for serious injury in the dark due to falling over an object or down stairs. Lack of light will make it very difficult to evaluate the injury and accomplish any first aid. A flashlight with fresh batteries should be immediately available on each floor of the house. It is also recommended that one be kept at bedside.

With loss of power, heating systems, air conditioning, refrigerators, and telephones that require an electrical source will stop working. A cellular phone will assist in ascertaining the nature of the power failure and expected duration. If the temperature is quite cold or hot, it may be necessary to make alternate living arrangements or use the emergency supplies described below. If an attempt is made to prepare hot food by using propane gas or other fuel, be certain the cooking area is well ventilated and the stove is placed securely so that it will not tip over.

Accidents and First Aid

Falls, solid and liquid poisoning, fires, and suffocation due to ingested objects are leading causes of deaths in homes. A disabling injury occurs every 5 seconds in homes in the United States. Prompt response and first aid can help prevent deaths or, in the case of an injury, help avoid further injury and speed healing of the injured part. It is recommended each person take a first aid course, such as the one offered by the American Red Cross. Each home should be equipped with a basic first aid kit, complete with instructions that should be reviewed by each family member. You can obtain AFirst Aid Fast@ from local chapters of the American Red Cross that provides first aid information and recommendations for a first aid kit. Recommendations of the American Red Cross and others for a basic first aid kit include the following:

- Analgesic, e.g. Acetaminophen, Ibuprofen
- Activated Charcoal (use only if instructed by Poison Control Center)
- Adhesive Tape
- Antiseptic Ointment
- Band-Aids (assorted sizes)
- Blanket
- Cold Pack
- Disposable gloves
- Eye pads
- Gauze Pads and Roller Gauze (assorted sizes)
- Hand Cleaner
- Plastic Bags
- Scissors and Tweezers
- Small Flashlight and Extra Batteries
- Syrup of Ipecac (use only if instructed by Poison Control Center)
- Triangular Bandage

Poisoning has always been one of the leading causes of fatalities in the home. Prompt action is essential in any poisoning, and a Poison Control Center can give rapid instruction on the best way to treat ingestion of a toxic substance. Telephone numbers of the Centers are listed in the emergency sections of most telephone directory books. Keep the number readily available if 911 in your area does not have direct contact with a Center. Tragically, *gun accidents* continue to cause deaths in children and adults. Guns must be kept secure to avoid any possible misuse. Accidents involving both children and adults continue to occur because the gun was thought to be unloaded. Gun safety is of crucial importance if weapons are to be kept in the home.

Cardio-Pulmonary Resuscitation (CPR) and the Heimlich Maneuver

The Red Cross and other organizations also offer *CPR courses*, and taking a course is strongly recommended. If infants are in the home, it is essential to take a course that includes the special instructions needed to respond to a problem in an infant or child. Prompt administration of CPR, even if done by only one person, can save a life. The *Heimlich maneuver* has been highly effective in restoring breathing to people choking on food or other object. As with CPR, it is essential to know how to do the *Heimlich* on children, who frequently choke on objects they have put in their mouths.

Floods and Other Conditions Requiring Turn Off of Water, Electricity, and Gas

If in a flood plain, the emergency escape plans discussed previously must include plans for rapid evacuation or other appropriate action should a flood occur. Even if not in an area with flood potential, a broken pipe, drain back-up, or similar problems can produce water hazards. Depending on location of the water and electrical equipment or outlets, a serious electrical hazard may result. Extinguishing of gas flame devices may result in release of gas if there is not an automatic shut-off device for such situations. It is important to consider such possibilities in developing emergency response plans and know how to shut off these services.

Emergency Survival Kits

In view of the potential for *natural* or *terrorist events* that may necessitate evacuating the home, consider obtaining or preparing a 72-hour kit to be used in such an emergency. The kit could also be used while staying in the home even if water, electricity, and natural gas were not available, e.g. after an earthquake. Experience during Katrina suggests it would be wise to plan for periods longer than 72 hours. Kits are available from commercial sources or can be prepared by individuals.

Preparation for Terrorism and Pandemics

The events of September 11, 2001 and the subsequent *anthrax* exposures have underscored our vulnerability to terrorist attacks. Although these events were tragic, our nation and its response agencies are now better prepared to respond to terrorist events. Additionally, health providers are now poised to recognize, and treat, a disease caused by *bioterrorism*. Early diagnosis and treatment during the anthrax exposures resulted in many fewer deaths than those projected from prior studies that noted a high fatality rate. Bioterrorism agents of primary concern to the Centers for Disease Control and Prevention are those producing *anthrax*, *botulism*, *pneumonic plague*, *smallpox*, *tularemia*, and *viral hemorrhagic fevers*. These agents are called Category A agents, the each one meets the following criteria:

- Easily disseminated or transmitted from person to person
- High mortality rates
- Major public health impacts
- Produce public panic and social disruption
- Require extensive, special public health action

Other terrorist agents are chemical, with the nerve gas used in the Tokyo subways as a classic example; radiological, including the "*dirty bomb*" or other dispersal of radioactive material; nuclear, with particular concern regarding "small" nuclear weapons; and explosive devices, as demonstrated on 9/11 in 2001. The overwhelming majority of terrorist devices to date have been explosive ones.

Should a terrorist event occur, local, state, and federal agencies would be rapidly involved and able to provide assistance. However, there are planning and other steps individuals can take to respond to the possible threats. These include the following:

1. Ensure all family members receive annual influenza immunizations. Respiratory symptoms are the initial manifestations of exposure to a number of biological agents. Preventing influenza will help reduce concerns in those that would have developed symptoms had they not had the immunizations. Similarly, a history of immunization will aid health providers in evaluating patients who do develop symptoms. (It is recognized that a specific person may still contract influenza even if immunized. However, large numbers of epidemiologic studies have clearly demonstrated that immunizations will dramatically reduce the number of people who contract influenza.)
2. Ensure all family members recognize the need to respond rapidly to unusual events, including:
   A. If in a shopping mall or other crowd situation, evacuate the area *immediately* and obtain medical evaluation if any of the following occurs (all are suggestive of exposure to a chemical agent or agents):
      - Sudden occurrence of an unusual odor that permeates the area.
      - Sudden onset of sneezing, coughing, watery eyes, nasal discharge, or shortness of breath.
      - Onset of itching or burning of the eyes or skin.
      - Onset of tremors, twitching of muscles, or other muscular symptoms.
      - Abrupt onset of nausea, vomiting, urination, defecation.
      - Flush eyes and skin with water if tearing or burning occurs. Remove all clothing with minimal handling to avoid ongoing or further contamination.

   B. Obtain prompt medical evaluation if any of the following develops:

- Fever, severe malaise, non-productive or minimally productive cough, headache, respiratory distress. (Several biological agents)
- Blurred vision, double vision, dry mouth, muscle weakness or paralysis. (Botulism)
- Unusual skin lesion or lesions, especially black, ulcerated lesions. (Cutaneous anthrax)
- High fever, prostration, headache followed by rash on face and extremities. (Smallpox)
- Other unusual or unusually severe symptoms.

C. Suspicious mail or packages, e.g. no, or unknown, return address, excessive postage, excessive tape or string, discolouration, odor, incorrect titles. (CDC recommendations)

- Do not shake or empty the contents.
- Do not carry the package or envelope, show it to others, or permit others to examine it.
- Put the package or envelope on a table or other stable surface.
- Do not touch, taste, or sniff any contents that may have come out of the envelope or package.
- Alert others in the area, depart the area, close doors. Turn off ventilation system if possible.
- Wash your hands promptly with soap and water.
- Notify police or security personnel.

What about gas masks (respirators)?

A properly fitted "*gas mask*" will protect against inhalation of bioterrorism agents as well as some chemical agents. However, such a mask must be "*fit tested*" by professionals to preclude leaks. The filtering cartridges must be kept current to assure effectiveness. Since bioterrorism agents cannot be seen, one would have to wear the mask 24 hours a day 7 days a week to be certain of effectiveness. As anyone who has used such a mask will attest, the masks are uncomfortable and 24/7 use is not practical. Additionally, many chemical agents are absorbed through the skin so the mask would not prevent toxic effects from such agents.

Preparing for Pandemics

Dr. Gerberding, Director of the Centers for Disease Control and Prevention (CDC), has appropriately commented, "It is not 'if' we have an influenza pandemic but 'when'.". Recent estimates are that an influenza pandemic of the severity of the 1918 outbreak would produce illness in 80 million people in the United States, with 45 million needing hospitalization and 2 million deaths. In Utah, 800,000 patients would be infected and 4,000 people would die.

Of course, the H5N1 Avian Flu outbreaks could present a new challenge. To date, almost all of the cases of this disease in humans have been the result of close contact with infected birds. However, the human mortality rate has been over 50%. Influenza viruses are known for their ability to mutate, and if the virus mutates to permit human-to-human transmission, the stage would be set for a serious pandemic. The 1918 influenza pandemic, as well as more recent ones, have been due to an avian flu variant.

The recent outbreak of Severe Acute Respiratory Syndrome (SARS) illustrates the threat from emerging infections. SARS spread rapidly around the world, and required a hospital in Toronto to close because it became a source of the disease. Fortunately, rapid public health action controlled the situation before widespread outbreaks occurred.

There are a number of steps that can be taken to respond to widespread respiratory disease outbreaks. It will be important to avoid crowds. Police, fire, hospitals, and business organizations may experience absentee rates of approximately 30%. Such absences will have a severe impact on the services that can be provided. It would be appropriate to increase home stores of food, water and other necessities to avoid having to visit locations with crowds. Currently, it is recommended that you plan to have such supplies available for periods of 2 to 4 weeks in preparing for a pandemic. You may wish to expand the other supplies in your "72-hour" kit. If possible, prepare to work from home to the extent possible and recognize that schools may be closed. Frequent hand washing and use of disposable tissues are of particular importance. Dust masks from local hardware or similar stores can provide some protection as will N-95 respirators obtained from medical supply houses. Government agencies have plans to provide additional instructions by television or radio.

13

Bioterrorism Working Group

Bioterrorism Readiness Planning

Healthcare facilities must be prepared to respond to *bioterrorism* (BT) attacks and threats. The Bioterrorism Readiness Working Group (BTWG) of the Association for Professionals in Infection Control and Epidemiology (APIC) offers this document as a summary of suggestions by APIC BT Advisors, ICPs, our members, and agency liaisons to facilitate preparation of BT readiness plans for individual and regional institutions.

These suggestions are not intended to provide an exhaustive reference on the topic of bioterrorism. Rather it is intended to serve as a tool for infection control (IC) professionals and healthcare epidemiologists to guide the development of practical and realistic response plans for their institutions in preparation for a real or suspected BT attack. In order for this document to serve its intended purpose, it must be adapted to fit your individual facility. Institution-specific response-plans should be prepared in partnership with local, state, and regional resources including health departments, emergency management, and first responders. Many of the facility BT planning components may be incorporated into existing disaster preparedness and other emergency management plans. These components also are useful for identifying and responding to other infectious disease outbreaks in the community. Individual facilities should determine the extent of their bioterrorism readiness needs, which may range from notification of local emergency networks and transfer of affected patients to appropriate acute care facilities, to activation of large, comprehensive communication and management networks.

Hospitals and *clinics* may have the first opportunity to recognize and initiate a response to a bioterrorism-related outbreak. Healthcare facilities should have IC policies in place authorizing the hospital epidemiologist, IC committee chairman, or designee to rapidly implement prevention and control measures in response to a suspected outbreak. If a *bioterrorism* event is suspected, a network of communication must be activated to involve emergency department (ED), emergency medical service (EMS) and IC personnel, hospital administration, local and state health departments, the Federal Bureau of Investigation (FBI) field office, local, state and federal emergency management and CDC (see Reporting Requirements and Contact Information below). Existing local emergency plans should be reviewed, and a multidisciplinary approach outlined that includes local EMS, police and fire departments, and media relations in addition to healthcare administrators and providers, and IC professionals.

In order to maximize the efficacy of your facility plan, annual disaster preparedness drills should incorporate a bioterrorism scenario to test and refine *Bioterrorism Readiness Plans* at each individual facility. An annual drill such as this would serve to meet the Joint Commission on Accreditation of Healthcare Organizations' (JCAHO) Environment of Care Standard EC. 2.9.1, which requires facilities to execute their disaster management plan by conducting emergency management drills.

An integral part of any mass casualty disaster plan includes the ability to dovetail with other civilian and military plans. One example of such an emergency management system is the Hospital Emergency Incident Command System (HEICS). HEICS is an emergency management system that employs a logical management structure, defined responsibilities, clear reporting channels, and a common nomenclature to help unify hospitals with other emergency responders. There are clear advantages to all hospitals using this particular emergency management system. Assessing your facility is a first step in developing a disaster response plan. One tool for such an assessment is the APIC Facility Mass Casualty Disaster Plan Checklist. This tool is designed to assist in the assessment process while encouraging dialogue with community resources.

Categorical Recommendations

Reporting Requirements and Contact Information

Healthcare facilities may be the initial site of recognition and response to bioterrorism attacks. If a bioterrorism attack is suspected, local emergency response systems should be activated. Notification should be immediate and include ED and infection control personnel, and the healthcare facility administration. There should be prompt communication with the local health department and FBI field office. This notification network includes local, state and regional health departments, FBI field office, local police, EMS, CDC, and the Federal Emergency Management Agency (FEMA). (In an overt BT event, the FBI is declared the lead agency, except in the situation of smallpox where FEMA becomes the lead agency.) It is important to note that given the best of communication, it is important to note that most cities/states will have to provide their own response for the first 48-72 hours.

Potential Agents

There are potentially thousands of agents that could be used in a *BT attack*. The CDC categorizes the agents of greatest threat into categories A, B and C. These agents are categorized based on the following criteria: ease of dissemination, potential for public health impact, and potential for public panic and social disruption. Recognizing this, six diseases with BT potential (*anthrax*, *botulism*, *plague*, *smallpox*, *tularemia*, and *viral hemorrhagic fever* [VHF]) and the agents responsible for them are already described. The CDC does not prioritize these agents in any order of importance or likelihood of use.

Subsequent revisions of this document may address additional agents with bioterrorism potential, including those that cause *brucellosis*, Q fever, viral encephalitis, and disease associated with *staphylococcal enterotoxin B*.

Detection of Outbreaks Caused by Agents of Bioterrorism

Bioterrorism may occur as covert events, in which persons are unknowingly exposed and an outbreak is suspected only upon recognition of unusual disease clusters or symptoms. Bioterrorism may also occur as announced events, in which persons are warned that an exposure has occurred. A number of announced BT events have occurred in the United States from 1998-2000, but these were determined to have been hoaxes; that is, there were no true exposures to *BT agents*. However, in 2001, bioterrorism events resulted in deaths due to inhalation of *Bacillus anthracis* spores sent through the US Postal Service.

As previously stated, JCAHO requires that every healthcare facility have a disaster plan that includes BT preparedness. A healthcare facility's *Bioterrorism Readiness Plan* should include details for management of both types of scenarios: suspicion of a BT outbreak possibly associated with a covert event and announced BT events or threats. Concerns about a suspected BT event should be evaluated with the assistance of the FBI and state health officials and emergency management agencies, including FEMA as previously indicated.

Syndrome-based criteria

Rapid response to a BT-related outbreak requires prompt identification of its onset. Because of the rapid progression to illness and potential for dissemination of some of these agents, it may not be practical to await diagnostic laboratory confirmation. Instead, it will be necessary to initiate a response based on the recognition of *high-risk syndromes*. Each of the agent-specific plans includes a syndrome description (i.e., typical combination of clinical features of the illness at presentation) that should alert healthcare practitioners to the possibility of a *BT-related outbreak*.

Epidemiologic features

Epidemiologic principles must be used to assess whether a patient's presentation is typical of an endemic disease or is an unusual event that should raise concern. Features that should alert healthcare providers to the possibility of a bioterrorism-related outbreak include:

1. A rapidly increasing disease incidence (e.g., within hours or days) in a normally healthy population.
2. An epidemic curve that rises and falls during a short period of time.
3. An unusual increase in the number of people seeking care, especially with fever, respiratory, or gastrointestinal complaints.
4. An endemic disease rapidly emerging at an uncharacteristic time or in an unusual pattern.
5. Lower attack rates among people who had been indoors, especially in areas with filtered air or closed ventilation systems, compared with people who had been outdoors.
6. Clusters of patients arriving from a single locale.
7. Large numbers of rapidly fatal cases
8. Any patient presenting with a disease that is relatively uncommon and has bioterrorism potential (e.g., *pulmonary anthrax*, *tularemia*, or *piague*).

Infection Control Practices for Patient Management

The management of patients following suspected or confirmed bioterrorism events must be well organized and rehearsed. Strong leadership and effective communication are paramount.

Isolation precautions

Many of the agents likely to be used in a BT attack are not transmitted from person to person and re-aerosolization of these agents is unlikely. All patients in healthcare facilities, including symptomatic patients with suspected or confirmed BT-related illnesses, should be managed utilizing *Standard Precautions*. Standard Precautions are designed to reduce transmission from both recognized and unrecognized sources of infection in healthcare facilities, and are recommended for all patients receiving care, regardless of their diagnosis or presumed infection status. For certain diseases or syndromes (e.g., smallpox and pneumonic plague), additional precautions may be needed to reduce the likelihood for transmission.

Standard Precautions prevent direct contact with all body fluids (including blood), secretions, excretions, nonintact skin (including rashes), and mucous membranes. Standard Precautions routinely practiced by healthcare providers include:

Handwashing / Hand hygiene

Hands are washed after touching blood, body fluids, excretions, secretions, or items contaminated with such body fluids, whether or not gloves are worn. Hands are washed immediately after gloves are removed, between patient contacts, and as appropriate to avoid transfer of microorganisms to other patients and the environment. Either plain or antimicrobial-containing soaps may be used according to facility policy. Alcohol based hand sanitizers are acceptable for all hand hygiene except when hands are visibly/grossly soiled or if the organisms contaminating the hands are hardy pathogens such as the spores of *Bacillus anthracis*. In the absence of running water, hand sanitizers may serve as an interim measure of hand hygiene.

Gloves

Clean, *non-sterile gloves* are worn when touching blood, body fluids, excretions, secretions, or items contaminated with such body fluids. *Clean gloves* are put on just before touching mucous membranes and nonintact skin. Gloves are changed between tasks and between procedures on the same patient if contact occurs with contaminated material. Hands are washed promptly after removing gloves and before leaving a patient care area.

Masks/Eye protection or Face shields

A mask and eye protection (or *face shield*) are worn to protect mucous membranes of the eyes, nose, and mouth while performing procedures and patient care activities that may cause splashes of blood, body fluids, excretions, or secretions.

Gowns

A *gown* is worn to protect skin and prevent soiling of clothing during procedures and patient-care activities that are likely to generate splashes or sprays of blood, body fluids, excretions, or secretions. Selection of gowns and gown materials should be suitable for the activity and amount of body fluid likely to be encountered. *Soiled gowns* are removed promptly and hands are washed to avoid transfer of microorganisms to other patients and environments.

Policies for the prevention of occupational injury and exposure to bloodborne pathogens (in accordance with Standard Precautions) should be in place within each healthcare facility. In the event a healthcare worker or other responder has an exposure to blood or other potentially infectious body fluids, post exposure management should be consistent with current Public Health Service recommendations.

Patient placement

In small-scale events, routine facility *patient placement* and infection control practices should be followed. However, when the number of patients presenting to a healthcare facility is too large to allow routine triage and isolation strategies (if required), it will be necessary to apply practical alternatives. These may include cohorting patients who present with similar syndromes, i.e., grouping affected patients into a designated section of a clinic or emergency department, or a designated ward or floor of a facility, or even setting up a response center at a separate building. Designated internal cohorting sites should be chosen in advance by the IC Committee (or other appropriate decision-making body), in consultation with ED and EMS personnel, and facility engineering staff; and should be based on patient arrival sites, patterns of airflow and ventilation, availability of adequate plumbing and waste disposal, and capacity to safely hold potentially large numbers of patients. Designated external cohorting sites should be coordinated through local, state and regional planning efforts. Any triage or cohort site should have controlled entry to minimize the possibility for transmission. At the same time, reasonable access to vital diagnostic services, e.g., radiography departments, should be maintained.

Patient transport

Most infections associated with BT agents cannot be transmitted from person-to-person. In general, the transport and movement of patients with BT-related infections, as for patients with any epidemiologically important infections (e.g., *pulmonary tuberculosis*, *chickenpox*, *measles*), should be limited to movement that is essential to provide patient care, thus reducing the opportunities for transmission of microorganisms within healthcare facilities.

Cleaning, disinfection, and sterilization of equipment and environment

Principles of *Standard Precautions* should be generally applied for the management of durable medical equipment and environmental infection control.

1. Used durable medical equipment soiled or potentially contaminated with blood, body fluids, secretions, or excretions should be handled in a manner that prevents exposures to skin and mucous membranes, avoids contamination of clothing, and minimizes the likelihood of transfer of microbes to other patients and environments.
2. Sterilization is required for all instruments or equipment that enter normally sterile tissues or through which blood flows.
3. Each facility should have in place adequate procedures for the routine care, cleaning, and disinfection of environmental surfaces, beds, bedrails, bedside equipment, and other frequently touched surfaces and equipment, and should ensure that these procedures are being followed.
4. With the exception of linens used on patients with actual or suspected smallpox and VHF, patient linens should be handled in accordance with Standard Precautions. Although linens may be contaminated, the risk of disease transmission is negligible if it is handled, transported, and laundered in a manner that avoids transfer of microorganisms to other patients, personnel and environments. Facility policy and local/state regulations should determine the methods for handling, transporting, and laundering soiled linen. It is important to include contract laundry facilities in the organization's BT response plan.
5. Rooms and bedside equipment of patients with bioterrorism-related infections should be cleaned using the same procedures that are used for all patients as a component of Standard Precautions, unless the infecting microorganism and the amount of environmental contamination indicates special cleaning. In addition to adequate cleaning, thorough disinfection of bedside equipment and environmental surfaces may be indicated for certain organisms that can survive in the inanimate environment for extended periods

of time. The methods and frequency of cleaning and the products used are determined by facility policy. It is essential to select an EPA-approved hospital grade germicidal product that is appropriate for the specific agent identified or suspected.

6. Policies should be in place to ensure that reusable equipment is not used for the care of another patient until it has been appropriately cleaned and reprocessed, and to ensure that single-use patient items are appropriately discarded.
7. EPA-registered facility-approved germicidal cleaning agents should be available in patient care areas to use for cleaning spills of contaminated material and disinfecting non-critical equipment.
8. Contaminated waste should be sorted and discarded in accordance with federal, state and local regulations.

Discharge management

Under most circumstances, patients with BT-related infections will not be discharged from the facility until they are deemed noninfectious. However, consideration should be given to developing home-care instructions and fact sheets in the event that large numbers of persons exposed may preclude admission of all infected patients. Depending on the exposure and illness, home care instructions may include recommendations for the use of appropriate barrier precautions, handwashing, waste management, and cleaning and disinfection of the environment and patient-care items.

Post-mortem care

Pathology departments and clinical laboratories should be informed of a potentially infectious outbreak prior to submitting any specimens for examination or disposal. All *autopsies* should be performed using all personal protective equipment and standards of practice in accordance with Standard Precautions, including the use of masks and eye protection whenever the splashes or splatter of body fluids are anticipated. Practices that generate fine aerosols, e.g., use of oscillating saws, should be undertaken using appropriate protective measures, including respirators and biosafety hoods. Instructions for funeral directors should be developed and incorporated into the *Bioterrorism Readiness Plan* for communication. In the event a large number of casualties has resulted from the BT event it is important to consider alternative morgue facilities within a healthcare organization, or even a community. Some possible solutions may include the use of refrigerated trucks or storage areas. Additionally, note suppliers of body bags and have alternate sources available. It is important to consider that a BT event could quickly overwhelm a community and for management/Public Health reasons, mass graves or cremation may have to be utilized. The State Public Health Department, CDC, and Mortuary Association will offer guidance in this event.

Post Exposure Management

Decontamination of patients and environment

The need for *decontamination* depends on the suspected exposure and in most cases will not be necessary. The goal of decontamination after a potential exposure to a BT agent is to reduce the extent of external contamination of the patient and contain the contamination to prevent further spread. Decisions regarding the need for decontamination should be made in consultation with local, state and regional health departments. Decontamination of exposed individuals prior to receiving them in the healthcare facility may be necessary to ensure the safety of patients and staff while providing care. When developing Bioterrorism Readiness Plans, facilities should consider available locations and procedures for patient decontamination prior to facility entry. Unlike the sequestering of runoff from chemical decontamination, containment of runoff from biological agent decontamination is usually not an emergent issue. This issue should be handled on a case-by-case basis.

According to the EPA, first responders are protected under the Comprehensive Environmental Response, Compensation and Liability Act (CERCLA) when undertaking necessary emergency actions to save lives and protect the public and themselves during a hazardous materials incident, including a bioterrorism attack. This applies to containment of contaminated runoff during the response to a crisis such as a bioterrorism attack. However, once the imminent threat to human health and life are addressed, all reasonable efforts should be made to contain the contamination and avoid or mitigate environmental consequences. It should be noted that CERCLA does not protect against intentional contamination such as washing hazardous materials down a storm-sewer as an alternative to a more costly and problematic disposal in order to save money or avoid extra effort.

Depending on the agent, the likelihood for re-aerosolization, or a risk associated with cutaneous exposure, clothing of exposed persons may need to be removed. After removal of contaminated clothing, patients should be instructed (or assisted, if necessary) to immediately shower with soap and water, to include the shampooing of hair. Potentially harmful practices, such as bathing patients with bleach solutions, are unnecessary and should be avoided. Clean water, saline solution, or commercial ophthalmic solutions are recommended for rinsing eyes. If removal is indicated, patient clothing should be handled only by personnel wearing appropriate personal protective equipment, and placed in an impervious bag to prevent further environmental contamination.

Development of *Bioterrorism Readiness Plans* should include coordination with the FBI field office and FEMA, as previously indicated. The FBI may require collection of exposed clothing and other potential evidence for submission to FBI or Department of Defense laboratories to assist in potential criminal investigations. Chain of custody documentation must accompany the specimen from the moment of collection.

Prophylaxis and post-exposure immunization

Recommendations for *prophylaxis* are subject to change. Current recommendations for postexposure *prophylaxis* and *immunization* are provided for relevant potential bioterrorism agents. However, up-to-date recommendations should be obtained in consultation with local, state and regional health departments and CDC. Facilities should ensure that policies are in place to identify and manage health care workers exposed to infectious patients. In general, maintenance of accurate occupational health records will facilitate identification, contact, assessment, and delivery of postexposure care to potentially exposed healthcare workers.

Consideration must be given to the facility's role in *mass prophylaxis*. This would include provisions for prophylaxis and/or immunization of healthcare workers and potentially, their household contacts. This is in addition to the role of the facility in community prophylaxis and/or immunization.

Triage and management of large scale exposures and suspected exposures

Each healthcare facility, with the involvement of the IC committee, administration, building engineering staff, and ED, laboratory, and nursing directors, should clarify in advance how they will best be able to deliver care in the event of a large scale exposure. Facilities should incorporate into their *Bioterrorism Readiness Plan* processes for triage and safe housing and care for potentially large numbers of affected individuals. Facility needs will vary with the size of the regional population served and the proximity to other healthcare facilities and external assistance. Triage and management planning for large-scale events may include:

1. Planning for the allocation or re-allocation of scarce equipment in the event of a large-scale event (e.g., duration of ventilator support of terminally ill individuals).
2. Developing discharge instructions for patients determined to be non-contagious or in need of additional on-site care, including medical follow-up.
3. With assistance from the Pathology service, identifying the institution's ability to manage a sudden increase in the number of cadavers on site.
4. Establishing networks of communication and lines of authority required to coordinate on-site care.
5. Determining availability and sources for additional medical equipment and supplies (e.g., ventilators) that may be needed for urgent large-scale care.
6. Identifying sources able to supply available vaccines, immune globulin, antibiotics, and antitoxin (with assistance from local, state and regional health departments).
7. Planning for cancellation of non-emergency services and procedures.
8. Planning for the efficient evaluation and discharge of patients.

Psychological aspects of bioterrorism

Following a BT-related event, fear and panic can be expected from both patients and healthcare providers. Psychological responses following a bioterrorism event may include horror, anger, panic, unrealistic concerns about infection, fear of contagion, paranoia, social isolation, or demoralization. IC professionals should develop prior working relationships with mental health support personnel (e.g., *psychiatrists*, *psychologists*, *social workers*, *clergy*, and *volunteer groups*) and assist in their collaboration with emergency response agencies and the media.

When developing the facility Bioterrorism Readiness Plan, consider the following to address patient and general public fears:

1. Minimize panic by clearly explaining risks, offering careful but rapid medical evaluation/treatment, and avoiding unnecessary isolation or quarantine.
2. Make available educational materials for the general public. These materials should be obtained *before* an incident and kept on hand for quick distribution following a known or suspected BT attack.
3. Provisions for medical intervention in unexposed persons who are experiencing somatic symptoms (e.g., with reassurance, or

medication as indicated for acute relief of those who do not respond to reassurance).

Consider the following to address healthcare worker fears:

1. Provide bioterrorism readiness education, including frank discussions of potential risks and plans for protecting healthcare providers.
2. Invite active, voluntary involvement in the bioterrorism readiness planning process.
3. Encourage participation in disaster drills.

Fearful or anxious healthcare workers may benefit from their usual sources of social support, or by being asked to fulfill a useful role (e.g., as a volunteer at the triage site).

Laboratory Support and Confirmation

This part of the document is subject to updates due to current work underway to improve the diagnostic capacity of laboratories to isolate and identify these agents. Facilities should work with local, state and federal public health services to tailor diagnostic strategies to specific events. Currently the Bioterrorism Emergency Number at CDC is at the Emergency Response Office, National Center for Environmental Health (NCEH), 770/488-7100.

The Laboratory Response Network (LRN) is also available to assist with support of the laboratory. The LRN is a product of the CDC with the goals being to provide an organized approach to the detection, recovery, and identification of suspected/suspicious biological agents. The LRN is divided into four levels (A, B, C, D). All non-public health laboratories are regarded as Level A. These laboratories have the primary responsibility of ruling out suspected agents and referring suspicious agents to the next Level (B, C, D) depending upon the nature of the agent. Laboratories that are designated as Levels B, C, or D all have unique diagnostic testing capabilities in addition to incremental safety levels. For example, Levels B and C have Biosafety Level 3 containment facilities. Level D has Biosafety Level 4 capabilities. Level A laboratories are not to handle or examine non-human specimens (i.e., environmental and animal specimens) but are to refer them to the next level following consultation with their state health laboratory. Level B and above, are responsible for "*ruling in*", performing genetic characterization, and archiving these agents.

Obtaining diagnostic samples

See specific recommendations for diagnostic sampling for each agent. Sampling should be performed in accordance with Standard

Precautions. In all cases of suspected BT, collect an acute phase serum sample to be analyzed, aliquotted, and saved for comparison to a later convalescent serum sample. Because samples may be considered evidence, it is important to have a protocol in place to address a chain of custody for any sample being used to diagnose a potential BT patient. As a general rule, these samples should not be sent through automated tube systems; samples should be hand carried to the lab.

Laboratory criteria for processing potential bioterrorism agents

To evaluate laboratory capacity in the United States, laboratories were grouped into one of four levels, according to their ability to support the diagnostic needs presented by an event. The laboratory levels are:

- Level A: Clinical laboratories—minimal identification, e.g., "rule-out" testing of Agents. Level A testing protocols are available via the site www.bt.cdc.gov and the American Society for Microbiology (ASM) site www.asmusa.org
- Level B: County/ State/ other laboratories—identification, confirmation, susceptibility testing
- Level C: State and other large facility laboratories with advanced capacity for testing—some molecular technologies
- Level D: CDC or select Department of Defense laboratories, such as U.S. Army Medical Research Institute of Infectious Diseases (USAMRIID)—Bio Safety Level (BSL) 3 and 4 labs with special surge capacity and advanced molecular typing techniques.

Transport requirements

Specimen packaging and transport must be coordinated with local, state and regional health departments, and the FBI. Chain of custody documents should accompany a specimen only if directed by the local or federal law enforcement agency. Chain of Custody does not apply to Level A laboratories because the Level A labs should not accept or analyze non-human specimens. Chain of Custody is appropriate for non-human specimens or items that are followed and examined for evidentiary purposes. Human specimens will not meet this requirement. Level A laboratories should, therefore, maintain a suspicious isolate or specimen until an event is deemed as credible. Further direction may be given by the local, state, or federal lead agency.

For specific instructions, contact the Bioterrorism Emergency Number at the CDC Emergency Response Office, 770/488-7100. Advance planning may include identification of appropriate packaging materials and transport media in collaboration with the clinical laboratory at individual facilities. When sending specimens or microbial isolates to the next level of testing, Level A laboratories must be compliant with current federal and/or *International Air Transport Association* (IATA) packaging and shipping guidelines. Only laboratory personnel specially trained in packaging and shipping are permitted to package and ship specimens to the next level laboratory.

Patient, Visitor, and Public Information

Clear, consistent, understandable information should be provided (e.g., via fact sheets) to patients, visitors, and the general public. During *bioterrorism-related outbreaks*, visitors may be strictly limited.

A well-designed healthcare facility *Bioterrorism Readiness Plan* should clarify the lines of authority and flow of communication. To minimize the anticipated responses of fear, confusion and anger, healthcare facilities should plan in advance the methods and channels of communications to be used to inform the public. IC professionals working with the IC committee and administration should coordinate in advance with local, state and regional health agencies, local emergency services, and local broadcast media systems to decide how communication and action across agencies will be accomplished. Failure to provide a public forum for information exchange may increase anxiety and misunderstanding, increasing fear among individuals who attribute non-specific symptoms to exposure to the BT agent.

Agent-Specific Recommendations

Anthrax

Description of agent/syndrome

Etiology

Anthrax is an acute infectious disease caused by *Bacillus anthracis*, a spore forming, gram-positive bacillus. Associated disease occurs most frequently in sheep, goats, and cattle, which acquire spores through ingestion of contaminated soil. Humans can become infected through contact with non-intact skin, ingestion, or inhalation of *B. anthracis* spores from infected animals or animal products (as in "*woolsorter's disease*" from exposure to goat hair). Person-to-person transmission of inhalational disease does not occur. Due to vesicular secretions of *cutaneous anthrax lesions*, Standard Precautions should be followed.

Clinical features

Human anthrax infection can occur in three forms: inhalational, cutaneous, or gastrointestinal, depending on the route of exposure. Of these forms, inhalational anthrax is associated with BT exposure to aerosolized spores. Clinical features for each form of anthrax include:

- Inhalational
  1. Non-specific prodrome of flu-like symptoms, specifically fever, follows inhalation of infectious spores.
  2. Possible brief interim improvement.
  3. Two to four days after initial symptoms, *abrupt onset of respiratory failure* and *hemodynamic collapse*, possibly accompanied by *thoracic edema* and a widened mediastinum on chest radiograph suggestive of mediastinal lymphadenopathy and hemorrhagic mediastinitis. The 2001 cases of inhalational anthrax demonstrated the usefulness of chest CAT scan instead of the standard chest x-ray alone.
  4. Gram-positive bacilli on blood culture, usually after the first two or three days of illness. Alert the lab that the sample may contain anthrax as gram-positive bacilli are generally considered to be contaminants. Confirmatory testing for *Bacillus anthracis* is usually available at state health department reference laboratories or other level B laboratory, although initial testing may have been performed using your facility's routine lab.
  5. Treatable in early prodromal stage. Mortality remains extremely high despite antibiotic treatment if it is initiated after onset of respiratory symptoms.
- Cutaneous
  1. Local skin involvement after direct contact with spores or bacilli.
  2. Commonly seen on the head, forearms or hands.
  3. Localized itching followed by a papular lesion that turns vesicular, and within 2-6 days develops into a depressed black eschar.
  4. Oftentimes, *Bacillus anthracis* may be cultured from lesion drainage. Confirmatory testing must be obtained from the state health department reference laboratory or other level B laboratory.
  5. Usually non-fatal if treated with antibiotics.
- Gastrointestinal
  1. Abdominal pain, nausea, vomiting, and fever following ingestion of contaminated food, usually meat.
  2. Bloody diarrhea, hematemesis.

3. Gram-positive bacilli on blood culture, usually after the first two or three days of illness.
4. Usually fatal after progression to toxemia and sepsis.

Modes of transmission

The spore form of *B. anthracis* is durable. As a bioterrorism agent, it could be delivered as an aerosol. The modes of transmission for anthrax include:

1. Inhalation of spores.
2. Cutaneous contact with spores or spore-contaminated materials.
3. Ingestion of contaminated food.

Incubation period

Based on limited scientific data, the incubation period following exposure to *B. anthracis* is estimated to range from 1 day to 8 weeks (average 5 days), depending on the exposure route and dose:

1. 1-5 days (may be as long as 60 days) following inhalational exposure.
2. 1-7 days (may be up to 15 days) following cutaneous exposure.
3. 2-7 days following ingestion.

Period of communicability

Transmission of anthrax infections from person to person is unlikely. Airborne transmission does not occur, but direct contact with skin lesions may result in cutaneous infection.

Preventive Measures

(a) *Vaccine availability*. Inactivated, cell-free anthrax vaccine—limited availability.

(b) *Immunization recommendations*. Routine vaccination of civilian populations is not currently recommended.

Infection control practices for patient management

Symptomatic patients with suspected or confirmed infections with *B. anthracis* should be managed according to current guidelines specific to their disease state. Recommendations for chemotherapy are beyond the scope of this document. CDC documents should be consulted for the most current information and recommendations for therapy.

Isolation precautions

Standard Precautions are used for the care of patients with infections associated with *B. anthracis*. Standard Precautions include the routine use of gloves for contact with non-intact skin, including rashes and skin lesions.

Patient placement

Private room placement for patients with anthrax is not necessary. Airborne transmission of anthrax does not occur. Skin lesions may be infectious, but requires direct skin contact. Patient room selection and care should be consistent with facility policy.

Patient transport

Standard Precautions should be used for transport and movement of patients with *B. anthracis* infections.

Cleaning, disinfection, and sterilization of equipment and environment

Principles of Standard Precautions should be generally applied for the management of patient-care equipment and for environmental control. Equipment and environmental surfaces that may have come into contact with drainage or secretions of a patient with cutaneous anthrax must be thoroughly cleaned and disinfected as soon as possible and prior to contact with other healthcare workers or patients. Decontaminate environmental surfaces using an EPA-registered, healthcare facility-approved disinfectant or 0.5% hypochlorite solution (one part household bleach added to nine parts water).

Discharge management

No special discharge instructions are indicated. Home care providers should be taught to use Standard Precautions for all patient care (e.g., dressing changes). If clothing was bagged at time of decontamination or admission and there is reasonable certainty that the clothing does not represent a risk for agent transmission, the following process can be used for laundering: wash in hot water (in a separate load from other clothing) with 1 cup bleach added, then dry in hot dryer. If it cannot be determined that clothing is without risk of agent transmission, follow instructions provided by public health authority.

Post-mortem care

Standard Precautions should be used for post-mortem care. Standard Precautions include wearing appropriate personal protective equipment, including masks and eye protection, when splashes or splatter of body fluids is anticipated. Procedures that generate fine aerosols, e.g., using oscillating saws, should be avoided or performed using appropriate safety devices, e.g., biosafety cabinets. If autopsies are performed, all related instruments and materials should be autoclaved or incinerated. Care should be taken to prevent cuts or other percutaneous injuries during post-mortem evaluation. Spills or splashes during post mortem evaluation should be cleaned promptly. In a mass casualty situation, consideration should be given to cremation.

Post exposure management

Decontamination of patients / environment

The risk for re-aerosolization of *B. anthracis* spores appears to be extremely low in settings where spores were released intentionally or occurred naturally. In situations of possible gross exposure to *B. anthracis* spores, cleansing of skin and potentially contaminated fomites (e.g. clothing or environmental surfaces) may be considered to reduce the risk for cutaneous and gastrointestinal forms of disease. The plan for decontaminating patients exposed to *anthrax* should include the following:

1. Instructing patients to remove contaminated clothing and store in labeled, plastic bags. Clothing may be considered to be evidence and should be safely stored for investigative purposes with an associated chain of custody document.
2. Handling clothing minimally to avoid agitation.
3. Instructing personnel regarding Standard Precautions and wearing appropriate barriers (e.g. gloves, gown, and respiratory protection) when handling contaminated clothing or other contaminated fomites.
4. Instructing patients to shower thoroughly with soap and water to include the shampooing of hair (and providing assistance if necessary).
5. Decontaminating environmental surfaces using an EPA-registered, healthcare facility-approved disinfectant or 0.5% hypochlorite solution (one part household bleach added to nine parts water).

Prophylaxis and post-exposure immunization

Recommendations for prophylaxis are subject to change. Up-to-date recommendations should be obtained in consultation with local, state and regional health departments and CDC. Prophylaxis should be initiated upon confirmation of an anthrax exposure or while a highly suspect exposure is being confirmed.

Following the events of 2001, new treatment regimens, including medications, length of treatment, and vaccination, and prophylactic therapy regimens are being re-evaluated. The CDC should be consulted for direction regarding continued prophylaxis, discontinuation of prophylaxis and immunization.

Triage and management of large scale exposures / potential exposures

Advance planning should include identification of:

1. Sources of bulk prophylactic antibiotics and planning for acquisition on short notice.

2. Locations, personnel needs and protocols for administering and monitoring prophylactic postexposure care to large numbers of potentially exposed individuals.
3. Means for providing telephone follow-up information and other public communications services.

Intensive care unit managers will need to consider in advance:

1. How limited numbers of ventilators will be distributed in the event of a large number of patients arriving with abrupt pulmonary decompensation.
2. How additional ventilators can be obtained. Note: Only Standard Precautions are needed for ventilated patients with inhalational anthrax. Therefore, special filters, maintenance of closed systems or other special handling and decontamination of equipment is not necessary.
3. In the event of severely limited ventilator availability, whether and when ventilator support will be discontinued for a terminally ill individual.

Laboratory support and confirmation

Diagnosis of anthrax is confirmed by aerobic culture performed in a BSL-2 laboratory.

Diagnostic samples

Diagnostic samples to obtain include:

1. Nasal swabs to test for the presence of anthrax are not to be used for diagnostic purposes, but may be used within the first 48 hours of exposure to determine possible exposure. *Note*: the absence of a positive anthrax nasal swab does not indicate the person was not exposed. The nasal swab should only be used as an epidemiology tool.
2. Cerebrospinal fluid culture if meningeal involvement is suspected.
3. Non-cotton (Dacron) swab culture of exudates, vesicle fluid or unroofed eschar if skin lesions are present.
4. Blood cultures.
5. Pleural fluid for culture.

Laboratory selection

Handling of clinical specimens should be coordinated with local, state and regional health departments, and undertaken in BSL -2 or -3 laboratories. Isolates are submitted to the laboratory response network (LRN) for confirmatory testing. The FBI will coordinate collection of evidence and delivery of forensic specimens to FBI or Department of Defense laboratories.

Transport requirements

Specimen packaging and transport must be coordinated with local, state and regional health departments, and the FBI. A chain of custody document should accompany the specimen from the time of collection. For specific instructions, contact the Bioterrorism Emergency Number at the CDC Emergency. Advance planning may include identification of appropriate packaging materials and transport media in collaboration with the clinical laboratory at individual facilities.

Patient, visitor, and public information

Fact sheets for distribution should be prepared, including explanation that people recently exposed to *B. anthracis* are not contagious, and antibiotics are available for prophylactic therapy along with the anthrax vaccine. Dosing information and potential side effects should be explained clearly. Decontamination procedures, i.e., showering thoroughly with soap and water to include shampooing hair; and environmental cleaning, i.e., with 0.5% hypochlorite solution (one part household bleach added to nine parts water), can be described.

Botulism

Description of agent/syndrome

Etiology

Clostridium botulinum is an anaerobic gram-positive bacillus that produces a potent *neurotoxin*, *botulinum toxin*. In humans, botulinum toxin inhibits the release of acetylcholine, resulting in characteristic flaccid paralysis. *C. botulinum* produces spores that are present in soil and marine sediment throughout the world. Foodborne botulism is the most common form of disease in adults. An inhalational form of botulism is also possible. Botulinum toxin exposure may occur in both forms as agents of bioterrorism.

Clinical features

Foodborne botulism is accompanied by gastrointestinal symptoms. Inhalational botulism and foodborne botulism are likely to share other symptoms including:

1. Responsive patient with absence of fever.
2. Symmetric cranial neuropathies (drooping eyelids, weakened jaw clench, difficulty swallowing or speaking).
3. Blurred vision and diplopia due to extra-ocular muscle palsies.

4. Symmetric descending weakness in a proximal to distal pattern (paralysis of arms first, followed by respiratory muscles, then legs).
5. Respiratory dysfunction from respiratory muscle paralysis or upper airway obstruction due to weakened glottis.
6. No sensory deficits.

Mode of transmission

Botulinum toxin is generally transmitted by ingestion of toxin-contaminated food. Aerosolization of botulinum toxin has been described and may be a mechanism for bioterrorism exposure.

Incubation period

1. Neurologic symptoms of foodborne botulism begin 12–36 hours after ingestion.
2. Neurologic symptoms of inhalational botulism begin 24-72 hours after aerosol exposure.

Period of communicability

Botulism is not transmitted from person to person. *Note*: While patients with suspected botulism are not infectious, those with flaccid paralysis from suspected meningitis require droplet precautions until meningitis has been ruled-out.

Preventive measures

(a) *Vaccine availability*. A pentavalent toxoid vaccine has been developed by the Department of Defense (DoD). This vaccine is available as an investigational new drug. Completion of a recommended schedule (0, 2, 12 weeks) has been shown to induce protective antitoxin levels detectable at 1-year post vaccination.

(b) *Immunization recommendations*. Routine vaccination of civilian populations not currently recommended.

Infection control practices for patient management

Symptomatic patients with suspected or confirmed botulism should be managed according to current guidelines. Recommendations for therapy are beyond the scope of this document. For up-to-date information and recommendations for therapy, contact CDC or state health department.

(a) *Isolation precautions*. Standard Precautions are used for the care of patients with botulism. *Note*: While patients with suspected botulism do not need to be isolated, those with flaccid paralysis from suspected meningitis require droplet precautions until meningitis has been ruled-out.

(b) *Patient placement*. Patient-to-patient transmission of botulism does not occur; private room placement is not necessary. Patient room selection and care should be consistent with facility policy.

(c) *Patient transport*. Standard Precautions should be used for transport and movement of patients with botulism.

(d) *Cleaning, disinfection, and sterilization of equipment and environment*. Principles of Standard Precautions should be generally applied for the management of patient-care equipment and for environmental control. Decontaminate environmental surfaces using an EPA-registered, healthcare facility-approved disinfectant or 0.5% hypochlorite solution.

(e) *Discharge management*. Since patients are not infectious, no special discharge instructions related to infection prevention and control are indicated.

(f) *Post-mortem care*. Standard Precautions should be used for post-mortem care. Standard Precautions include wearing appropriate personal protective equipment, including masks and eye protection, when splashes or splatter of body fluids is anticipated.

Post Exposure Management

Suspicion of even single cases of botulism should immediately raise concerns of an outbreak potentially associated with shared contaminated food. In collaboration with CDC and local, state and regional health departments, attempts should be made to locate the contaminated food source and identify other persons who may have been exposed. Any individuals suspected to have been exposed to botulinum toxin should be carefully monitored for evidence of respiratory compromise.

Decontamination of patients / environment

Contamination with botulinum toxin does not place persons at risk for dermal exposure or risk associated with re-aerosolization. Therefore, decontamination of patients is not required. If exposure is known, the patient should shower with soap and water. Clothing worn by patient during the time of suspected exposure may be laundered using usual household procedures.

Prophylaxis and post-exposure immunization

Trivalent botulinum antitoxin is available by contacting state health departments or by contacting CDC. This horse serum product has a <9% percent rate of hypersensitivity reactions. Skin testing should be performed according to the package insert prior to administration.

Triage and management of large scale exposures / potential exposures

Patients affected by botulinum toxin are at risk for respiratory dysfunction that may necessitate mechanical ventilation. Ventilatory support is required, on average, for 2 to 3 months before neuromuscular recovery allows unassisted breathing. Large-scale exposures to botulinum toxin may overwhelm an institution's available resources for mechanical ventilation. Sources of auxiliary support and means to transport patients to auxiliary sites, if necessary should be planned in advance with coordination among neighbouring facilities.

Advance planning should include identification of:

1. In the event of severely limited ventilator availability, whether and when ventilator support will be discontinued for a terminally ill individual.
2. How additional ventilators can be obtained. Note: Only Standard Precautions are needed for ventilated patients with botulism. Therefore, special filters, maintenance of closed systems or other special handling and decontamination of equipment is not necessary.
3. Means for providing telephone follow-up information and other public communications services. Intensive care unit managers will need to consider in advance.
4. How limited numbers of ventilators will be distributed in the event of a large number of patients arriving with abrupt pulmonary decompensation.

Laboratory support and confirmation

Obtaining diagnostic samples

Routine laboratory tests are of limited value in the diagnosis of botulism. Detection of toxin is possible from serum, stool samples, or gastric secretions. For advice regarding the appropriate diagnostic specimens to obtain, contact state health authorities or CDC.

Laboratory selection

Handling of clinical specimens should be coordinated with local, state and regional health departments. The FBI will coordinate collection of evidence and delivery of forensic specimens to FBI or Department of Defense laboratories. Specimens for the detection of *botulism toxin* are to be sent to the designated Level B laboratory. The Laboratory should contact their state health department to identify the closest Level B laboratory that tests for *botulinum toxin*. Not all state health department laboratories test for this toxin.

Transport requirements

Specimen packaging and transport must be coordinated with local, state and regional health departments, and the FBI. A chain of custody document should accompany the specimen from the moment of collection. Advance planning may include identification of appropriate packaging materials and transport media in collaboration with the clinical laboratory at individual facilities.

Patient, visitor, and public information

Fact sheets for distribution should be prepared, including explanation that people exposed to botulinum toxin are not contagious. A clear description of symptoms including blurred vision, drooping eyelids, and shortness of breath should be provided with instructions to report for evaluation and care if such symptoms develop.

Plague

Description of agent/syndrome

Etiology

Plague is an acute bacterial disease caused by the gram-negative bacillus *Yersinia pestis*, which is usually transmitted by infected fleas, resulting in lymphatic and blood infections (*bubonic* and *septicemic plague*). A BT-related outbreak may be expected to be airborne, causing a pulmonary variant, pneumonic plague, although an outbreak of bubonic plague could be encountered following the release of infected fleas.

Clinical features of pneumonic plague

1. Fever, cough, chest pain.
2. Hemoptysis.
3. Mucopurulent or watery sputum with gram-negative rods on gram stain.
4. Radiographic evidence of bronchopneumonia.

Modes of transmission

1. Plague is normally transmitted from an infected rodent to man by infected fleas.
2. Bioterrorism-related outbreaks are likely to be transmitted through dispersion of an aerosol.
3. Person-to-person transmission of pneumonic plague is possible via large aerosol droplets

Incubation period

The incubation period for plague is normally 2–8 days if due to fleaborne transmission. The incubation period may be shorter for pulmonary exposure (1-3 days).

Period of communicability

Patients with pneumonic plague may have coughs productive of infectious particle droplets. Droplet precautions, including the use of a mask for patient care, should be implemented until the patient has completed 72 hours of appropriate antimicrobial therapy.

Preventive measures

(a) *Vaccine availability*. Formalin-killed vaccine exists for bubonic plague, but has not been proven to be effective for pneumonic plague. It is not currently available in the United States.

(b) *Immunization recommendations*. Vaccination requires multiple doses given over several weeks. Routine vaccination of civilian populations is not currently recommended. Post-exposure immunization has no utility.

Infection control practices for patient management

Symptomatic patients with suspected or confirmed plague should be managed according to current guidelines. Recommendations for specific therapy are beyond the scope of this document. For up-to-date information and recommendations for therapy, contact CDC or state health department.

Isolation precautions

For *pneumonic plague*, *Droplet Precautions* should be used in addition to Standard Precautions.

1. Droplet Precautions are used for patients known or suspected to be infected with microorganisms transmitted by large particle droplets, generally larger than 5 μ in size, that can be generated by the infected patient during coughing, sneezing, talking, or during respiratory-care procedures.
2. Droplet Precautions require healthcare providers and others to wear a surgical-type mask when within 3 feet of the infected patient. Based on local policy, some healthcare facilities require a mask be worn to enter the room of a patient on Droplet Precautions.
3. Droplet Precautions should be maintained until patient has completed 72 hours of appropriate antimicrobial therapy. Susceptibility patterns should be confirmed to ensure adequate antibiotic coverage before discontinuation of isolation due to the risk of a genetically altered strain being used in a BT attack.

Patient placement

Patients suspected or confirmed to have pneumonic plague require *Droplet Precautions*. Patient placement recommendations for Droplet Precautions include:

1. Placing infected patient in a private room.
2. Cohort symptomatic patients with similar symptoms and the same presumptive diagnosis (i.e. pneumonic plague) when private rooms are not available.
3. Maintaining spatial separation of at least 3 feet between infected patients and others when cohorting is not achievable.
4. Avoiding placement of patient requiring *Droplet Precautions* in the same room with an immunocompromised patient.
5. Staff needs to wear a surgical mask when caring for infected patients.
6. Special air handling is not necessary and doors may remain open.

Patient transport

1. Limit the movement and transport of patients on Droplet Precautions to essential medical purposes only.
2. Minimize dispersal of droplets by placing a surgical-type mask on the patient when transport is necessary.

Cleaning, disinfection, and sterilization of equipment and environment

Principles of Standard Precautions should be generally applied to the management of patientcare equipment and for environmental control. Decontaminate environmental surfaces using an EPA-registered, healthcare facility-approved disinfectant or 0.5% hypochlorite solution (one part household bleach added to nine parts water).

Discharge management

Ideally, patients with pneumonic plague would not be discharged from a healthcare facility until no longer infectious (completion of 72 hours of appropriate antimicrobial therapy) and would require no special discharge instructions. In the event of a large bioterrorism exposure with patients receiving care in their homes, home care providers should be taught to use *Standard* and *Droplet Precautions* for all patient care.

Post-mortem care

Standard Precautions and *Droplet Precautions* should be used for post-mortem care. Aerosol generating procedures, such as surgery or autopsies, are not recommended due to the risk of secondary transmission. If such aerosol generating procedures are necessary, airborne precautions are required (HEPA-filters for recirculated air, N-95 masks and negative pressure room).

Post exposure management

Decontamination of patients / environment

The risk for re-aerosolization of *Y. pestis* from the contaminated clothing of exposed persons is low. In situations where there may have been gross exposure to *Y. pestis*, decontamination of skin and potentially contaminated fomites (e.g. clothing or environmental surfaces) may be considered to reduce the risk for cutaneous or bubonic forms of the disease. The plan for decontaminating patients may include:

1. Instructing patients to remove contaminated clothing and store in labeled, plastic bags. Clothing may be considered to be evidence and should be safely stored for investigative purposes with an associated chain of custody document.
2. Handling clothing minimally to avoid agitation.
3. Instructing personnel regarding Standard Precautions and wearing appropriate barriers (e.g. gloves, gown, and respiratory protection) when handling contaminated clothing or other contaminated fomites.
4. Instructing patients to shower thoroughly with soap and water to include the shampooing of hair (and providing assistance if necessary).
5. Decontaminating environmental surfaces using an EPA-registered, healthcare facility-approved disinfectant or 0.5% hypochlorite solution (one part household bleach added to nine parts water).

Prophylaxis and post exposure immunization

Recommendations for prophylaxis are subject to change. Up-to-date recommendations should be obtained in consultation with local, state and regional health departments and CDC.

Post-exposure prophylaxis should be initiated following confirmed or suspected bioterrorism *Y. pestis* exposure, and for post-exposure management of healthcare workers and others who had unprotected face-to-face contact with symptomatic patients.

Prophylaxis should continue for 7 days after last known or suspected *Y. pestis* exposure, or until exposure has been excluded.

Facilities should ensure that policies are in place to identify and manage health care workers exposed to infectious patients. In general, maintenance of accurate occupational health records will facilitate identification, contact, assessment, and delivery of post-exposure care to potentially exposed healthcare workers.

Triage and management of large scale exposures/potential exposures

Advance planning should include identification of sources for appropriate masks to facilitate adherence to Droplet Precautions for potentially large numbers of patients and staff. Instruction and reiteration of requirements for Droplet Precautions (as opposed to Airborne Precautions) will be necessary to promote compliance and minimize fear and panic related to an aerosol exposure.

Advance planning should also include identification of:

1. Sources of bulk prophylactic antibiotics and planning for acquisition on short notice.
2. Locations, personnel needs and protocols for administering and monitoring prophylactic postexposure care to large numbers of potentially exposed individuals.
3. Means for providing telephone follow-up information and other public communications services.

Laboratory support and confirmation

Laboratory confirmation of plague is by standard microbiologic culture, but slow growth and misidentification in automated systems are likely to delay diagnosis. For decisions regarding obtaining and processing diagnostic specimens, contact state laboratory authorities or CDC.

Diagnostic samples

Diagnostic samples to obtain depend on the form of illness encountered (*bubonic*, *pneumonic* or *septicemic*) and should be handled in an evidentiary manner and accompanied by the chain of command documentation. Samples to be collected include:

1. Serum for capsular antigen testing.
2. Blood or bubo cultures.
3. Sputum or tracheal aspirates for Gram's, Wayson's, and fluorescent antibody staining.
4. Sputum or tracheal aspirates for culture.

Laboratory selection

Handling of clinical specimens should be coordinated with local, state and regional health departments, and undertaken in BSL -2 or -3 laboratories. Isolates are submitted to the laboratory response network (LRN) for confirmatory testing. The FBI will coordinate collection of evidence and delivery of forensic specimens to FBI or Department of Defense laboratories.

Transport requirements

Specimen packaging and transport must be coordinated with local, state and regional health departments, and the FBI. A chain of custody document should accompany the specimen from the moment of collection. For specific instructions, contact the Bioterrorism Emergency Number at the CDC Emergency Response Office, 770/488-7100. Advance planning may include identification of appropriate packaging materials and transport media in collaboration with the clinical laboratory at individual facilities.

Patient, visitor, and public information

Fact sheets for distribution should be prepared, including a clear description of Droplet Precautions, symptoms of plague, and instructions to report for evaluation and care if such symptoms are recognized. The difference between prophylactic antimicrobial therapy and treatment of an actual infection should be clarified. Decontamination by showering thoroughly with soap and water can be recommended.

Smallpox

Description of agent/syndrome

Etiology

Smallpox is an acute viral illness caused by the *variola virus*. Smallpox is a BT threat due to its potential to cause severe morbidity in a non-immune population and because it can be transmitted via the airborne route. A single case is considered a public health emergency.

Clinical features

Acute clinical symptoms of *smallpox* resemble other acute viral illnesses, such as influenza. Skin lesions appear, quickly progressing from macules to papules to vesicles. Other clinical symptoms to aid in identification of smallpox include:

1. 2-4 day, non-specific prodrome of fever, prostration and lower back pain.
2. Rash most prominent on face and extremities (including palms and soles) in contrast to the truncal distribution of varicella.
3. Rash scabs over in 1-2 weeks.
4. In contrast to the rash of varicella, which arises in "*crops*," variola rash has a synchronous onset.

Modes of transmission

Smallpox is transmitted via large and small respiratory droplets as well as from contact with skin lesions and items contaminated with drainage from lesions. In addition, scabs contain viral particles and may be contagious. Patients are considered more infectious if coughing or if they have a hemorrhagic form of smallpox.

Incubation period

The incubation period for smallpox is 7-17 days; the average is 12 days.

Period of communicability

Unlike varicella, which is contagious before the rash is apparent, patients with smallpox become infectious at the onset of the rash and remain infectious until their scabs separate (approximately 3 weeks). The period of communicability begins with the onset of the first lesion. However, the initial lesions may not be readily apparent (i.e., inside the mouth or other less visible location).

Preventive measures

Vaccine availability

A live-virus intradermal vaccination for the prevention of *smallpox* exists, but is not currently available to the general public without authorized release from the CDC. Routine vaccination and production of vaccine was discontinued in the US in 1972 following worldwide eradication of smallpox. Due to the threat of smallpox as a biological weapon, production of new vaccine has been initiated as well as research studies examining methods of diluting current vaccine stocks.

Immunization recommendations

Routine vaccination of civilian populations is not currently recommended. Length of immunity following vaccination is not known. Therefore, even previously vaccinated persons should be considered susceptible to smallpox. All personnel working directly with patients with confirmed smallpox must be vaccinated. Individuals with contraindications to smallpox vaccination, e.g., persons with altered immune states, pregnant women or those with a history of eczema or other forms of chronic dermatitis, should not be selected to provide care to smallpox patients.

Vaccinations will be provided first to individuals who have never been vaccinated followed by those individuals who have been immunized previously.

Ring Vaccination Strategy

Ring vaccination involves isolation of confirmed and suspected smallpox cases with tracing, vaccination, and close surveillance of contacts to these cases as well as vaccination of the household contacts of the contacts. Vaccinating and monitoring a "*ring*" of people around each case and contact is designed to help protect those at greatest risk for contracting the disease as well as form a buffer of immune individuals to prevent the spread of disease. This strategy is more desirable than indiscriminate mass vaccination.

Infection control practices for patient management

Symptomatic patients with suspected or confirmed smallpox should be managed according to current guidelines. Recommendations for specific therapy are beyond the scope of this document. For up-to-date information and recommendations for therapy, contact the CDC or state health department.

Isolation precautions

For patients with suspected or confirmed smallpox, both Airborne and Contact Precautions should be used in addition to Standard Precautions.

1. Airborne Precautions are used for patients known or suspected to be infected with microorganisms transmitted by airborne droplet nuclei (small particle residue, 5 μ or smaller in size) of evaporated droplets containing microorganisms that can remain suspended in air and can be widely dispersed by air currents.
2. Airborne Precautions require healthcare providers and others to wear respiratory protection when entering the patient room. (Appropriate respiratory protection must meet the minimal NIOSH standards for particulate respirators, e.g., N95).
3. Contact Precautions are used for patients known or suspected to be infected or colonized with epidemiologically important organisms that can be transmitted by direct contact with the patient or indirect contact with potentially contaminated surfaces in the patient's care area.
4. Contact precautions require healthcare providers and others to:
   - Wear clean gloves upon entry into patient room.
   - Wear gown for all patient contact and for all contact with the patient's environment. Based on local policy, some healthcare facilities require a gown be worn to enter the room of a patient on Contact Precautions. Gown must be removed before leaving the patient's room.
   - Wash hands using an antimicrobial agent.

Patient placement

Patient placement depends upon clinical presentation and physical plant capabilities of the facility. Each of the following groups of patients has specific isolation considerations.

1. Known or Presumed Infectious Individuals (Type C = Contagious Facility):
   - Persons with a compatible illness and laboratory confirmation of smallpox (Confirmed case)
   - Persons with a compatible illness following suspected/known exposure with pending laboratory confirmation (Probable case)
   - Persons referred by a consultant as suspected cases of smallpox but who do not have a typical clinical presentation
2. Febrile Contacts without Rash (Type C or Type X Facility):
   - Vaccinated contacts under surveillance who become febrile with oral temperatures ≥101°F (38°C) on two successive readings (but do not have a rash)
3. Asymptomatic Contacts (Type R = Residential Facility):
   - Afebrile vaccinated contacts
   - Afebrile vaccinated individuals who were with a smallpox patient 10-18 days before the onset of the patient's rash (possible common exposure)
   - Contacts who refuse vaccination

Specific types of facilities may be used for housing patients during a *smallpox emergency*. These include:

1. Type C Facility to house cases of smallpox and minimize the exposure of susceptible individuals to contagious individuals. All persons admitted to or entering a Type C facility must be vaccinated including those that are considered to be smallpox cases, as errors in diagnosis are possible.
2. Type X Facility to house *febrile* contacts during the observation period for further development of symptoms of *smallpox* (rash).
3. Type R Facility may be the person's own home. This is for asymptomatic (noninfectious) contacts.

In order to limit the number of Type C Facilities, it is important to consider methods for triaging patients in a location outside of a healthcare facility that is not already designated as a Type C Facility. This can be accomplished by triaging suspected smallpox patients outside of the facility (i.e., decontamination areas or vehicles).

Hospitalized smallpox patients require placement in rooms that meet the ventilation and engineering requirements for Airborne Precautions, which include:

1. Monitored negative air pressure relative to the corridor and surrounding areas.
2. 6-12 air exchanges per hour.
3. Appropriate discharge of air to the outdoors, or use of monitored high-efficiency particulate air (HEPA) filtration prior to circulation to other areas in the healthcare facility.
4. A door that must remain closed.
5. Working knowledge of facility heat, ventilation and air conditioning system (HVAC) is critical to determining airflow within a facility. Therefore, proper functioning of HVAC systems, including negative air flow and proper maintenance of HEPA filters, is essential to prevention of transmission of *smallpox*. Circumstances that will alter the balance of supply and exhausted air will disrupt continuous negative airflow. Examples of altered airflow and balance include activation of the fire alarm systems, elevator shaft work, changes in ventilation dampers, changing of large bag filters and shutting down portions of a ventilation system. These factors must be integral to your facility plan.

Healthcare facilities without patient rooms appropriate for Airborne Precautions should have a plan for transfer of suspected or confirmed smallpox patients to other facilities with appropriate isolation environments.

Patient placement in a private room is preferred. However, in the event of a large outbreak, patients who have active infections with the same disease (i.e., smallpox) may be cohorted in rooms that meet appropriate ventilation and airflow requirements for Airborne Precautions.

Patient transport

1. Limit the movement and transport of patients with suspected or confirmed smallpox to essential medical purposes only.
2. When transport is necessary, minimize the dispersal of respiratory droplets by placing a mask on the patient, if possible.

Cleaning, disinfection, and sterilization of equipment and environment

A component of Contact Precautions is careful management of potentially contaminated equipment and environmental surfaces.

1. When possible, noncritical patient care equipment should be dedicated to a single patient (or cohort of patients with the same illness).
2. If use of common items is unavoidable, all potentially contaminated, reusable equipment should not be used for the care of another patient until it has been appropriately cleaned and reprocessed. Policies should be in place and monitored for compliance.
3. EPA-approved hospital grade germicides easily kill variola virus.

Linen and regulated medical waste

All bodily fluids are safely disposed of via the sanitary sewer. It is anticipated that the US Public Health Service will determine handling procedures for linens and definitions of regulated medical waste.

Discharge management

In general, patients with smallpox will not be discharged from a healthcare facility until determined they are no longer infectious or are sent to another designated facility. Therefore, no special discharge instructions are required.

Post-mortem care

Airborne and *Contact Precautions* should be used for post-mortem care. Cremation is preferable for the remains of smallpox victims. Provisions for immunization of mortuary employees should be considered in the prioritization of those receiving vaccination.

Post exposure management

Decontamination of patients/environment

Patient decontamination after exposure to smallpox is not indicated unless there is evidence of a recent overt release. If an overt release is suspected or known, the plan for decontaminating patients exposed to smallpox should include the following:

1. Instructing patients to remove contaminated clothing and store in labeled, plastic bags. Clothing may be considered to be evidence and should be safely stored for investigative purposes with an associated chain of custody document.
2. Handling clothing minimally to avoid agitation.
3. Instructing personnel regarding Contact Precautions and wearing appropriate barriers (e.g. gloves, gown, and respiratory protection) when handling contaminated clothing or other contaminated fomites.
4. Instructing patients to shower thoroughly with soap and water to include the shampooing of hair.

5. Decontaminating environmental surfaces using an EPA-registered, healthcare facility-approved disinfectant or 0.5% hypochlorite solution (one part household bleach added to nine parts water).

Prophylaxis and post-exposure immunization

Recommendations for prophylaxis are subject to change. Up-to-date recommendations should be obtained in consultation with local, state and regional health departments and CDC.

Post-exposure immunization with *smallpox* vaccine (*vaccinia virus*) is effective, but is not currently available to the general public without authorized release from the CDC. Vaccination alone is recommended if given within 3-5 days of exposure. *Passive immunization* is also available in the form of vaccinia immune-globulin (VIG) (0.6 ml/kg IM). VIG is maintained at USAMRIID: (301)619-2833. Vaccination is generally contraindicated in pregnant women, and persons with immunosuppression, HIV–infection, and eczema, who are at risk for disseminated vaccinia disease. However, the risk of smallpox vaccination should be weighed against the likelihood for developing smallpox following a known exposure. VIG should be given concomitantly with vaccination in these patients.

High-risk groups prioritized for vaccination

1. Because of the potential for the greater spread of smallpox in a hospital setting due to aerosolization of the virus from a severely ill patient, consideration should be given to vaccination of all individuals present in the hospital during the time a case was present and not isolated in an appropriate manner in a room with ventilation separate from other areas of the hospital.
2. Personnel selected for direct medical or public health evaluation, care, or transportation of confirmed, probable or suspected smallpox patients.
3. Laboratory personnel selected for the collection or processing of clinical specimens from confirmed, probable or suspected smallpox cases.
4. Persons with face-to-face, household, or close proximity contact (within 3 feet), with a confirmed or suspected smallpox patient after the patient developed fever and until all scabs have separated.
5. Other groups whose unhindered function is deemed essential to the support of response activities and who are not otherwise involved in patient care activities but who have a reasonable probability of contact with smallpox patients or infectious materials, e.g., law enforcement, EMS, military.

6. Persons exposed to the initial release of the virus.
7. Other persons with increased likelihood of contact with infectious materials from a smallpox patient such as laundry or medical waste handlers for a facility where smallpox patients are admitted.

Indications for VIG use:

1. The recommended dosage of VIG for treatment of complications due to vaccinia vaccination is 0.6 mL/kg of body weight. VIG must be administered intramuscularly (IM) and should be administered as early as possible after the onset of symptoms.
2. Because the therapeutic dose of VIG may be large (e.g., 42 mL for a 70 kg person), the product should be given in divided doses over a 24-36 hour period. Doses may be repeated at 2-3 day intervals until no new lesions.

Post-vaccination complications for which VIG may be indicated include:

1. Eczema vaccinatum
2. Progressive vaccinia (vaccinia necrosum)
3. Severe generalized vaccinia if the patient has a toxic condition or serious
4. Underlying illness.
5. Inadvertent inoculation of the eye or eyelid without vaccinial keratitis

*VIG is not indicated for the treatment of post-vaccination encephalitis and is contraindicated for vaccinial keratitis.

The currently limited supplies of VIG do not allow for its concomitant administration with vaccine for the prevention of potential complications. VIG use should be reserved for treatment of the most serious or life-threatening complications.

Following prophylactic care, exposed individuals should be instructed to monitor themselves for development of flu-like symptoms (most notably, fever) or rash during the incubation period (i.e., for 17 days after exposure) and immediately report to designated care sites selected to minimize the risk of exposure to others.

Facilities should ensure that policies are in place to identify and manage health care workers exposed to infectious patients. In general, maintenance of accurate occupational health records will facilitate identification, contact, assessment, and delivery of post-exposure care to potentially exposed healthcare workers. Occupational health records should include smallpox immunization history for all employees. Note:

Routine childhood vaccination for smallpox ceased in approximately 1972 in the USA.

Triage and management of large scale exposures/potential exposures

Advance planning must involve IC professionals in cooperation with building engineering staff, to identify sites within the facility that can provide necessary parameters for Airborne Precautions.

Laboratory support and confirmation

Diagnostic samples

For decisions regarding obtaining and processing diagnostic specimens, contact state laboratory authorities or CDC.

Laboratory selection

Handling of clinical specimens must be coordinated with state health departments, CDC, and USAMRIID. Testing can be performed only in BSL-4 laboratories. The FBI will coordinate collection of evidence and delivery of forensic specimens to FBI or Department of Defense laboratories.

Transport requirements

Specimen packaging and transport must be coordinated with local, state and regional health departments, and the FBI. A chain of custody document should accompany the specimen from the moment of collection. Advance planning may include identification of appropriate packaging materials and transport media in collaboration with the clinical laboratory at individual facilities.

Patient, visitor, and public information

Fact sheets for distribution should be prepared, including a clear description of symptoms and where to report for evaluation and care if such symptoms are recognized. Details about the type and duration of isolation should be provided. Vaccination information that details who should receive the vaccine and possible side effects should be provided. Extreme measures such as burning or boiling potentially exposed materials should be discouraged.

Tularemia

Description of agent/syndrome

Etiology

Tularemia is an acute infectious disease caused by *Francisella tularensis*, small aerobic nonmotile, catalase-positive gram-negative coccobacilli. The organism is naturally occurring in a wide range of animal hosts, and can be recovered from contaminated water, soil and vegetation. *F. tularensis* are very infectious pathogenic bacteria, requiring inhalation or inoculation of as few as 10 organisms to cause infection.

Also referred to as rabbit fever or deerfly fever, *tularemia* primarily causes disease in many animals, most commonly rabbits, beaver, and squirrels. The disease does occur in humans, primarily through tick bites and exposure due to handling infected animals. There is a peak of cases in the summer months when outdoor activity is most common, and another peak in winter reflecting hunting-associated cases. Inhalational *tularemia* infections have occurred only in rural areas; cases occurring in urban dwellers or in those with no other risk factors should alert healthcare personnel to the possibility of a BT attack.

Clinical features

Clinical manifestations of *tularemia* are varied depending on the portal of entry, immune status of the human host, and the virulence of the strain. Diagnosis is difficult and relies on clinical suspicion.

Tularemia starts abruptly with onset of fever, chills, headache, malaise, anorexia, and fatigue. Other symptoms may include cough, myalgias, chest discomfort, sore throat, vomiting, abdominal pain, and diarrhea.

There are six forms of *tularemia*:

1. *Ulceroglandular*—21% to 87% of naturally occurring cases; generally starts as a red painful papule which necroses, resulting in a tender ulcer with raised border; often associated with localized lymphadenopathy.
2. *Glandular*—3-20% of cases; presentation as tender regional lymphadenopathy, but without cutaneous lesion.
3. *Oculoglandular*—up to 5% of cases occurs when organism gains entry through conjunctiva from contaminated fingers or direct splashes into eye. Presents as painful conjunctivitis with lid edema and often associated with local tender lymphadenopathy.
4. *Pharyngeal*—up to 12% of case, occurs as a result of entry into the oropharyx such as through eating contaminated foods or water; presents with severe throat pain accompanied by exudative, sometimes ulcerative, pharyngitis or tonsillitis.
5. *Pneumonic*—7-20% of all naturally occurring cases, but may be the most common presentation associated with a BT attack due to an aerosol release. Occurs as a result of direct inhalation of

organism or secondary hematogenous spread to the lungs. Enlargement of hilar nodes is the principle finding on chest x-ray.

6. *Typhoidal*—5 to 30% of cases occurs as a result of any mode of transmission and presents as acute febrile illness, and is the most difficult to diagnose. Loose watery diarrhea often accompanies typhoidal tularemia. Some sources combine typhoidal and pneumonic tularemia into the same category with chest X-ray changes being the differentiating criteria between the two.

Within 2 weeks of initial symptoms, up to 35% of tularemia infections result in secondary skin rashes appearing as diffuse maculopapular or vesiculopapular eruptions.

Modes of transmission

1. *Tularemia* is normally transmitted through the bite of an insect, most commonly ticks in the U.S.; or by direct contact with a contaminated animal during skinning or dressing.
2. *Bioterrorism*-related outbreaks are likely to be transmitted through dispersion and inhalation of aerosol droplets resulting in typhoidal or pneumonic tularemia.
3. *Person-to-person transmission* does not occur, although secondary transmission has been known to occur in the laboratory setting.

Incubation period

The incubation period for tularemia averages 3–5 days.

Period of communicability

Tularemia is not transmitted from person to person.

Preventive measures

Vaccine availability

A live attenuated vaccine was developed that provided partial protection against some strains of tularemia, and has been used to immunize laboratory workers routinely handling *F. tularensis*. This vaccine is currently under review by the US Food and Drug Administration but is not currently available to the general public.

Immunization recommendations

Routine vaccination of civilian populations is not currently recommended. Post-exposure immunization has no utility.

Infection control practices for patient management

Symptomatic patients with suspected or confirmed tularemia should be managed according to current guidelines. Recommendations for specific therapy are beyond the scope of this document. For up-to-date information and recommendations for therapy, contact CDC or state health department.

Isolation precautions

Standard Precautions are used for the care of patients with *tularemia*. Standard Precautions include the routine use of gloves for contact with non-intact skin, including rashes and skin lesions.

Although special isolation precautions are not indicated for patient care, infection prevention strategies in the laboratory (e.g. opening cultures only in BSL-2 safety cabinets) are crucial to protect laboratory personnel from infection. The lab must be notified if tularemia is suspected since cultures of *F. tularensis* are highly infectious and represent a laboratory hazard if not contained. Examination of cultures suspected as *F. tularensis* should be done in an appropriate biosafety cabinet.

Patient placement

Patient-to-patient transmission of tularemia does not occur; private room placement is not necessary. Patient room selection and care should be consistent with facility policy.

Patient transport

Standard Precautions should be used for the transport and movement of patients with *F. tularensis* infections.

Cleaning, disinfection, and sterilization of equipment and environment

Principles of Standard Precautions should be generally applied for the management of patient-care equipment and for environmental control. Decontaminate environmental surfaces using an EPA-registered, healthcare facility-approved disinfectant or 0.5% hypochlorite solution (one part household bleach added to nine parts water).

Discharge management

Since patients are not infectious, no special discharge instructions related to infection prevention and control are indicated. Home care providers should be taught to use Standard Precautions for all patient care (e.g., dressing changes).

Post-mortem care

Standard Precautions should be used for post-mortem care. Standard Precautions include wearing appropriate personal protective equipment, including masks and eye protection, when splashes or splatter of body fluids is anticipated.

Post exposure management

Decontamination of patients/environment

There is no risk for re-aerosolization of *F. tularensis* from contaminated clothing of exposed persons. In situations where there may have been gross exposure to *F. tularensis*, decontamination of skin and potentially contaminated fomites (e.g. clothing or environmental surfaces) may be considered to reduce the risk for ulceroglandular, glandular or ocular forms of the disease. The plan for decontaminating patients may include:

1. Instructing patients to shower thoroughly with soap and water to include the shampooing of hair (and providing assistance if necessary).
2. Instructing patients to avoid touching eyes; handwashing should be done as soon as possible, and after touching potentially contaminated items.
3. Decontaminating environmental surfaces using an EPA-registered, healthcare facility-approved disinfectant or 0.5% hypochlorite solution (one part household bleach added to nine parts water).
4. Instructing patients to remove contaminated clothing and store in labeled, plastic bags. Clothing may be considered to be evidence and should be safely stored for investigative purposes with an associated chain of custody document.
5. Instructing personnel regarding Standard Precautions and wearing appropriate barriers (e.g. gloves, gown, and respiratory protection) when handling contaminated clothing or other contaminated fomites.
6. Handling clothing minimally to avoid agitation.

Prophylaxis and post-exposure immunization

Recommendations for prophylaxis are subject to change. Up-to-date recommendations should be obtained in consultation with local, state and regional health departments and CDC. Post-exposure prophylaxis should be initiated following confirmed or suspected bioterrorism exposure, and for postexposure management of healthcare workers and others who had unprotected face-to-face contact with symptomatic patients.

Triage and management of large scale exposures/potential exposures

Since rapid diagnosis for tularemia is not widely available, a cluster of persons presenting with atypical pneumonia, pleuritis, and hilar lymphadenopathy should alert personnel to potential BT attack due to *F. tularensis*.

Advance planning should include identification of:

1. Sources of bulk prophylactic antibiotics and planning for acquisition on short notice.
2. Locations, personnel needs and protocols for administering and monitoring prophylactic postexposure care to large numbers of potentially exposed individuals.
3. Means for providing telephone follow-up information and other public communications services.

Laboratory support and confirmation

Because only a small inhaled dose is sufficient to cause infection, laboratory personnel must be notified if tularemia infection is suspected. Laboratory workers are especially vulnerable to infection through inhalation or accidental inoculation. Examination of open culture plates can cause infection.

The organism *F. tularensis* is rarely seen on Gram stained smears or in tissue biopsies, and does not grow on routine cultures. Using supportive media (e.g. cysteine enriched broth, cysteine heart blood agar), *F. tularensis* can be recovered from pleural fluid, lymph nodes, wounds, pharyngeal washings, and sputum. It is only occasionally isolated from blood. Laboratory confirmation of tularemia is by culture.

For decisions regarding obtaining and processing diagnostic specimens, contact state laboratory authorities or CDC.

Diagnostic samples

Clinical suspicion of tularemia should prompt the physician to notify the laboratory and obtain specimens of:

1. Respiratory secretions for culture
2. Blood cultures
3. Sputum or other secretions or biopsy specimens for direct fluorescent antibody staining.

Laboratory selection

Handling of clinical specimens should be coordinated with local, state and regional health departments, and undertaken in BSL -2 or -3 laboratories. Isolates are submitted to the laboratory response network (LRN) for confirmatory testing.

Transport requirements

Specimen packaging and transport must be coordinated with local, state and regional health departments, and the FBI. A chain of custody document should accompany the specimen from the moment of collection.

Advance planning may include identification of appropriate packaging materials and transport media in collaboration with the clinical laboratory at individual facilities.

Patient, visitor, and public information

Fact sheets for distribution should be prepared, including a clear description of symptoms of tularemia, and instructions to report for evaluation and care if such symptoms are recognized. The difference between prophylactic antimicrobial therapy and treatment of an actual infection should be clarified. Decontamination by showering thoroughly with soap and water for persons with a known exposure can be recommended.

Viral Hemorrhagic Fevers

Description of agents/syndrome

Etiology

Viral hemorrhagic fevers (VHF) are a mixed group of syndromes caused by viruses including representatives of the families *Filoviridae* (e.g., ebola and marburg), *Arenaviridae* (e.g., Lassa fever), and *Bunyviridae* (e.g., Crimean-Congo hemorrhagic fever). Each causes a febrile syndrome characterized by hemorrhagic complications, but mortality rates, incubation periods and susceptibility to antiviral therapy vary depending on the etiologic agent. These organisms pose a BT threat due to their potential to cause severe morbidity and because transmission can occur from person to person.

Clinical features

Acute clinical symptoms of *VHF* resemble other acute viral illnesses, such as influenza, with headache, myalgia, and fever. Affected patients develop petechiae, mucosal bleeding (epistaxis, gingival bleeding, gastrointestinal bleeding), capillary leakage and hypovolemic shock.

Modes of transmission

VHF is transmitted by percutaneous or mucosal exposure to infectious body substances. Potentially infectious body substances include respiratory secretions, saliva, blood, vomitus, stool, semen, and sweat. Transmission is mostly due to direct contact and droplet exposures, though limited animal studies have shown that airborne transmission can be engineered using a fine aerosol.

Incubation period

The incubation period varies by virus type and ranges from 2-21 days.

Period of communicability

VHF patients are most communicable during late stage disease, when individuals are most likely to manifest hemorrhagic complications.

Preventive measures

(a) *Vaccine availability*. Neither vaccines nor post exposure prophylaxis are currently available for *VHF*.

(b) *Immunization recommendations*. Vaccination does not currently exist for *VHF*.

Infection control practices for patient management

Patients with suspected or confirmed VHF should be managed according to current guidelines. Recommendations for specific therapy are beyond the scope of this document. For up-to-date information and recommendations for therapy, contact the CDC or state health department.

Isolation precautions

VHF is transmitted by percutaneous or mucosal exposure to infectious body substances. Potentially infectious body substances include respiratory secretions, saliva, blood, vomitus, stool, semen, and sweat. Transmission is mostly due to direct contact and droplet exposures, though limited animal studies have shown that airborne transmission can be engineered using a fine aerosol.

For patients with suspected or confirmed *VHF*, both Droplet and Contact Precautions should be used in addition to Standard Precautions.

1. Droplet Precautions require healthcare providers and others to wear a surgical-type mask when within 3 feet of the infected patient. Based on local policy, some healthcare facilities require a mask be worn to enter the room of a patient on *Droplet Precautions*.
2. Contact precautions require healthcare providers and others to:
   - Wear clean gloves upon entry into patient room.
   - Wear gown for all patient contact and for all contact with the patient's environment. Based on local policy, some healthcare facilities require a gown be worn to enter the room of a patient on *Contact Precautions*. Gown must be removed before leaving the patient's room.
   - Wash hands using an antimicrobial agent.

Patient placement

Patient placement recommendations for *Droplet* and *Contact Precautions* include:

1. Placing infected patient in a private room.
2. Cohort symptomatic patients with similar symptoms and the same presumptive diagnosis (i.e. *VHF*) when private rooms are not available.
3. Maintaining spatial separation of at least 3 feet between infected patients and others when cohorting is not achievable.
4. Avoiding placement of patient requiring Droplet Precautions in the same room with an immunocompromised patient.

Special air handling is not necessary and doors may remain open.

Patient transport

1. Limit the movement and transport of patients to essential medical purposes only.
2. Minimize dispersal of droplets by placing a surgical-type mask on the patient when transport is necessary.

Cleaning, disinfection, and sterilization of equipment and environment

Principles of Standard Precautions should be generally applied to the management of patientcare equipment and for environmental control.

The germicidal agents of choice when VHF is known or suspected include chlorine-based or phenolics.

Discharge management

Patients with *VHF* may be discharged home when clinically able following appropriate consultation with public health authorities. However, depending on the etiologic agent, some patients may shed virus in semen for a protracted time after clinical recovery.

Post-mortem care

Droplet and Contact Precautions should be used for post-mortem care. Post mortem examinations should not be done unless epidemiologically indicated. If done, special precautions should be performed to prevent exposure to patient body fluids. Cremation is preferable for the remains of VHF victims.

Post exposure management

Decontamination of patients/environment

Following an intentional exposure, the risk for contracting of *VHF* from the contaminated clothing of exposed persons is unknown. Items soiled with infectious body substances, e.g., vomitus, may pose a transmission risk and should be handled appropriately. The plan for decontaminating patients may include:

1. The germicidal agents of choice for decontamination of environmental surfaces when VHF is known or suspected include EPA-registered, healthcare-facility-approved chlorine based products or phenolics.
2. Instructing patients to remove contaminated clothing and store in labeled, plastic bags. Clothing may be considered to be evidence and should be safely stored for investigative purposes with an associated chain of custody document.
3. Instructing personnel regarding Standard Precautions and wearing appropriate barriers (e.g. gloves, gown, and respiratory protection) when handling contaminated clothing or other contaminated fomites.
4. Instructing patients to shower thoroughly with soap and water to include the shampooing of hair (and providing assistance if necessary).
5. Handling clothing minimally to avoid agitation.

Prophylaxis and post-exposure immunization

Following suspected exposure, individuals should be instructed to monitor themselves for development of flu-like symptoms or fever during the incubation period (i.e., for 21 days after exposure) and immediately report to designated care sites selected to minimize the risk of exposure to others.

Facilities should ensure that policies are in place to identify and manage health care workers exposed to infectious patients.

Triage and management of large scale exposures/potential exposures

Advance planning must involve ED, ICU and nursing staff, and IC to identify sites within the facility best suited to providing appropriate infection control capability.

Laboratory support and confirmation

Diagnostic samples to obtain

For decisions regarding obtaining and processing diagnostic specimens, contact local, state, and regional laboratory authorities or CDC.

Laboratory selection

Handling of clinical specimens must be coordinated with state health departments and CDC. Testing can be performed only in BSL-4 laboratories. The FBI will coordinate collection of evidence and delivery of forensic specimens to FBI or Department of Defense laboratories.

Transport requirements

Specimen packaging and transport must be coordinated with local, state and regional health departments, and the FBI. A chain of custody document should accompany the specimen from the moment of collection. Advance planning may include identification of appropriate packaging materials and transport media in collaboration with the clinical laboratory at individual facilities.

Patient, visitor, and public information

Fact sheets for distribution should be prepared, including a clear description of symptoms and where to report for evaluation and care if such symptoms are recognized. Details about the type and duration of isolation should be provided. Extreme measures such as burning or boiling potentially exposed materials should be discouraged.

14

Bioterrorism Threats with Interior Plants

Since September 11, 2001 the odds of a biological chemical attack in America have greatly increased. An attack such as this could be devastating to a massive number of Americans while having severe economic consequences. The most likely approach terrorists might use is to employ an aerosolizer to release biological and chemical warfare agents into a building's ventilation ducts. Once dispersed, aerosolized toxic substances will rapidly find their way into buildings adjacent to the release area.

For example, though thousands were killed at Ground Zero, many more may be suffering chronic respiratory problems from breathing toxic dust and chemical vapours that entered schools and other nearby buildings through air intake ducts after the Twin Towers collapsed.

No reliable means currently exists for detecting biological agents released into the atmosphere; agents would probably go unrecognized until building occupants began to exhibit symptoms.

Most buildings bring in fresh air through an outside duct and mix it with recirculated air. Since the 1970s "*energy crisis*," new buildings have been built with a tighter envelope for reducing energy consumption. As a result, more and more buildings have *indoor air quality* (IAQ) problems due to a buildup of pollutants released from building materials and furnishings.

Building occupants are increasingly exhibiting symptoms indicative of "*sick building syndrome*." In an effort to combat IAQ problems, the American Society of Heating, Refrigerating and Air- Conditioning

Engineers (ASHRAE) has continually recommended increasing ventilation rates in an effort to purge the air. This approach has three inherent problems: reduced energy efficiency, an assumption of clean outside air, and increased vulnerability to bioterrorism.

Today, most buildings use only dust filters without "*treating*" air at all, primarily because it is cost prohibitive. Even if cost were not an issue, high-efficiency particulate filters (HEPA) cannot filter chemical agents. They can only trap biological agents, and cannot destroy them. Some buildings use standard gaseous adsorbent media, such as treated activated carbon, to trap chemical pollutants. Once the HEPA filter or gaseous adsorbent media has been saturated with pathogenic microbes and/or toxic chemicals, how can they be disposed of? If saturated filters or filter media are not changed immediately, they begin to release the chemical pollutants back into the building.

Tommy Thompson, Secretary of Health and Human Services, stated that he is becoming increasingly concerned that ventilation systems in buildings around the country remain too vulnerable to bioterrorists. Public health experts have urged our government to address this major vulnerability in the nation's security. Tom Ridge, Director of Homeland Security, stated that we must invent innovative ways to protect ourselves against bioterrorism threats in the U.S.

Innovative Method

As a scientist with the Department of Defense (DOD) in defense of chemical and biological warfare, one can appreciate the challenges currently facing the building industry. Later, at NASA, our goal was to develop a completely closed ecological life support system for long-term space habitation. In space, ventilation is obviously not an option. Quite early in our research it became apparent that an earth-like ecosystem capable of treating human waste, purifying and revitalizing the air, and producing food would need to work in concert with mechanical devices to produce long-term sustainability and redundancy. On Earth, a building only needs to purify and revitalize the air, but the same concept applies.

Plants and Their Influence on Human Health and Well-Being

For many years now, plants have been placed in hotels, restaurants, offices, and homes to enhance ambiance. While the aesthetic value of interior plants is important, scientists in the U.S., Japan and several European countries have proven during recent years that plants play a far more significant role in our lives than just decoration. Many physiological and psychological health benefits can be derived from the presence of plants in an indoor environment. The presence of plants has been proven to increase the healing process among the sick. Plants in offices significantly improve worker productivity and reduce sick leave when compared to environments without plants. The interior plantscaping industry has been promoting plants for their non-aesthetic qualities, and the public has quickly grasped the concept. The building industry, however, has been slow to accept the role of plants as anything other than a way to fill an empty corner.

Plant Ecosystems

One of nature's most powerful tools for cleaning the environment stems from the synergistic reactions taking place between plants and their root microbes. This biotechnology is called *phytoremediation*.

During the last 30 years, scientists have made many discoveries leading to an understanding of how plants can purify both air and water. DOD studies showing plant ecosystems' abilities to remove toxic chemicals from contaminated water were first published in 1973. NASA first published studies in 1984 showing how interior plants could remove *volatile organic chemicals* (VOCs) from sealed test chambers. These findings received widespread publicity, and were quite readily accepted by the plant industry and general public. However, the *Environmental Protection Agency* (EPA) and the building industry were skeptical that plants could play any significant role in solving serious IAQ problems in buildings. They contended that sealed, "*static*" tests could not be extrapolated into "*real world*" conditions. To address these issues, NASA and the Associated Landscape Contractors of America (ALCA) initiated a joint program to conduct further studies with plants commonly used by the interior plantscaping industry.

A small, 800 square-foot, tightly sealed structure termed "the *Biohome*" was constructed to accommodate one person. The Biohome was fabricated and furnished with synthetic materials and had an insulation "*R-rating*" of 45. Complex chemical analyses of air samples from within the building showed high levels of a variety of VOCs. Upon entering the building, individuals exhibited common symptoms associated with "*sick building syndrome*," including watering eyes, burning throat and respiratory discomfort.

Several containers of plants and one small, fan-assisted planter using a mixture of activated carbon and potting soil were placed in the Biohome. After several days, chemical analyses confirmed that most of the VOCs had been removed. More importantly, upon entering the building, no one experienced any discomfort, proving that interior plants and high-efficiency plant filters can purify and revitalize air in nonventilated, hermetically sealed buildings. Additional studies in a home environment showed that plants actually reduce the number of mold spores and other airborne microbes instead of increasing them. Further studies have shown that plants' ability to remove VOCs increases with exposure time due to microbial adaptation, and that microbes in the rhizosphere (root area) play a major role in the chemical removal process.

Colleagues conducted the early studies at NASA and later studies at privately owned company. However, scientists in Germany, Australia and Japan have recently confirmed these findings and added new knowledge in the field. There is now sufficient scientific evidence to support the concept of using interior plants to provide good IAQ in hermetically sealed buildings having little or no mechanical ventilation.

Having many plants in an indoor environment is a common occurrence in hotels, offices, and restaurants. A visit to Opryland Hotel in Nashville or hotel chains such as Embassy Suites will confirm the euphoric indoor environment created by interior plants. The missing link, however, is that the clean air from the plant-filled spaces is not normally introduced into the surrounding rooms.

Hospitals in Japan are adding plants to take advantage of their air-cleaning properties. In many instances, existing buildings such as these need only modifications to their HVAC systems to create a closed internal air recirculating system, thus reducing their vulnerability to bioterrorism. Additionally, high-efficiency, plant-based filters can increase internal air purification and create a small positive pressure, if needed.

High-efficiency plant-based filters employ the adsorption properties of activated carbon, germicidal irradiation of ultraviolet light, and chemical degrading properties of plants and their root microbes to create a bioregenerating (self-sustaining) filter system. This process increases the filtering ability of each plant by several hundred times. Actree Corporation (Japan) is designing and will manufacture modular, built-in units for use in larger buildings. A small, portable unit is currently on the market in Japan. In our post 9-11 world, *bioterrorism* is an imminent threat that we must prepare to counteract. Can the building industry continue to ignore the promising role interior plants can play in creating a safer, healthier indoor environment?

15

Terrorism in North Dakota

Many of us prefer not to think about bad things happening. And most of us don't believe we will ever be affected by a terrorist attack, not here in North Dakota. It's true, terrorism may be a remote possibility, but other emergencies do happen. With the Minot anhydrous ammonia spill in 2002, we saw that it doesn't take a terrorist act to cause a public health emergency. Every day, trucks and trains carry potentially hazardous material through our state. Our residents travel the world and could be faced with terrorist situations while in other states or countries. No matter where we live or travel, we should always be ready to expect the unexpected.

What is North Dakota Doing About Terrorism?

The North Dakota Department of Health (NDDoH) has received federal funding to help the state prepare for terrorism events. We are using those funds to:

1. Educate the public.
2. Train health-care professionals.
3. Expand the ability of local public health units to respond quickly to emergencies.
4. Design and remodel our laboratory facilities, enhancing our ability to detect terrorism agents.
5. Increase our communication abilities.
6. Prepare to receive medicines and other medical supplies from the Strategic National Stockpile.
7. Develop partnerships with hospitals and local public health units to implement an enhanced disease surveillance system that would rapidly identify unusual disease events that may occur.

The benefit to these terrorism preparations is that we are becoming better able to respond quickly and efficiently to any health-related event.

How can WE "Be Aware and Prepare"?

The best way for you to be safe is to be as prepared as possible for any potential disaster. This booklet will help you learn about what kinds of terrorist threats are possible, prepare you to protect your home and family in case of an emergency, answer some basic terrorism questions and introduce you to other resources for learning about terrorism and general emergency preparations.

TERRORISM AGENTS AND THREATS

Radiological

A *radiological threat* could come in the form of a nuclear blast or a dirty bomb. A dirty bomb would involve the use of explosives to spread radioactive contamination over a targeted area. It is not a nuclear blast. The best way to protect yourself from a dirty bomb is to:

1. Cover your nose and mouth, and leave the immediate area on foot.
2. Go inside the nearest building.
3. Remove your clothes as soon as possible, and seal them in a plastic bag.
4. Take a shower or wash yourself as best you can.

Chemical

A *chemical attack* is the deliberate release of a toxic gas, liquid or solid to poison people and the environment. Nerve agents such as sarin and tabin are high on the list of suspected chemical threats. Signs of a chemical attack would include many people suffering from watery eyes, choking and having trouble breathing and many sick or dead birds, fish or small animals. If you suspect a chemical attack has occurred:

1. Avoid the contaminated area. Either get away from the area or shelter in place, using the option that minimizes your exposure to the chemical.
2. Wash with soap and water immediately if you were exposed to a chemical.
3. Seek medical attention.
4. Notify local law enforcement or health authorities.

Biological

A *biological attack* is the deliberate release of biological substances that can make you sick. Some agents, like anthrax, are not contagious while others, like smallpox, can be transmitted to other people. A biological attack may not be immediately obvious. Patterns of unusual illnesses or a surge of sick people seeking medical treatment may be the first sign of an attack. If you believe there has been a suspicious release of biological substances:

1. Quickly get away from the area.
2. Cover your mouth and nose with layers of fabric, such as a t-shirt or towel.
3. Wash with soap and water.
4. Contact local law enforcement or health authorities.

The CDC has listed the following agents as Category A agents, meaning they pose the greatest potential public health threat: anthrax, botulism, plague, smallpox, tularemia and viral hemorrhagic fevers.

Frequently Asked Questions About Terrorism

Q. *In an emergency, should we shelter in place or evacuate?*

Depending on the type of emergency, you may be instructed by authorities to either shelter in place or evacuate. Authorities base their decisions on what would cause the least harm to individuals. Even though leaving your home may seem like the best thing to do, there are times when staying inside and sealing doors and windows may provide you with the most protection. Listen to your TV or radio for instructions from local authorities or public health officials.

Q. *Could our water supply be a bioterrorism target?*

Most bioterrorism experts agree that municipal water systems are an unlikely target for bioterrorists. Methods already in place to filter and clean the drinking water supply are considered effective against most biological agents. Chlorine, for example, protects drinking water from water-borne bacteria and would neutralize most biological agents.

Q. *Should we buy a gas mask to protect myself against bioterrorism?*

A gas mask would only be helpful if it was specially fitted and you were wearing it at the exact moment that a bioterrorist attack occurred. A biological agent would likely be released without anyone's knowledge.

Q. *Will sealing windows with plastic sheeting and duct tape protect us during a biological or chemical emergency?*

There have been varying opinions publicized about the use of duct tape and plastic sheeting. While sealing your home will probably not be effective against a biological agent, sealing your windows and doors after a chemical release may provide temporary protection from exposure to the chemical.

Q. *Should we store my own supply of antibiotics for use after a bioterrorist attack?*

A bioterrorist might use several different germs. Although many antibiotics are effective for a variety of diseases, no single antibiotic is effective against all diseases. In addition, no antibiotics are effective against viruses. Antibiotics should be taken only with medical guidance.

Q. *How will we know that a terrorism event or emergency has occurred?*

In the event of an emergency, local, state and federal agencies will quickly respond and inform the public about what to do and where to go. You generally will hear of an emergency through your local radio, television and newspaper media. State health officials will coordinate with law enforcement, fire departments, hospitals, emergency management, local public health units and other local, state and federal agencies, developing plans to minimize the risk to the public and to treat those who may become ill.

Q. *What is North Dakota doing to prepare for a possible smallpox attack?*

Although the probability of an intentional release of smallpox is low, the consequences are so great that we must be prepared. North Dakota is not often thought of as a target for the release of smallpox, but it's possible that our residents could be exposed to a release of smallpox elsewhere or could be exposed to someone who is infected and develop symptoms upon returning home.

The North Dakota Department of Health has worked closely with local public health units, hospitals, the medical community and federal emergency response partners to implement the state's voluntary smallpox vaccination program as part of a national bioterrorism preparedness initiative. The benefit of this voluntary program is a prepared professional work force across the state that will be able to respond in case of a smallpox emergency. North Dakota has pre-event and post-event smallpox response plans in place.

National researchers continue working to develop a safer and more effective smallpox vaccine.

Q. *If we see suspicious activity, whom should I call?*

In an emergency, call 9-1-1. If you notice someone or something suspicious, contact your local law enforcement agency.

Make a Plan and Build a Kit

In an emergency or natural disaster, you are the real "*first responder.*" You will be the first one there for your family and your neighbours. Emergency personnel will be able to help but may not initially be able to reach you. Therefore, you must be prepared.

Give your Family the Gift of Security

You fix the leaky roof, rotate the tires on the car and change the batteries in your smoke detectors, all to protect your family and your home. Why not make this weekend's home improvement project a "*life improvement*" project? Prepare your family emergency plan and emergency supplies kit today. Here are some checklists to get you started.

Family Emergency Plan

1. Identify a relative or friend whom all family members can call if they are not together during an emergency. Make sure this person lives far enough away not to be affected by the same emergency, preferably outside of the state.
2. Help your children and elderly relatives or neighbours identify your community's warning system siren and tell them what to do if they hear it.
3. Hold a family meeting about emergencies and decide what to do in case of fire, severe weather, a hazardous chemical spill or a terrorist event.
4. Make sure the adults in your family know how to turn off water, gas and electricity at main switches. (Remember to turn off gas only if instructed to do so. You must have a professional turn your gas back on.)
5. Teach children how and when to dial 9-1-1 or 1-0-0.
6. Establish a meeting place away from your home where you can go if the area in which you live has been evacuated.

7. Determine escape routes from your home. Find two ways out of each room.
8. Practice fire drills and emergency evacuations.
9. Learn the emergency plans at schools and workplaces.
10. Teach responsible family members how to use your fire extinguisher.
11. Teach children how to call long distance and how to use a cell phone.
12. Put family records in a safe deposit box or fireproof, waterproof safe.
13. Take a basic first aid and CPR class.
14. Post emergency numbers near your telephones.
15. Have a plan for your pets during an emergency.

Emergency Supplies Kit

Listed below are recommended items for your emergency supplies kit. Store these items in a plastic storage container or backpack, something you could easily grab and take with if you have to evacuate.

1. Battery-operated portable radio and flashlight
2. First aid kit
3. An extra set of car and house keys
4. Pocket knife, tape, plastic bags with ties, scissors, whistle
5. Candles and waterproof matches
6. List of important phone numbers
7. Plastic tableware and a non-electric can opener
8. Entertainment (i.e., toys, playing cards, games, books)

Store the following occasionally used items near your emergency supplies kit so you know where they are.

1. Sleeping bags and blankets
2. Rain gear
3. Tarp and plastic sheeting

Keep the following items in or near your pantry and replenish them as they are used. Make it a habit to check dates on food, water and batteries whenever you change batteries in your smoke detectors.

1. Water—three gallons per person (enough for three days)
2. A three-to five-day supply of non-perishable food (i.e., canned foods and juices, granola bars, dried meats)
3. Extra batteries for your portable radio and flashlight

Keep a list of the following regularly used items taped to the inside of your pantry or broom closet. Be prepared to gather these items quickly in case you have to evacuate.

1. Special items for infants and elderly or disabled family members (i.e., diapers, formula, baby food, insulin)
2. Special items for pets (i.e., food, pet carrier, cat litter, leash)
3. Sturdy shoes or boots and gloves
4. A change of clothing for each family member
5. Medications and important medical information
6. Toilet paper and personal toiletries
7. Extra eye glasses or contact lenses and solution

In an emergency or a biological or chemical attack

1. Remain calm and be patient.
2. Listen to the radio or television news for instructions.
3. If your family is separated, make one phone call – to your family contact.
4. Follow the advice of local emergency officials about whether to shelter in place or evacuate.
5. If you evacuate:
   - Take identification, credit cards, cash and important documents, including home insurance information.
   - Wear protective clothing and sturdy shoes.
   - Take your emergency supplies kit, cell phone and other items you may need.
   - Take your pets.
   - Lock your home.
   - Use travel routes designated by authorities.
   - Shut off water and electricity if instructed to do so before leaving.

Strategies National Stockpile Ready

The U.S. Centers for Disease Control and Prevention (CDC), in consultation with other partners in bioterrorism preparedness, has developed a Strategic National Stockpile (SNS) program to respond to biological or chemical terrorism emergencies. The stockpile is made up of life-saving antibiotics, chemical antidotes and other medical supplies and equipment that are meant to be available when medical supplies at the local level are exhausted. Stockpiles are stored in strategic locations to ensure rapid delivery (two to 12 hours) anywhere in the country. In addition to the medical supplies already set aside, the federal government has an agreement with drug manufacturers to make large amounts of additional emergency medicine available.

The North Dakota Department of Health currently is working in conjunction with the Division of Emergency Management and other city, county and state agencies to develop a plan to receive and distribute items from the national stockpile. North Dakota has adopted an "*all hazards preparation*" approach to emergency planning, meaning we will be prepared to use stockpile items in the case of any disaster or public health emergency.

The planning process involves recruiting and training a group of qualified personnel (doctors, nurses, pharmacists, etc.) who would receive and distribute any needed antibiotics or other medical supplies. A computer database also is being developed that will track and inventory all received and distributed stockpile items.

The Department of Health, along with other healthcare institutions and government agencies, will work to protect the health of North Dakota's citizens. If a terrorist event or other emergency occurred, the public would be informed through the news media about what to do to protect themselves and their families. If antibiotics or vaccines were recommended, instructions would be provided locally about who should receive them and where the distribution sites would be located.

North Dakota Health Alert Network

The North Dakota Health Alert Network (NDHAN) website is your source for current information about health emergencies. Developed in cooperation with the U.S. Centers for Disease Control and Prevention, the NDHAN is part of the North Dakota Department of Health's Emergency Preparedness and Response program. Visit the website for:

- Health alerts.
- Preparation and safety guidelines.
- Emerging health issues.
- Terrorism agents and threats.
- Whom to contact in an emergency.
- Other resources of information about health-related issues.
- County-specific health information.
- Schedules of Department of Health webcasts and training.
- News releases from the Department of Health.

Volunteers Needed to Help During an Emergency

Every emergency response is a coordinated effort. Officials and volunteers must work together to save lives and protect property. Emergency officials all agree volunteers are absolutely necessary in the event of an emergency.

During a public health emergency—such as a terrorist event—help might be needed at central locations. At these clinics, we may need people to:

- Distribute information.
- Help patients complete paperwork.
- Direct traffic.
- Staff an informational hotline.
- Load and unload supplies.
- Provide child care.
- Prepare meals.
- Provide security.
- Distribute medications.
- Give vaccinations.

If you would like to be an asset to your neighbourhood or community in an emergency, consider joining the Public Health Emergency Volunteer Reserve. You do not need to be a health-care professional to join.

16

ATTACK ON BIOTERRORISM

Newly designed molecules that bind to and capture biowarfare agents are on the drawing board at Livermore. The goal is for these molecules to quickly and efficiently detect such deadly pathogens as botulinum toxin, anthrax spores, or smallpox. Using synthetic chemistry, scientists produce these new molecules that bind to unique sites on the surface of the toxin or organism. Their two-pronged, or bidentate, structure is critical. When a small molecule binds to a protein, the attachment is usually weak, and the interaction between the two is short-lived. If, however, two or more small molecules that bind to the protein are linked together, their binding to the same protein may be thousands, even millions, of times stronger. By targeting specific proteins, the synthetic molecules will mimic some of the behaviour in our immune system where antibodies recognize molecular foreign entities in our bodies and abnormalities such as cancer cells.

A single detector armed with many of these synthetic targeting molecules could simultaneously recognize an equal number of harmful biological agents that might be used in a terrorist attack. Assays using antibodies, known as immunoassays, are widely used to identify pathogens in the laboratory and form the basis for many biowarfare detection systems fielded to date. However, only seven good antibodies are currently available for pathogen detection. Other detectors depend on recognizing the bioagent's DNA. "But some pathogens, such as viruses, require human exposure to only a small number of organisms to be acutely toxic," says Livermore biochemist Rod Balhorn. "With so little DNA present in each virus and given the rapid variation that occurs in the base sequences that make up the DNA, those pathogens are typically very difficult to detect."

Similarly designed targeting molecules could zero in on defective or overactive proteins in our bodies and poison them, just as our natural antibodies do. These antibody-like molecules can lock on to cancer cells or other pathogens and kill them—and only them. By targeting unique sites on other proteins that cause disease—for example, the proteases that cause inflammation in arthritis or enable HIV to function—the synthetic molecules would block the activity of the protein without entering its active site. The active site is a cavity on the surface of a protein that is used by the protein to perform its function. Similar active sites can be present in many proteins, both those that are essential to cell function and others that cause disease.

The pharmaceutical industry has already begun using this approach to develop drugs that function as intended without blocking the activity of healthy cells or proteins. Molecules that target unique sites on the surfaces of specific proteins may soon lead to a new generation of drugs that have minimal side effects.

Balhorn is leading the program at Livermore to design synthetic molecules for bioagent detection and cancer treatment. He and a team of Livermore investigators are collaborating with scientists at Brookhaven and Sandia national laboratories and the University of California at Davis Cancer Center. Together, they are developing the methods needed to produce the first of these synthetic antibodylike molecules. "Terminology is a little tricky," he notes. "It is tempting to call our new molecules 'synthetic antibodies.' But we are designing small molecules that function like antibodies, not large proteins that are synthetic versions of antibodies. So we use the term 'high-affinity ligands' to describe our molecules."

"*Ligand*" is a general term used to describe a small molecule that binds to proteins or other large molecules. The higher the affinity a ligand has for a specific protein, the more tightly it binds to it. Research by others has demonstrated that bidentate ligands have a vastly increased affinity for the target protein, anywhere from thousands to millions of times greater. Polyvalent ligands—molecules that bind to multiple sites on the surface of a protein—are observed in many biological interactions that require very tight binding. The seek-and-destroy antibodies of our immune system, which normally operate quite successfully, are one example.

"What we're doing is searching for two molecules that bind to two sites next to each other on the surface of a protein," says Balhorn. "Then our synthetic chemist joins them together using a third molecule, called a linker. The linker must be both flexible and robust, or the new molecule will fall apart. This new synthetic ligand will then behave pretty much like an antibody, binding tightly to the protein."

The new bidentate molecules, called high-affinity ligands (HALs), will have several advantages over naturally occurring antibodies. They can be totally inorganic (nonprotein) and can be synthesized in large quantities using methods to ensure that each batch is structurally and functionally identical. They will also be stable over a long period, making them excellent candidates for long-term deployment in detectors for agents of biological warfare.

Toxic Targets

As bioagent detectors, HALs can be designed to target protein toxins produced by pathogens as well as any major protein component of pathogenic organisms. For the National Nuclear Security Administration's Chemical and Biological National Security Program, work is under way to develop HALs that bind to the *Clostridium* neurotoxins, which include botulinum and tetanus, the most toxic substances known. The *Clostridium* toxins attack the central nervous system and cause spastic paralysis in the case of tetanus and flaccid paralysis in the case of botulinum.

Balhorn's team is laying the groundwork for future development of HALs to target the *Staphylococcus* enterotoxins, which cause acute intestinal symptoms such as those associated with food poisoning, and ricin, a residue of castor bean processing that causes major intestinal or respiratory complications. The body's response to toxic quantities of either of these substances is swift and often fatal.

Work is also scheduled to begin in the near future on HALs that bind to proteins in the spores of *Bacillus anthracis* (anthrax) and in *Yersinia pestis* (plague). Once these HALs are completed, efforts will focus on the next highest priority agents: smallpox, *Francisella tularensis* (a plaguelike illness), and *Brucella melitensis* (an organism whose infections, often called *Mediterranean fever*, cause spontaneous abortions). Creating synthetic ligands even for proteins with a known structure is still a research project. Work began in 2000, and Balhorn estimates that high-affinity ligands for these eight bacterial toxins and threat organisms can be delivered in about 2005.

Got Structure?

If the structure of the target protein is known, the team uses that structure to develop a HAL. Work on these molecules is a logical progression from Livermore's protein structure and computational biology effort, with which Balhorn has been involved since its inception. Using x-ray crystallography and nuclear magnetic resonance (NMR) spectroscopy, high-resolution structures for many proteins have been determined at laboratories around the world, including Livermore. These include several types of *Clostridium* toxins (botulinum and tetanus) and the *Staphylococcus* enterotoxins.

All toxins in the *Clostridium* family have three parts. The targeting (or binding) domain, which binds to receptor molecules on the nerve cell membrane, and the translocation domain, which makes a pore in the cell through which the toxin passes, together make up what is known as the heavy chain. The light chain, which contains the catalytic domain, is a protease that is injected into the nerve cell and disrupts its functioning.

For the *Clostridium* neurotoxins, the team is developing a HAL to bind to the targeting domain, that fragment of the protein that recognizes and binds to motor neurons. Of these neurotoxins, botulinum is considered a greater threat than tetanus, but tetanus is easier to work with. Fortunately, its targeting domain is sufficiently similar in structure to botulinum's that it serves as a model for botulinum.

In 1998, Livermore's x-ray crystallography group completed a high-resolution structure of the binding domain of the tetanus toxin. Researchers then computationally calculated the molecular surface of the protein to identify sites where binding is likely to occur. "We look for pockets on the surface of the folded protein, places where another molecule would be able to fit tightly," says computational chemist Felice Lightstone. For the tetanus toxin, Lightstone found two appropriate sites adjacent to one another on the binding domain.

For a HAL to be effective, the sites designated for binding must be on a part of the toxin that is "*conserved*," meaning that these regions remain essentially identical across all strains of a toxin. When bioagents are being genetically engineered, areas such as these are difficult to modify without altering the toxicity of the agent. Ideally, a high-affinity ligand for tetanus toxin will be able to recognize engineered and other unknown or related *Clostridium* toxins.

The next step involved selecting compounds that might fit into the two sites. All of the 300,000 compounds in the Available Chemicals Database, a listing of all commercially available compounds, were computationally inserted (docked) into each site. The potential fit and interactions were then assessed. The top 1,000 compounds were run again using a range of structures for each compound representing the different bond orientations and shapes, known as *conformations*, that each molecule is likely to adopt. In this manner, the top 100 compounds were identified. The calculations for each site took about 3 weeks on a Linux cluster of 40 dual-processor personal computers.

Sandia National Laboratories in Livermore has recently written new programs to expedite this time-consuming process. Each compound is tested in 10 different conformations to see which fits best into the rigid protein. This provides a more realistic test of binding, because many of these small molecules are not rigid and can adopt different conformations. "Computational docking projects typically have success rates of anywhere from 10 to 40 percent," says Lightstone. "Even before we started using our new version of this program, our success rate of identifying molecules that actually bind to the protein was in the 40- to 65-percent range. Now, the likelihood of getting a fit may be even greater."

Into the Laboratory

Once possible ligands have been identified computationally, they must be tested in the laboratory to see whether binding actually occurs. *Mass spectrometry* (MS) and *NMR spectroscopy* are both effective for testing ligand–protein binding. NMR examines binding in the solution state, while MS looks at binding in the gas phase. MS typically requires much smaller samples, but it cannot handle certain compounds or chemical buffers. NMR can examine mixtures of compounds more easily and determine which combinations bind best in solution. Both techniques can identify where on the target protein binding is occurring.

The initial computational screening process to find new compounds that bind to tetanus neurotoxins resulted in 100 possible ligands that were predicted to bind to one of two sites on the tetanus neurotoxin's targeting domain. Experiments using *electrospray ionization*–mass spectrometry (ESI–MS) suggested that 7 of the first 13 tested compounds bound to the toxin. With ESI–MS, ligand binding is confirmed when a new mass peak appears at the expected mass-to-charge ratio for the ligand–tetanus complex.

The antitumour drug doxorubicin was discovered to be the best fit at site 1. The binding of this ligand to site 1 was later confirmed by x-ray crystallography of doxorubicin–tetanus toxin and doxorubicin–botulinum toxin complexes. For site 2, the same MS method was used to screen 1 of 100 compounds, six of which were observed to bind. The figure above shows one of these ligands, lavendustin A, docked into site 2 in the predicted structure of the tetanus–lavendustin A complex. The six ligands predicted to bind to site 2 were then screened for binding to the targeting domain using NMR. The six molecules were tested individually, as mixtures of different combinations of the compounds, and in the presence or absence of the known site 1 binder, doxorubicin.

When examined by NMR, small molecules exhibit weak, negative signals referred to as NOEs (*nuclear Overhauser effects*). Large molecules such as proteins exhibit strong, positive NOEs. When small molecules bind to proteins, the characteristics of the NOE for the large molecule are transferred to the small molecule. Thus, strong NOEs are detected for ligands that bind to the protein.

The NMR screening of mixtures containing the six predicted site 2 ligands confirmed that four bind to tetanus toxin in solution. Using a novel transfer NOE (trNOE) competition assay, researchers have determined that three of these ligands bind in the same site, presumably at site 2. The fourth ligand was determined to bind in a third site distinct from site 1 and site 2.

NMR experiments were also performed to evaluate how possible structural changes induced by the binding of one ligand in site 1 could influence the binding of the second ligand in another site. In these experiments, doxorubicin, which was added first, remained bound to site 1 throughout the additions of all six of the predicted site 2 ligands. The mixture containing doxorubicin and lavendustin A produced the strongest positive trNOE signal in the presence of the tetanus toxin. This experiment confirmed that both lavendustin A and doxorubicin bind simultaneously to the toxin, indicating that each must bind to a different site. "Unfortunately, this assay cannot define the location of the binding site," says physical chemist Monique Cosman, leader of the NMR group at Livermore. "But since doxorubicin is known to bind to site 1, we know that lavendustin A must bind to a different site, which may be site 2.

By performing these trNOE binding experiments with pairs of molecules that were determined to compete for binding to the same site, Cosman developed a new NMR method for identifying the relative strength of binding of each ligand to a particular site on the protein. MP-biocytin, another molecule that binds to site 2, did so with a relatively lower affinity than lavendustin A. The affinity of the third ligand is similar to that of lavendustin A, but it was not studied further because it is too perishable.

Mass spectrometry was then used to verify where the molecules are binding. Chemist Sharon Shields developed a new method that combines MS with proteolysis, a process in which a protein is digested by enzymes. "This is unique," she notes. "Now we can study solution-phase biological processes using a gas-phase mass spectrometric method."

She first treated the targeting domain of tetanus toxin with proteases that make clips in the amino acid chain either alone or on the tetanus–doxorubicin complex using various ratios of doxorubicin to the neurotoxin. Then she used matrix-assisted laser desorption ionization and ESI–MS to determine the pattern of enzymatic degradation that had occurred. In the tetanus–doxorubicin combinations, doxorubicin prevented the enzyme from digesting the protein at the binding site by limiting access to the amino acids located in that region.

Map of peptides (amino acid chains) produced by digesting the tetanus–doxorubicin complex compared to the tetanus toxin alone. In this experiment, Shields used the enzyme trypsin. The decreased abundance of peptides indicates the location where binding is occurring. That location contains amino acids 299–304, 351–376, and 394–434. Molecular docking calculations had predicted that doxorubicin would reside near amino acids 356, 358, 359, 407, 409, 419, 427, and 437. These predictions are a close match to MS results. Comparable locational experiments using other enzymes had similar results.

Shields also found that the presence of doxorubicin induces subtle changes in the tetanus toxin's three-dimensional structure, suggesting that the protein may envelope, or wrap around, doxorubicin when it binds. Further experiments are needed to confirm these results.

Creating a New Molecule

Synthetic chemist Julie Perkins has the job of linking the two molecules that bind to sites 1 and 2 to create a new HAL. This is the critical step. She is experimenting with linkers that will connect doxorubicin and MP-biocytin as well as doxorubicin and lavendustin A. "We know that each of these compounds binds individually to sites 1 and 2, but because they bind weakly, they can also float away," Perkins says. "When the compounds are linked together, they are much more likely to stay bound.

She is starting with the amino acid lysine as a linker. Lysine is an ideal building block because it has three distinct functional groups upon which she can perform synthetic chemistry experiments. Many derivatives of lysine are commercially available as well. The molecules that have been identified to bind into site 1 and site 2 can either be attached directly to lysine, resulting in their close proximity, or with a linker, which increases the distance between them. Increasing the distance between the two compounds with a flexible chain may also help increase the affinity of the ligand for the protein.

"To achieve maximum affinity of the ligand for the protein, we have to find the optimal length and rigidity of the linker," says Perkins, "and that can only be done experimentally." She is experimenting with a flexible glycol chain that can be attached to the lysine to increase the distance separating the two ligands.

Once she has synthesized each new compound containing the two linked ligands, conventional binding studies will identify the highest affinity and most selective ligand combinations. These studies will determine how tightly the HALs bind and confirm that they selectively bind only to *Clostridium* neurotoxins.

Targeting Cancer

For cancer therapy, the challenge is to synthesize molecules that bind with high affinity to each cancer cell without themselves generating an immune reaction from the body. Targeting molecules therefore must be smaller and more specific and have higher affinities than natural antibodies. They should also not be made of proteins, which elicit an immune response from the body.

The goal is to use these small, exceptionally high-affinity molecules to deliver a lethal radiation dose directly to a tumour. In this case, the HALs would be tagged with radioactive isotopes and introduced into the body. Research all over the world is focused on this new technique, known as isotopically enhanced molecular targeting.

To create new HALs for cancer treatment, Livermore is using the same process developed for producing HALs that bind to toxins and pathogens. The first project will be a HAL for a receptor protein found on the surface of non-Hodgkin's lymphoma, HLA-DR10. The crystal structures of four HLA-DR molecules are known, and unique binding sites on the HLA-DR10 protein have been identified using computer models of the protein generated by computational biochemists Adam Zemla and Daniel Barsky. Computational docking experiments are under way.

The HAL developed for binding HLA-DR10 and targeting human lymphomas will be designed to rapidly pass through the liver and kidney and thus minimize the systemic damage that can occur when antibodies carry radionuclides. "We are striving to convert the meaning of the word 'cancer' from 'fear, pain, suffering, and death' to 'just another treatable disease,'" says Balhorn.

Targets of Unknown Structure

When a target protein's structure is not known, the team will use a different route to design and synthesize HALs. Computers cannot be used to predict the binding of molecules to sites on these proteins. But NMR and MS processes that are being developed and fine-tuned now for identifying ligands that bind to known protein structures will identify ligands that bind to unknown structures.

Libraries of molecules will be experimentally screened for their ability to bind to the protein using a combination of Cosman's NMR technique and mass spectrometry methods being developed by chemist Lori Zeller. The molecules that bind will be segregated into sets that bind to different sites. Perkins will then synthesize all possible combinations of pairs of these small molecules using a series of different- size linkers. With Livermore's new Fourier transform ion cyclotron resonance mass spectrometer, mixtures of the HALs and protein can be quickly screened to identify the particular combination of ligands and linkers that produce HALs that bind to the protein. This approach should work well for creating detection reagents for pathogens. In collaboration with groups at Porton Down Defense Science and Technology Laboratory in England, Livermore researchers will design the first HAL for a protein with an unknown structure to bind to a protein on the coat of the anthrax spore.

Measuring Success

The Livermore team will soon produce its first HAL for the *Clostridium* neurotoxins. To know whether this work has been successful—whether the ligand works as designed in a bioagent detector—the team will send its results to the Department of Defense's Critical Reagent Program to be assessed for quality and specificity.

In the war against bioterrorism, the best defense begins with having the best possible data. Work has begun on docking studies to identify binding sites on the light chain of botulinum toxin. In this case, the goal is to synthesize HALs that can distinguish between the different types of *Clostridium* neurotoxins. That kind of fine-tuning is essential for accurate bioagent detection and identification during a crisis.

17

Bioterrorism Consequences Management

Before September 11, 2001, most Americans had never heard of anthrax, let alone cutaneous or inhalational *anthrax*. But these words became etched into the vocabulary of millions of people after Bob Stevens, photo editor for American Media Inc.—the parent company of the supermarket tabloids *The National Enquirer* and *The Globe*—died of inhalational anthrax on October 5, 2001. Suddenly, the threat of *biological warfare* was no longer theorctical, but a clear and present reality.

In the late 1990s there had been much debate about the threat of biological warfare. The media was filled with so-called experts crowing that an attack was imminent, while others claimed that rogue nations did not possess the delivery systems necessary to strike the United States. In fact, there were commentators who derided the whole notion of a threat to the U.S. from rogue nations using weapons of mass destruction as a way for consultants to make money. One of the most common statistics cited was that more people were killed falling off ladders then by acts of terrorism.

Today, however, the fear of *biological terrorism* is much greater than almost any other form of terrorism. Some of this fear is justified and some is exaggerated. The most frightening aspect of bioterrorism is that a biological agent can invade the body of an unsuspecting victim and that person would not know how or when it happened. We fear things that we cannot see, hear, feel or taste. A *microbial attack* by state-sponsored militaries or terrorists has the potential to sicken and kill thousands of individuals quickly—the essential definition of *catastrophic terrorism*. The effect of a biological attack could be equally or more devastating than a nuclear or chemical attack, due to its clandestine nature and the specific challenges it offers analysts, the medical community, law enforcement, and intelligence experts in identification and response. The consequences of the weaponization of a microbial agent are frightful, as the symptoms could be misidentified, mimicking other types of illnesses, and if contagious, spread quickly. Further, a response that is not timely could have grave consequences. One terrorist could execute a successful biological attack, and if it is a communicable disease, the outbreak could last for some time before it is identified, treated and eradicated. A biological attack could quickly overwhelm community or state-level emergency resources.

The anthrax attacks of 2001 demonstrated that the U.S. had miscalculated its ability to respond to a biological attack. Strategies were based on a one-size-fits-all approach—a chem/bio plan. Much emphasis was placed on the First Responders (police, fire and Emergency Medical Services [EMS]) and very little attention was paid to the health care community. In fact, the infectious disease community and public health departments were woefully under-funded and lacked not only resources but also the manpower to respond adequately.

In the early weeks after the first anthrax letter, infectious disease experts were not called upon to disseminate information to the public or to the media. The result was a deluge of so-called experts who spewed misinformation on TV and other media outlets. The best example is the "*expert*" who claimed that because Mr. Stevens was an avid outdoorsman, he most likely contracted anthrax by drinking contaminated water. Additionally, treatment and post-exposure prophylaxis including issues surrounding the pre-planned drug of choice, ciprofloxacin, were debated in public. The decision to use "*cipro*" was actually based on the fact that it was the only drug tested on animals, not because of its proven efficacy on humans. In fact, it was later found that penicillin was also a potentially effective treatment. The next issue that the U.S. faced was finding out where it could get large quantities of drugs in a timely manner.

National Pharmaceutical Stockpile

The *national pharmaceutical stockpile* (NPS) program was created by the U.S. Department of Health and Human Services' Center for Disease Control (CDC) and Prevention and the National Center for Environmental Health, a key component in the CDC's Bioterrorism

Response Initiative. The aim of the program is to ensure the timely distribution of lifesaving medication, including antidotes, supplies, vaccines and medical equipment needed to counter the effects of microbial pathogens, chemical and nerve agents. Because most communities will not have adequate supplies and medications available immediately following a disaster, the NPS provides governments at the federal, state and local levels immediate access to large quantities of medical supplies and pharmaceuticals. The NPS has designed push packages, ("*push packs*"), which cumulatively contain approximately 50 tons' worth of medications and medical supplies. These push packs are located in undisclosed locations throughout the country. In the event of a biological or chemical attack on a civilian population, the federal decision is made to deploy the push packs, and the NPS delivers them to any location in the U.S. within 12 hours. At this point, it is up to the state receiving the push pack to divide the medication that has arrived in bulk quantities and distribute it to the public.

The NPS program's response was tested for the first time in the hours and days following the World Trade Center attacks of September 11, 2001. New York State and local officials requested logistical assistance and mass quantities of medical supplies. Working in conjunction with local and state emergency response and public health agencies, the program was executed successfully. Following the World Trade Center and Pentagon attacks, the NPS was mobilized again to support the cities affected by the anthrax attacks of October and November.

Points of Distribution (POD)

The next issue was how to distribute the medicine. Fortunately, the New York City Office of Emergency Management (NYC-OEM) had developed a strategy for the mass distribution of medications to the city's population of eight million people. This strategy included the selection and use of hundreds of *Points of Distribution* (PODs) located strategically throughout the five boroughs. In addition, working with NYC-OEM as the project lead, the U.S. Army's Soldier, Biological, Chemical Command had established the Biological Weapons Improved Response Plan in the late 1990s. The theoretical plan included PODs for the mass distribution of drugs to a potentially affected population. PODs are the most efficient way to provide large quantities of prophylactic antibiotics to the general public in the shortest period of time. Using a high-throughput model, thousands of people can theoretically receive medication in a matter of hours. PODs are community-based facilities with large open areas. The staff needed consists of approximately 80 people, most with minimal or no prior medical training. Individuals are screened, or triaged, as they enter the facility. An oral triage assessment is used and is made up of approximately 12 questions. The main questions cover allergies and side-effects to medications, foods, etc. The triage process can be performed by either *Emergency Medical Service* personnel (EMTs and paramedics), or other medical practitioners such as nurses or physicians. Numerous cities throughout the U.S. had attempted to test this concept but most did not meet the needs of large numbers of people receiving medicine in a very short period of time.

In May of 2002, NYC-OEM conducted a real-time exercise called Operation TriPOD (*Trial Point of Dispensing*). The purpose of this six-hour simulation was to test New York City's capability for dispensing *prophylactic antibiotic* medication in the event of a biological attack; it was the first test of its kind in the U.S. The trial sought to determine whether New York City could handle a throughput rate of dispensing medication to 1,000 people per hour. The resulting data showed the city could handle approximately 4,000 people in three hours, indicating that the exercise was a success. The trial exceeded expectations by affirming that the city could handle approximately 1,500 people in one hour. TriPOD also helped New York City agencies familiarize themselves with the program and ultimately assist in the development of future planning.

Health and Human Services

The department of health and Human Services (HHS) has taken a crucial lead in preparing the nation and its public health infrastructure in epidemic and bioterrorism preparedness plans. In the event of a biological release, HHS would play a significant and lead role in the detection and investigation of the outbreak, as well as the dissemination of pharmaceuticals (*antibiotics* and *vaccines*) to the public. In addition, HHS works with the private sector and other federal agencies to develop the capabilities for response to a biological attack.

So far this year [2002], the federal government has approved a $350 million HHS spending package to be used for preparedness and response plans to a biological attack. HHS has begun to develop a five-year plan for enhancing the nation's ability to prepare for potential bioterrorism attacks. The plan will delineate specific requirements and strategies for all agencies on the federal, state and local level, as well as medical response for bioterrorism. The intent of this plan is to address issues such as disease surveillance, the public health network, medical consequence management, the national pharmaceutical stockpile, research and development, and deterrence.

Syndromic Surveillance

Early recognition is the front-line defense against biological terrorism. Unlike *chemical agents*, which act quickly, the effects of *biological agents* are inherently delayed due to their incubation periods as well as other environmental factors present during the release of the agent. These factors include meteorological indicators such as wind speed and direction, time of day and temperature, which all have an effect on inversion layers which, in turn, affect the ability of the agent to remain airborne. A narrow window of opportunity exists when aggressive medical treatment, including prophylaxis (for bacterial agents), can positively affect the outcome of the disease.

To ensure that an outbreak is recognized early, physicians, nurses, EMS personnel and relevant medical staff who are the most likely to observe an emerging disease incident must be trained to recognize the signs and symptoms of the diseases considered to be the result of a bioterrorism threat. The goal of this training is to raise the index of suspicion when considering differential diagnoses surrounding an unusual infectious disease or fever of unknown etiology. The seven individuals in New York City who contracted anthrax were never reported to the medical surveillance system.

In addition to *passive surveillance*, in which trained medical practitioners watch for signs of an event through their patients, an active surveillance system is one that is designed to identify an outbreak early by the aggressive monitoring and analysis of health and medical indicators. A critical indicator in American surveillance is Emergency Medical Service (EMS) demand. In the U.S., EMS serves as a gateway to health care for many Americans, especially in densely populated urban areas. Ambulance run data is often associated with both naturally and unnaturally occurring events, which may affect the general population. This would include summer heat and winter weather extremes and certain unusual disease outbreaks. Ambulance service data is an excellent barometer for assessing and analyzing the health of a given population. Other general data include hospital emergency department statistics as well as medical examiner and coroner death data. Once a baseline is established for a specified area (i.e., a city, township or county), the daily evaluation of current indicators against the baseline is made extremely feasible.

Surveillance is needed at the regional level if early recognition of a *biological terrorism* incident is to occur. This is essential in metropolitan areas where cities share populations. New York City for example, shares a population of 12 million with the surrounding suburban areas. While 8 million reside within the city limits, an additional 4 million commuters travel to the city every workday. Add in thousands of tourists who visit the city every day and one gets a sense of the enormity of the population. When considering the potential for an incident to occur in a city, with the effects being transmitted throughout the surrounding suburban communities, the need for regional surveillance becomes clear. Advanced surveillance can also be conducted by analyzing medical data in more specific terms. Given that most biological agents present as an influenza-like illness, monitoring hospital and ambulance data targeted at the signs and symptoms of influenza, influenza-like syndrome and even respiratory illnesses can help in early detection.

While we have learned much over the past few years about planning, responding to and recovering from biological terrorism, the events of the autumn of 2001 have left us with a number of unanswered questions. Now more than ever, we see the need for more research, as well as a greater need for technological development and intergovernmental and international cooperation in the areas of intelligence and emergency planning. Proper focus and funding can help us ensure that if there is a next time, the world's governments can respond with alacrity and efficiency.

A Security Study

From the interwar era through the end of World War II, Japan and major powers competed to develop and weaponize various *biological agents*. In general, however, the use of biological weapons (BW) was restrained in *World War II*, especially in contrast to *World War I*, when opposing camps used large amounts of chemical agents against one another.

During the Cold War, nuclear weapons dominated the interests and concerns of decision-makers, strategists and peace activists. Major powers such as the United States and the United Kingdom had gradually begun to regard BW as an insignificant factor in war planning. This devaluation was driven by two factors. One was the emerging international consensus that BW was too inhumane for anyone to consider using seriously. The other, from the military's point of view, was the relative ineffectiveness of BW on the modern battlefield, where armed forces rarely came into contact with one another and where conventional weapons could be used from miles away. The United Nations General Assembly adopted a resolution to ban chemical and biological weapons in 1969. In the same year, by executive order, the Nixon administration unilaterally proclaimed the renunciation of offensive biological programs. This declaration was supported by other Western countries. Subsequently, the *Biological* and *Toxic Weapons Convention* (BWC) was signed in 1972 (enacted in 1975) and instituted the first total disarmament of a specific category of Weapons of Mass Destruction. In this way BW disappeared from many countries' defense and deterrence policies.

However, BW never really disappeared. It became clear that, despite its being a signatory to the BWC, the Soviet Union had continued to develop and deploy BW as a strategic weapon. BW was attractive to countries that could not develop nuclear weapons (because of costs and technology that were out of their reach) but had the ambition to obtain an offensive card. In addition, some regarded BW as a convenient terrorism tool (in the 1970s, Bulgarian secret agents assassinated a defector living abroad by using the deadly toxin ricin).

Now that the U.S.-Soviet symmetrical nuclear arms race is over, BW has come to the surface again, this time in a new era of terrorism. U.S. National Defense University's comprehensive survey, *Bioterrorism* and *Biocrimes*, shows that out of a total 142 cases of bioterrorism or biocrime in the past 100 years across the globe, 115 occurred in the 1990s. Over the past decade, bioterrorism has become a growing international security concern for the U.S. and its allies. However, some worry that "*security experts*" in Japan have not paid enough attention to bioterrorism.

How Japan is changing its stance to address the threat from bioterrorism is the primary focus of this section. First we'll consider two recent bioterrorism cases and explore how they have influenced Japan's bioterrorism policy. We'll also examine how Japan's perceptions of anti-terrorism and nonproliferation are affecting national policymaking on bioterrorism, and why debate on bioterrorism policy has not advanced in Japan. Finally, we'll explore how the threat of bioterrorism can be averted in the context of U.S.-Japan cooperation.

Lessons Learned from Aum Shinrikyo

Aum Shinrikyo, a Japanese doomsday cult with international interests, produced and dispersed botulinum toxin for the first time in 1990, targeting the Yokosuka Naval Base, Narita International Airport and the Japanese Parliament building. No casualties were reported. The cult is said to have obtained the botulism-causing germ in a forest near Tokachi River in Hokkaido. As further evidence of Aum's interest in BW, the cult dispatched a medical mission to Zaire in 1992, most likely to acquire strains of the deadly Ebola virus.

In June 1993, Aum sprayed anthrax from inside their headquarters building in Kameido, a downtown Tokyo district. The *noxious odor* created a furor among the residents, but no one became sick. By this time, Aum was already notorious because leader Shoko Asahara and his followers had appeared on television many times and had been causing trouble in cities and villages where their main complex and branches were located. The Japanese media treated the Kameido affair as a light human interest story. Aum explained the incident away by claiming that soybean oil and perfume, boiled to purify the building, had caused the smell. Since the local authorities were prohibited from entering the building, nobody at that time discovered the real cause of the smell or the true motive behind the cult's activity.

On March 15, 1995, three briefcase-style devices for disseminating a virus were placed at Kasumigaseki subway station, a hub of the Tokyo subway system, and the station closest to several central government buildings .Again, no casualties were reported. No one has been arrested in relation to this ominous incident, though it may have been connected to Aum Shinrikyo. In retrospect, it could have been a hint at the sarin attacks in the same station five days later. That attack killed a total of 12 commuters and station employees and injured some 5,000 others.

Immediately after the Tokyo subway attacks on March 20, 1995, many Aum followers were arrested for various crimes but none were arrested or indicted on charges of using biological weapons. This was due largely to the fact that, at the time, there was no Japanese law to punish terrorist activities related to biological agents. No trials related to bioterrorism were opened, and the details of the incident were not made public. One thing that is certain is that Seiichi Endo, a former microbiologist at the Graduate School of Kyoto University and the cult's designated "Minister of Health and Welfare," played an essential role in the plan. Police began to investigate covert biological weapons-related activities from 1995, but this investigation has not been made public.

Ask a Japanese person which word comes to mind when they hear "*Aum Shinrikyo*," and almost every answer, even from children, will be "sarin," the deadly nerve gas. However, it could just as easily be "*anthrax*" or simply "*terrorism.*" The Japanese should draw lessons from Aum Shinrikyo's wanton plan of biological terrorism. But unfortunately they have not done so because of the serious lack of information about these forms of terrorism.

What measures did Japan take after all of these Aum-related incidents? In the first instance, greater efforts were made to prevent chemical, rather than biological, terrorism. Later, the Japanese government began to use the term NBC (*nuclear*, *biological*, *chemical*) terrorism, which indicated that the government did not focus only on biological terrorism, but rather expanded the concept of terrorism to include such acts as covert attacks on nuclear power plants as well as on crowded subways.

It is the *National Police Agency* (NPA) that has been paying particular attention to the threat of NBC terrorism. NPA established a new post called "*Special Advisor on Terrorism*" in the Security Bureau in April 2000. This official's job is to enhance and coordinate the response capability not only for NBC terrorism, but also for hijacking, hostage-taking abroad and attacks on larger, international events (i.e., the World Cup soccer tournament). Aum is one of the driving factors that helped to establish the post. Further, NPA examined the anti-bioterrorism policies of other G8 countries in 1999, and established counter-NBC terrorism special units in the police agencies of the two largest cities in Japan, Tokyo and Osaka. Meanwhile, the Japan Defense Agency (JDA) organized a roundtable conference on biological weapons in 2000. The report from the roundtable of non-governmental experts was made public in April 2001. It gave recommendations on how to tackle biological weapons; however, it also revealed how far behind Japan's defense program is, compared with the U.S. Relevant agencies composed a manual for first responders to use for rescue, identification of bio/chemical agents and decontamination purposes. Meanwhile, the Cabinet Secretariat for National Security and Crisis Management organized a Consequence Management (CM) manual in April 2001 to replace the previous one.

Looking back on the years since 1995, it is clear that Japan did not consider bioterrorism a top national security priority. In fact, bioterrorism did not become a hot issue in security dialogue until 2001. While there were those who were interested in bioterrorism from an epidemiological, microbiological or emergency medical treatment standpoint, almost no one examined it from a security studies point of view. The questions of who is likely to commit acts of bioterrorism and how a state deters and prevents those acts must be answered. These answers must be linked to foreign policy, arms control arrangements and an overall anti-terrorism strategy. This task is the responsibility of security experts.

Ultimately, Aum Shinrikyo was not a wake-up call for the Japanese. Policy discussion on the implications of Aum's actions was not active, and almost no one considered the attacks "a case study of proliferation of weapons of mass destruction by non-state actors," as U.S. Senate committees described it in October 1995. In fact, Aum was a prototype for a new brand of terrorism that is now posing a threat to international society. Unprepared for future crises, Japan was forced to look more seriously at the threat bioterrorism posed in the autumn of 2001.

Anthrax Letters and their Impact on Japan

On October 5, 2001, Robert Stevens, a photo editor in Florida, was killed by inhalation anthrax (spores in the form of a powder). For almost two months, the U.S. was in the grips of this invisible threat. In the end, five people were killed and 22 infected. Although the FBI could trace the spores to a post office in New Jersey and identified "*persons of interest*," including a former army researcher, no one has been arrested in connection with the letters so far.

A biological attack was predicted by terrorism experts long before September 11. In fact, even as early as the late 1990s, experts were repeatedly warning that an occurrence was a matter of "not if, but when." The Clinton administration recognized the immediate threat of bioterrorism and considered it one of its top national security priorities in 1998. Before 2001, there were many hoaxes that inured terrorism experts to the threat of bioterrorism. In the case of the anthrax attacks, however, the method of dissemination (through the U.S. Postal Service) is what caught many experts off guard.

Although the shock experienced by other countries was much less serious than that of the U.S., the anthrax mail raised concerns among the Japanese people and within Japan's government.

While the Japanese public's interest focused mainly on the situation in Afghanistan and when and how the Bush administration would start its "*War on Terror*," the Japanese Ministry of Foreign Affairs (MOFA) reported in September 2001 that the next act of global terrorism would likely be a biological one. Based on this conclusion, MOFA began to coordinate with other relevant agencies. The Ministry of Health also issued urgent warnings to local governments and cities.

On October 12, 2001, an inter-agency meeting created a "Priority List on Domestic Anti-Terrorism Policies," which included ways to strengthen responses to NBC terrorism. In accordance with the list, each agency took the following measures: the NPA strengthened its six new NBC terrorism investigation units; the JDA increased production of antibiotics and bolstered the emergency medical system; the National Fire Department organized its own NBC terrorism units; the Ministry of Education arranged for protective suits to be delivered to National University Hospitals; the Maritime Safety Agency also arranged for protective materials to be sent to hospitals; and the Ministry of Health began to create a vaccine stockpile and prepared for decontamination units to be deployed to Emergency Relief Centers. These consequence management (CM) measures were put in place to manage the results of a large-scale incident, to prevent panic and to minimize casualties. CM is doubtlessly much easier for the Japanese to address than daily anti-terrorism operations. CM is similar to disaster management, and the Japanese have extensive experience dealing with natural disasters, especially earthquakes and volcanic eruptions. In this sense, CM is a socially and politically acceptable concept. On the other hand, daily anti-terrorism measures, including the collection of information, containment of unstable variables and prosecution of terrorist organizations, is much more difficult because it requires comprehensive foreign relations and security strategies, which Japan is not accustomed to devising.

Compared to the situation before 2001, it was remarkable to see police and fire departments conducting drills for chemical and biological terrorism. Planning for the 2002 FIFA World Cup cohosted by South Korea and Japan was a factor in the increased frequency of those drills.

According to a statement by the Minister of Public Safety, over 1,000 anthrax-related hoaxes occurred in Japan in the first two months after the first anthrax-laced letter appeared in the U.S. These hoaxes caused anxiety and anger throughout Japan. The government and media bear a heavy responsibility in determining what information should be released to the public and how it should be released, as well as the importance of public relations efforts.

It is worth noting that in the face of the anthrax incident in the U.S., Japan decided to ratify the U.N. Convention to Suppress Terrorist Bombings, which was adopted in December 1997 and came into effect in May 2001. Although Japan signed it in April 1998, it had not been ratified. The reason for the delay was that the Japanese legal code lacked the proper law that would allow the Convention to be observed. Finally, in November 2001, Japan revised its existing laws to enable the government to punish those who perpetrate acts of bioterrorism, thus allowing for ratification of the Convention. Had the events of September 11 and the anthrax letters not occurred, the political will to ratify the Convention would not have materialized.

Coupled with the flood of coverage of terrorism, many books on bioterrorism, as well as nuclear and chemical terrorism, were published in Japan. Some were translated into Japanese after the events of 2001. However, the phenomenon was temporary, and after some time, many were pulled out of bookstores.

Has Japan changed its course to combat terrorism? I believe it has. The question is will these efforts continue and how will agencies coordinate themselves for maximum efficiency? It will take several years to accurately assess Japanese preparedness. Most Japanese security experts have been talking about the impact of September 11 on international politics and regional security, but only a handful of them have examined the equally important problem of how bioterrorism affects national and international security.

Japan's Anti-Terrorism Efforts

Besides Aum Shinrikyo and the attacks of September 11, there have been many terrorism incidents involving Japanese both on domestic soil and abroad. Despite these circumstances, Japanese *anti-terrorism policy* is still incoherent. In reviewing what we know, we may be able to find out why Japanese bioterrorism policy is so far behind its contemporaries.

First, Japan does not recognize the importance of defining terrorism. Most experts believe that a definition is necessary in order to distinguish between terrorism and other kinds of violence. Without a definition, it is difficult to identify and regulate terrorism on a case-by-case basis. In other words, a definition of terrorism should be imperative in anti-terrorism laws and policy. In reality, neither the MOFA nor the JDA has definitions of terrorism; the NPA has an obsolete one used for its targets mainly among the domestic far-left wing. This definition shows clearly how the NPA did not consider international terrorism a grave threat.

International relations scholars have not paid attention to international terrorism either, much less its definition. For example, a representative international relations researcher described in the current *Dictionary of Modern Politics* that terrorism is a "*political assassination.*" There are several terrorism books in which the history of assassination is described in great detail. Needless to say, assassination is only one of several methods of terrorism. In practice, the NPA and the JDA do not differentiate between terrorism and guerrilla tactics. It is clear that for those who only see the topic from such present-day examples as September 11 or Palestinian suicide bombings, it is not necessary to define what terrorism is. But it is difficult, for example, to block money to terrorists without applying some definition of what constitutes a terrorist and terrorism in general. Japan risks being regarded by the rest of the international community as a country less eager to combat terrorism if it continues to put off defining what terrorism is.

Second, unlike the U.S., Japan has no proclaimed principles against terrorism. The U.S. Department of State confirms its tenets in its annual *Patterns of Global Terrorism*. Japan, in lieu of such tenets, lives by a different credo: "Respect human life; seek a peaceful solution." This mentality clearly expresses the Japanese sentiment that the use of force should be avoided at all costs. The phrase is repeatedly heard by government officials, some members of the media and in public opinion. Those who subscribe to this motto wanted, for example, to deter the Peruvian government from bursting into the Japanese ambassador's residence in Lima during the 1997 hostage crisis. This "*no force*" philosophy was used more recently to criticize the U.S. bombing campaign in Afghanistan in 2001. This is certainly a praiseworthy norm, but a "*peaceful solution*" does not tell us how to punish groups who have committed crimes once the incidents are over. In order to declare national principles that can be applied on a daily basis, we must amend our laws to cover at least general contingencies.

Third, unlike the U.S., the UK and other countries, Japan does not designate Foreign Terrorist Organizations (FTOs). In the U.S., the secretary of state, with assistance from the Office of the Coordinator for Counterterrorism and in accordance with the Anti-terrorism and Effective Death Penalty Act of 1996, has the right and responsibility to designate FTOs whose members are inadmissible to and removable from the U.S. The secretary of state can also ban or restrict fundraising activities by FTOs and their members. These responsibilities explicitly show the resolve of the U.S. to the international community, and send a warning signal to terrorists and their supporters. Japan, on the other hand, has avoided tackling terrorist organizations. Once hostages are returned safely, the predicament is deemed solved. Japan does not attempt to pursue, contain, or bring the perpetrators to justice or prosecute the offending organizations by means of international cooperation.

Although definitions, principles and FTOs are the pillars of antiterrorism policy, they are hardly discussed among security experts in Japan. Of course, definitions and principles are no panacea since new types of terrorism may not fall within those definitions, and practice does not always follow principle. But to clarify definitions and principles and to identify terrorist organizations would allow Japan to express its efforts and posture to the world community. Terrorism is not only an emergency matter but also a chronic, ongoing one. Therefore, prevention and deterrence strategies well-coordinated with foreign and domestic policies are as important as CM measures in combating terrorism.

Worst-case scenarios are less debated in Japan than in the U.S. Some experts study American scenario exercises on Weapons of Mass Destruction (WMD) terrorism such as Wild Atom, Dark Winter, Top Off and others, but in general, Japanese do not like to think of worst-case scenarios from the political and military points of view, and tend to avoid public discussion of their own scenarios for fear that the press or peace movement groups will criticize them. Worst-case scenarios, if any, are discussed and played as a game only in back rooms.

Attitudes Toward WMD Proliferation

How has Japan positioned itself on the WMD proliferation problem and BW in particular? There is a mutual relationship between nonproliferation and anti-terrorism. That is, if a country truly combats bioterrorism, it should necessarily pay attention to BW proliferation in the world.

How a country stands on the Iraqi problem is now the typical indicator of where it stands on WMD proliferation. The real problem for the international community regarding Iraq is how to respond to a dictatorial government that makes biological and chemical weapons in direct violation of international agreements and mandates. With regard to biological agents only, it was already clear in 1995 that the Iraqi government had produced at least 19,000 liters of botulinum toxin, 8,500 liters of anthrax and 2,200 liters of aflatoxin. Since the end of the *Gulf War*, the U.S. and the United Nations have been addressing this problem.

In 2002, the security dialogue in Japan, as in other nations, has centered on Iraq. The discussions in Japan, however, have focused only on whether and how Japan should support the U.S. military's use of force under the current law, or if a new law is necessary. These discussions are no doubt of vital importance to this dialogue, but at the same time it is unfortunate that hardly anyone has suggested a way to curb BW proliferation in Iraq.

Japan's reactive posture on matters of both domestic and international security is nowhere more evident than in the diplomatic brouhaha surrounding the U.S. Operations Infinite Reach and Desert Fox in the summer and winter of 1998 respectively. To retaliate against the terrorist bombings of the U.S. embassies in Kenya and Tanzania, the U.S. launched Operation Infinite Reach, attacking Osama bin Laden's terror camps in Afghanistan as well as a "*chemical weapons factory*" in Sudan. When asked to comment on the U.S.'s military action, then Prime Minister Obuchi stated that Japan could "*understand*" the reasons for the U.S. bombing. Given the heightened intensity of cooperation among G8 nations at the time, Obuchi's comment sounded flat and uninspired. The U.S. was naturally disappointed with Japan's response, which appeared to lack conviction to fight terrorism with its allies and the rest of the international community, despite Japan's 25-point promise to the G8 to do so. Later, in the winter, Japan had an opportunity to save face with the international community when the U.S. and the UK embarked on Operation Desert Fox, a series of bombing raids against Iraq, in response to violations of UN resolutions. Japan, remembering the reaction of the U.S. after Operation Infinite Reach, ended up supporting Desert Fox for fear of committing another political *faux pas* against Washington.

Desert Fox, which promoted counter-proliferation, was different from Infinite Reach, which focused on counter-terrorism. But from the Japanese perspective, both were seen as American military operations, which Japan must support. Close relations with allies are vitally important, but it is also critical that Japan concentrate on the core issues of anti-terrorism and anti-proliferation, regardless of international politics, not only in times of crisis but also on a more comprehensive and consistent basis. In the four years that have passed since Desert Fox, Japan has missed several opportunities to establish its own WMD non-proliferation policy.

Japan missed another opportunity to demonstrate its commitment to anti-terrorism efforts through WMD non-proliferation when the former Soviet Union (FSU) announced that it would dismantle its stores of WMD. The Soviets violated the Biological and Toxic Weapons Convention during the Cold War. In 1992, President Boris Yeltsin confessed to producing and deploying various biological weapons on a large scale. After disclosure of the violation, it became urgent to dismantle the arsenal. In 2001, it was confirmed that a huge amount of anthrax was still left on Vozrozhdeniye, an island in the Aral Sea, despite the fact that the U.S. and Uzbekistan had already agreed to remove anthrax from the island for fear of worsening the environment and of supplying terrorists with biological agents. Russia's insufficient safeguards for nuclear materials have resulted in what are often described as "*Loose Nukes*." This instance, then, can appropriately be dubbed "*Loose Bio*." Japan could have supplied funds and human resources to the containment and disposal effort; this move would certainly have been looked upon favourably by the international community as a forward-thinking measure against international terrorism.

Japan has spent money to dismantle nuclear submarines but has paid no attention to biological weapons. It is imperative that Japanese government policy reflect a link between WMD proliferation and terrorism.

Japan's uninterested posture towards Iraq and towards the FSU in terms of WMD proliferation seems to reveal its reluctance to solve these international security issues. Moreover, very few in the security studies field mention proliferation of biological weapons as well as bioterrorism as co-existing threats to international security.

While nuclear weapons and missiles have been the subject of controversy, little attention has been given to chemical and biological weapons. Since the end of *World War II*, the Japanese government has been promoting the annihilation of nuclear weapons as a goal of foreign policy. As norms to ban other weapons of mass-murder are shared widely, Japan should expand its mission goal to include chemical and biological weapons.

As mentioned above, though Japan took some measures to combat bioterrorism in 2001, the Japanese government and people essentially view bioterrorism as an emergency issue, something like a natural disaster. This perception of terrorism is only half-accurate. Terrorism cannot happen without terrorists who prepare their attacks over a long period of time. If we become preoccupied with only the emergency aspects, we will certainly miss the opportunities to prevent those attacks.

It has been over a year since September 11, 2001, and during that time Japan has passed some anti-terrorism legislation, but it is insufficient. The largest obstacle to creating effective policy may be Japan's own unchanged perception of terrorism, which will most probably not see significant change in the near future.

Prevention of Bioterrorism

At Japan society's July 2002 bioterrorism roundtable conference held in New York, a Japanese participant stated that there was nothing the U.S. and Japan could reasonably do to cooperate on anti-bioterrorism efforts. Although this opinion may not be representative of other participants, it may sadly reflect the feeling of most security experts in Japan. In October 2000, at Japan Society's first roundtable on terrorism, one U.S. participant asked irritably why Japanese anti-terrorism policy was so lax in light of the suffering caused by Aum Shinrikyo.

As these views demonstrate, it is obvious that there is a gap between Japan and the U.S. in terms of threat perception and assessment. In general, any nation's security policy originates from its so-called "*strategic culture.*" Strategic culture is thought to influence a nation's long-term security policy goals, policymaking processes, use of force and decision-makers' behaviour in times of crisis. According to Alan Macmillan and Ken Booth, both scholars in international politics, sources of strategic culture are a nation's geography and resources, history and experience, and political structure and defense organization. This means that each nation has its own unique strategic culture. The concept of terrorism, among other things, is based on culture. The word "*terrorism*" is used to denounce to the strongest degree possible an enemy's malicious action. In this sense, terrorism does not reflect any objective reality, but rather it expresses a subjective image of evil collectively shared by one particular society.

There is no doubt that a difference of strategic cultures exists between Japan and the U.S. As a result, anti-terrorism policies are also different in laws, institutions and threat perception, even if both nations seemingly share common interests. Such a perception gap between allies, especially when terrorism is increasingly becoming a matter of international security, is not desirable. To bridge the gap, Japan should re-think its passive stance and match its threat perception to that of the U.S.

Consequence management (CM) goes part and parcel with anti-terrorism policy. Although there is no universally accepted definition, its importance is widely recognized among the antiterrorism community under the circumstantial umbrella "*Catastrophic Terrorism.*" As important as CM is in a nation's fight against terrorism, prevention is critical as well.

Prevention of bioterrorism can be thought of not only in terms of regulating access to biological agents but also in terms of broader national security strategies. First, Japan should categorize non-state actors into three groups: those who have the capacity to commit bioterrorism; those who have the motive to commit bioterrorism; and those who have committed acts of mass murder on a domestic and/or international scale.

Individuals and organizations who have the capacity are, of course, not necessarily potential terrorists. Moreover, we cannot stop the proliferation of information. Today, thanks to the Internet and self-help manuals, it is easy to attain the know-how behind making biological weapons used to "*wipe out cities.*" Therefore, 100 percent prevention is impossible from the outset. But this fact does not preclude the necessity for strict measures to deter "*amateur terrorists.*" In particular, we can pre-empt R.I.S.E-like terrorist groups by preventing them from gaining deadly agents. R.I.S.E. was an eco-terrorist group from Chicago, composed of 19- and 20-year-old youths, who in the early 1970s succeeded in procuring biological agents from the University of Illinois Hospital where one of the boys worked as a part-time research assistant. They attempted to commit acts of bioterrorism indiscriminately.

The second category is for those who intend to commit acts of bioterrorism and who would immediately do so if given the biological agents and technology to disseminate them. This category includes many fundamentalist organizations that have been branded as terrorists; Al-Qaeda is a typical example. They leave indirect evidence that they are inclined to bioterrorism. It is relatively easy to maintain surveillance of these groups by watching what they claim on the Internet, television and by other means. It is important for the various national and international agencies to exchange information among themselves about the results of their surveillance.

The third category is for groups who have already committed acts of mass murder. Perhaps many of the groups in this category would have used bioterrorism and other WMD terrorism if they had had appropriate agents. Splinter groups of national armies, *guerrilla* and *fanatical terrorist* organizations are most likely to be in this category.

Based on the information gathered on terrorist organizations and radical factions all over the world, the threat of biological terrorism can be analyzed in three categories: capability, intention and record of mass murder. The assessment should be conducted under the strict coordination of intelligence, foreign, defense and police agencies. Furthermore, it is necessary to share information among like-minded countries and draw common lessons from bioterrorism incidents.

The history of bioterrorism shows that small groups and individuals cannot be ignored. In addition to the R.I.S.E. example cited above, in the 1990s, members of the Minnesota Patriots Council, a right-wing militia, were convicted of conspiracy charges for planning to use ricin to assassinate IRS agents and others. In Oregon, members of the relatively large cult Bhagwan Shree Rajneesh poisoned food at 10 restaurants by spraying salmonella on salad bars, sickening 751 people.

In general, wherever bioterrorism occurs, it is important that individual nations think of it as their own problem. In the new globalized world, disease observes no national boundary. In addition, theories of terrorism show us that terrorists learn from past incidents, and imitate or go beyond their predecessors to get what they want. Radicals are similar to one another despite the fact that their groups' character and goals may be entirely different. Rightwing militias, religious cults and far left-wing groups seem to have nothing in common. But they are all characterized by their reliance on conspiracy theories to frame their world view. They express delusional objectives that are difficult for ordinary citizens to understand. Thus, transnational cooperation is required to combat the borderless nature of terrorism.

Japan and the U.S. should construct a comprehensive anti-terrorism scheme that includes everything from sharing information about terrorists, to joint research and development, to funding and training friendly nations how to fight terrorist groups, to disrupting the movement of terrorists and transfer of their weapons, to developing an international regime to punish terrorists. This kind of bilateral agreement is not rare—recently the U.S.-India Counterterrorism Joint Working Group accomplished and expanded various types of cooperation.

So-called track-two meetings with regard to bioterrorism should be held frequently in both countries. Local government officials should participate in such conferences. If bioterrorism happens in either country, both should exchange information and review response. Communication between the U.S. armed forces, diplomats in Japan and various Japanese agencies such as the Maritime Safety Agency, the Ministry of Health, the Ministry of Land and Transportation and others should be close and should be expanded during peacetime.

On the Japanese side, social scientists should pay much more attention to bioterrorism. They tend to regard this issue as a matter of emergency medical treatment. Social scientists may not be able to contribute to research on viruses and diseases, but terrorism is a man-made phenomenon, and we must remember that we are combating terrorists within an international society. Security studies have an important role to play in helping to solve this problem, as they did in helping to formulate nuclear strategy and disarmament policy during the *Cold War*. Cooperation on all fronts is essential to stopping bioterrorism before it undermines the very fabric of our societies.

Management

Japan society hosted a roundtable of Japanese and American experts in professions related to national and local response to bioterrorism in New York City on July 15 and 16, 2000. The purpose of the roundtable was to advance the collective understanding of issues related to bioterrorism preparedness affecting both Japan and the United States, and to explore ways to enhance bilateral cooperation. The roundtable also provided a forum for discussing recent events related to the release of anthrax through the postal system in the U.S.

The roundtable began with participants working through a pair of hypothetical scenarios involving the release of plague bacterium in both Japan and the U.S. The exercise was followed by a discussion of key topics related to crisis and consequence management of the hypothetical bioterrorism events. Roundtable participants included representatives of the respective ministries of foreign affairs, health and emergency management, as well as nationally recognized authorities from the media, law enforcement, hospital administration and academia. Some participants had attended an earlier Japan Society roundtable in Tokyo in October of 2000, which sought to expand bilateral cooperation in the fight against terrorism by focusing on prevention and preparedness.

Since September 11, 2001 the expansion of terrorist activity into the area of weapons of mass destruction has added new urgency to the need for international cooperation in consequence management. Japan has increased its engagement in regional and international preparedness for bioterrorism. Tokyo's participation in the G7 plus Mexico Health Security Summits, in Ottawa in 2001 and in London in 2002, has furthered Japan's international collaborations in bioterrorism preparedness.

Washington, as part of its "*war on terrorism*," has also accelerated national efforts to respond to bioterrorism. The U.S. is seeking to restructure its public health service, re-align functional components of government related to national security, and integrate intelligence and law enforcement activities for the purpose of improving national readiness to respond to terrorism. During the past year, for example, the U.S. Department of Health and Human Services' budget for health and medical aspects of bioterrorism preparedness increased by more than $3 billion, and other governmental agencies are equally engaged.

The Japan-U.S. alliance remains a central component to the security of the Asia-Pacific region. Globalization of the economy and advances in bioscience make this relationship more vital than ever in responding to threats of bioterrorism.

The roundtable in New York in July began with the presentation of two brief "thought experiments" involving imaginary bioterrorist attacks. A scenario from the American perspective depicted a hypothetical assault on an inter-city train on the East Coast of the U.S.A parallel scenario, from the Japanese perspective, portrayed a similar attack on an inter-city train on Japan's main island of Honshu.

The scenarios were used to highlight important points related to crisis and consequence management following a bioterrorism event. They also served to focus technical and policy discussions while allowing other issues relevant to both countries to emerge. Following the "*thought experiments*," discussions by participants were channeled into three broad categories: jurisdiction and infrastructure; medical preparedness; and psychosocial issues.

Thought Experiment: A Plague in New York and Tokyo

The agent of plague is a bacterium called *Yersinia pestis*. Under natural conditions, it is endemic to rodents in many areas throughout the world, including the southwest U.S., with transmission occurring through flea bites. From a bioterrorists' perspective, the most infectious variety of plague is the *pneumonic form*, which can be spread as an aerosol and infects people, causing pneumonia (*pneumonic plague*) one to six days after exposure. Patients who develop pneumonic plague can infect others through respiratory droplets.

Throughout history there have been large outbreaks of pneumonic plague. Before the development of effective antibiotic treatment, virtually all victims died. Ill patients require prompt treatment within 24 hours for the best chance of survival. Those exposed to *pneumonic plague* should receive antibiotic treatment for seven days to prevent them from acquiring the disease.

New York City

The American Scenario simulated the national and local response to a release of plague on board a commuter train traveling from Philadelphia to New York City on December 23. The scenario focused on the early cases of a suspicious disease in individuals from the affected train who presented at clinics and emergency rooms over a wide geographic area. Typical responses likely to occur during such a national emergency were outlined. Emergency responses are complicated because the first cases are reported by three different state health departments (Pennsylvania, New Jersey and New York) on December 25, a national holiday. Inclement weather makes the transfer of specimens to the Centers for Disease Control and Prevention (CDC) in Atlanta and other federal laboratories more difficult than usual. A determination as to whether the outbreak is natural or deliberate relies heavily on laboratory analysis, with federal confirmation at CDC, the Department of Defense and the FBI. This analysis affects initial federal decisions regarding the initial emergency response.

As the scenario progresses, local pharmacies begin to report spot shortages of certain antibiotics known to prevent or treat plague. The issue of quarantine is quickly reviewed and some states take steps to prevent the spread of disease by closing points of assembly and transportation and aggressively pursuing those who were exposed. The media and congressional delegations from affected states demand more information from the relevant federal organizations. Some confusion develops between law enforcement and the public health community concerning who is "*in charge*" of exactly which aspects of the outbreak, and how information should be disseminated to the media.

By day six of the outbreak, the disease seems to be under control. Approximately 50 people have been hospitalized and 20 have died from pneumonic plague. Nearly 40,000 people have received antibiotics to prevent plague.

Following this presentation, the most important initial point made by participants was concern that health providers would fail to recognize and report the initial cases of pneumonic plague and that this would hasten spread of disease. The issue of laboratory confirmation to support the initial diagnosis of plague was raised. While many state public health laboratories are capable of handling plague as part of the Laboratory Response Network (using tests supplied by CDC), individual hospital labs or physicians' offices might not be equipped or trained to identify plague organisms. Many in the group felt that federal authorities would hesitate to make public statements about the course of the disease until the biological agent had been confirmed in their laboratories and their staff was "*on the ground*" in the affected sites. This would delay the "*official response*" by at least 24 hours.

Significant discussion centered on dealing with the media and the importance of maintaining effective communications throughout the course of the outbreak. The participants felt that other nations would interdict travel from the U.S. to their countries until the epidemic was controlled. This would result in thousands of international travelers being stranded at U.S. airports alongside people who potentially could have been infected on the Philadelphia-New York City commuter train, potentially contributing to the spread of the disease.

Finally, there was concern regarding who in the U.S. would inform allies such as Japan, and whether formal channels of diplomatic and law enforcement communication would provide an adequate characterization of the technical aspects of the outbreak to allow Japanese officials to take effective public health measures.

Tokyo

The second scenario simulated a covert strike on Japan from an aerosol release of plague on a Shinkansen ("Bullet") train traveling between Osaka and Tokyo. The attack occurs nine days after the announcement of the outbreak in the U.S. Because the U.S. was the target of a highly visible bioterror attack, Japan is able to intensify its preparedness efforts, with the prime minister directing his ministers to prepare contingency plans. All medical facilities in Japan receive clinical and diagnostic information regarding pneumonic plague at the direction of the Ministry of Health, Labor and Welfare (MHLW). In addition, information from the World Health Organization (WHO) and the U.S. Department of Health and Human Services is provided to the relevant Japanese authorities. The MHLW directs all national quarantine stations to implement their active surveillance systems at international airports, and orders prefectural governors to institute passive surveillance at health centers. The MHLW, National Police Agency (NPA), Japan Defense Agency (JDA) and other related agencies develop a special headquarters for planning and coordination. The media was relentless in covering the outbreak in the U.S. and, as a result, many city officials in Japan have gained some knowledge of the disease.

The attack in Japan occurs on January 4, in a crowded compartment of a commuter train. On January 5 the first victim checks into a Tokyo hospital with severe respiratory illness and is diagnosed with unspecified pneumonia. On January 6, 10 additional patients from the ill-fated train are hospitalized, in Kyoto, Nagoya and Tokyo. Certain medical facilities are beginning to experience an increase in patients with similar symptoms. On January 7, an infectious disease expert affiliated with one of the admitting hospitals makes the presumptive diagnosis of pneumonic plague. She notifies the hospital authorities, who initiate control measures to prevent the spread of the disease. People exposed to ill patients with suspected pneumonic plague are given antibiotics. Hospital authorities report their findings to the Tokyo Metropolitan Government. Tokyo notifies the MHLW and ultimately the prime minister's office is alerted along with the deputy chief cabinet for crisis management, who summons the directors general of the relevant ministries for a crisis meeting.

Nationwide surveillance expands to all health centers and hospitals. The National Institute for Infectious Diseases initiates an epidemic investigation focusing on the affected sites. Confusion is compounded when the prefectural governors of Tokyo, Aichi and Kyoto attempt to make public announcements independent from the national-level announcements made by the MHLW. While law enforcement officials begin an exhaustive search of laboratories and medical institutes around the country to determine the source of the *plague*, the media begins to report that a plague epidemic has occurred in Japan.

The prime minister states there is a possibility that a bioterrorist attack has occurred, and immediately Japan is at the center of a worldwide crisis. The nation experiences some degree of panic, reflected in health centers that cannot deal with the overwhelming numbers of inquiries and "*worried well.*"

On January 8, it is discovered that the illness broke out in cities along the railway line between Osaka and Tokyo. The strain of plague is determined to be different from the strain in the U.S., suggesting there is no single source (or single person or group responsible) for the biological agent affecting both countries. Antibiotic production is increased nationwide due to a request by the MHLW. Hospital overcrowding becomes an issue in some areas. There is some debate as to who—politicians, law enforcement officials or medical personnel—should take the lead in educating the public about the outbreak and how this will be coordinated.

By January 11 the epidemic is under control, but not until 15 people have died and 150 have become ill. Throughout Japan, more than 3,000 people have been given antibiotics to prevent infection.

Eventually, a suspect is arrested who is thought to be acting without any connection to the bioterrorism perpetrators in the U.S. Many citizens with acute stress disorder are developing lingering psychological afflictions.

Based on discussions by roundtable participants there were many common factors between the two countries in their responses to a bioterrorism emergency. In both countries the "*thought experiment*" progressed from a local emergency to national crisis almost as soon as the outbreak was recognized. One important difference between Japan and the U.S. was the fact that Japan was already on high alert for a bioterrorism attack due to the preceding attack in the U.S.A number of measures had been implemented beforehand to assure timely detection of an unusual outbreak and to deal in advance with some leadership issues concerning the response.

Jurisdiction and Emergency Response Infrastructure

The discussion of jurisdiction focused on definitions of bioterrorism and the public health authorities necessary to control an epidemic. There is no international definition of bioterrorism that adequately informs law enforcement, public health officials and the media. One law enforcement participant defined bioterrorism as the malicious use of a *biological agent* or *pathogen*. It was clear that nuances of intent and scale of attack were important in evaluating a threat from biological agents. While the urgency of a smallpox outbreak might speak for itself (bioterrorism would be the only explanation for its appearance), the use of pathogens that are less deadly and more removed from our everyday awareness demands a more concise definition as to what constitutes bioterrorism.

For the sake of discussion, participants agreed to think of bioterrorism as consisting of situations where viruses, bacteria or their toxic by-products were used to harm or threaten large populations. Many attendees agreed that there is still much work to be done in both Japan and the U.S. to educate the public adequately concerning the real threats posed by infectious agents, and that there is a need to demonstrate how bioterrorism is different from other non-contagious terrorist threats to public safety.

Several points related to the rights of individuals versus the authority of government were discussed. In response to *bioterrorism*, these concerns included the potential for the violation of individual civil liberties in the pursuit of epidemic control measures when the overall public's safety is threatened. Such measures might include activities related to patient confidentiality, such as the reporting of new cases to the authorities and the active search by authorities throughout the community for those individuals who might have been in contact with these contagious cases. Few participants knew exactly which government officials from their respective countries would be in charge of shutting down certain critical infrastructures such as transportation or business, or who would be responsible for enforcing quarantine measures to protect public health.

Some participants pointed out that in the U.S., legal organizations in collaboration with the CDC have developed templates for state-level health laws that give state and local jurisdictions the power of quarantine and other actions to protect the public and control the spread of disease during a crisis. Participants felt these templates attempted to preserve individual civil liberties while allowing public health authorities to implement steps to control the spread of disease within the population. Using these templates as a guide, more than 30 states have upgraded their public health laws. With regard to the implementation of actual control measures (e.g., patient isolation, closure of schools), roundtable participants agreed that the most important authorities in both countries are at the local level. As such, developing transparent and coherent response plans well in advance of any bioterrorism attack is crucial, so that adequate review and planning by pertinent implementing agencies can be achieved.

Internationally, the World Health Organization (WHO) develops and maintains International Health Regulations to protect individual countries against certain contagious diseases, including plague. However, current regulations date from 1971 and do not cover newer diseases like *ebola*. Ironically, *smallpox* was removed from reporting in 1981. Nonetheless, once the WHO is notified of a contagious outbreak, a series of actions unfold, including alerting the world's quarantine authorities. The role of the WHO following a bioterrorism attack was thought to be important, since a serious epidemic in any one country can have global implications. Many roundtable participants supported the notion that individual nations should strengthen their ties with the WHO regarding emerging infectious disease preparedness.

Discussants also suggested that Japan and the U.S. maintain a number of WHO Collaborating Centers where experts can focus on certain diseases, including plague, and whose expertise could be used during an international crisis. However, few of these centers have been included in national or international contingency plans for bioterrorism and remain underdeveloped as an emergency response resource. The infrastructure aspect of this discussion focused on the importance of dealing effectively with the media. The participants were concerned about the identification of a primary national spokesperson during a bioterrorism crisis. Most felt that a leading political figure at the local level, such as the mayor or governor, should be the spokesperson in the event of an attack contained within a city. A wider national emergency would ultimately involve the central government and its leadership. Experts from both countries were concerned during the "*thought experiment*" about the potential for strained relationships between investigative officials and the media. Police pursue crimes under special forensic guidelines while the media pursues information for publication. It was felt that the role of public health must be balanced somewhere between these two extremes.

During the recent anthrax investigation in the U.S., it was unclear which information in possession by law enforcement officials should be shared with the media and the public. The ability to rapidly convey critical health information was felt to be crucial to the success of an effective risk communications infrastructure. Key political officials were thought to have had a difficult time communicating with the media during the *anthrax* outbreak for several reasons. First, the bioscience information involved was complex and follow-up communication by credible health authorities was necessary to support and refine such an effort. Second, the risk communications infrastructure necessary to quickly assemble public health information and disseminate it to the media during a crisis was underdeveloped. Third, those from the media (and their public) strongly desired to hear health information from competent health officials rather than from political figures. Lastly, it was emphasized by those participants from the media and emergency management that the time to develop a strategy for dealing with the media is before a disaster—not during or after one.

Japanese participants mentioned the power of the Press Club and its role in society as an important player in disseminating information to the public. Overall, participants felt that many underestimated the beneficial aspects of the media during the recent national emergency (both the September 11 attack and the anthrax letters) and that the media proved its worthiness by providing continuous public health and emergency information in a calm and responsible manner.

The consensus of nearly everyone at the roundtable was that every major city should have an emergency communications plan. This plan should detail how information will be collected, managed and disseminated during a crisis. The plan should include a "*staging area*" where journalists can be briefed on the situation as information becomes available. Most present thought that New York City's past mayor, Rudolph Giuliani, was an example of a good crisis communicator following September 11 and the subsequent anthrax attacks. Giuliani was immediately active in responding to the events, communicating information to the public, and also had the support of a well-structured Office of Emergency Management team, fire department and law enforcement infrastructure, which all quickly acted together to restore the flow of real-time information to the mayor and his staff. Both American and Japanese experts felt that a strong political leader with a clear and authoritative message to the public was key to maintaining order and minimizing panic.

Discussants noted that there were major differences between the coverage of the attack on the World Trade Center in New York City and the anthrax attacks in four states in the eastern U.S. The transparency of government officials during the anthrax investigation was nowhere near the transparency and openness of the U.S. government following the attack on the World Trade Center. There was less of a central locus in the multi-state anthrax outbreak, which involved an unseen enemy. The most visible images were the contaminated buildings, grieving relatives and angry federal postal employees. Consequently, it was unclear to the public whether the government was doing enough to address the situation. The lack of a consistent central national organization, department, agency or spokesperson capable of framing this response in a positive light on behalf of all federal entities responding to this event did little to assuage the public's fears.

Finally, both U.S. and Japanese experts recognized that there is no special dialogue or formal system of exchange of "*biosecurity*" information between Washington and Tokyo. While an informal exchange may exist between scientists who collaborate on technical projects, a formal system between the two governments would be critical for early warning and coordination. Japan would probably learn about the plague attack in the U.S. through unofficial means, such as personal e-mails or the media, long before any pertinent material would be provided through diplomatic or official public health channels.

Practical recommendations included communication between senior public health and law enforcement authorities of both countries during the early phase of a bioterrorism emergency. Once the crisis peaks, a system of ongoing dialogue was thought to be needed to adequately inform officials in both Japan and the U.S. It was pointed out that the U.S. and Japan have a long history of joint military training to further their mutual defense against conventional enemies, but that little has been done in comparable sectors such as health to further mutual security against asymmetric threats like bioterrorism.

MEDICAL PREPAREDNESS

Laboratory Maintenance, Vaccine Development and Disease

Based on the scenario, it is imperative that Japanese authorities be able to determine quickly if an outbreak is the result of an act of bioterrorism perpetrated in Japan, or if the disease has been brought into the country by infected travelers from the U.S. It was clear that Japan required information about the bacterial plague strains affecting the U.S. even before cases were detected in Japan. Until Japan had exact information on the strain and other characteristics concerning the bacterium in the U.S., it would have been difficult or impossible to determine whether the outbreaks were related and to organize appropriate readiness measures. Roundtable participants felt certain that the laboratory specimens in the U.S. would be considered foremost as forensic evidence, and law enforcement procedures and international security concerns would hinder an open exchange of public health information. American participants felt that the identification and diagnosis of plague in the scenario would not have happened so quickly, particularly in the winter months, at the peak of flu season. Also, they felt there would have been a longer delay in sending specimens to CDC headquarters in Atlanta and from there to CDC's labs in Fort Collins, Colorado for specialized confirmatory testing. Consequently, U.S. authorities would not be able to rapidly collate laboratory and forensic data from multiple sites and quickly transmit such "*breaking*" information to Japanese authorities at the time of crisis. It is far more likely that such activities would transpire over days or perhaps weeks before reliable diplomatic-level information moved between nations. This observation raised the question of whether or not an international laboratory network was needed to accelerate international response.

Vaccine is critical to preventing certain illnesses, and in some cases can be used to prevent disease after exposure to a biological agent. However, currently there is not much incentive for vaccine production by manufacturers, since many potentially needed vaccines associated with bioterrorism preparedness would not be commercially viable if developed. Roundtable participants from both countries expressed the need for governmental incentives to stimulate development and production of new vaccines and medications by the private sector. Currently, the opportunities for international collaboration in maintaining and sharing vaccine and medication stockpiles are limited because neither Japan nor the U.S. has enough vaccine to meet the projected needs of its own citizens in the event of a bioterrorism attack, much less citizens of other countries. However, in the future, it is clear that the development of new vaccines and expertise concerning the ability to plan and rapidly implement emergency mass vaccination programs at the community level would greatly benefit both countries. Moreover, since the cost of developing new vaccines is extremely expensive, collaboration by Japan and the U.S. on select vaccine development projects would provide a strategic economy of scale while fitting into already existing long-term bilateral science and technology collaborations.

Based on the U.S. experience with anthrax, consequence management following a bioterrorism attack tends to be information intensive. Surveillance systems in Japan have been developed to track 70 different infectious diseases in four different categories. The Japanese experts were satisfied that a system was in place, but stated that it needed improvement to ensure timeliness. Once a diagnosis is made, reports are sent by paper, which can create a time delay. Most localities in the U.S. are still in the process of developing surveillance systems for bioterrorism. New York City is at the forefront, having developed a rapid reporting prototype that uses a geographic and cluster analysis method to collate information from emergency department triage records. Nationally, the public health infrastructure in the U.S. is weak and lacks advanced technology and a well-trained epidemiology workforce. Critical components of a *bioterrorism surveillance* system that need to be addressed for both countries are timeliness, accuracy and the ability to be stand-alone and automatic so as not to disrupt routine patient care activities. Currently, such an ideal system does not exist anywhere in the world. It was suggested by the meeting attendees that surveillance collaborations on early detection of bioterrorism would greatly facilitate the communication of critical public health information between the two nations.

Clinical Surge

Participant noted that medical preparedness requires concern for both hospital beds as well as the need for specialized staff such as nurses or infectious disease consultants. In the plague scenarios presented, questions were quickly raised concerning the availability of isolation beds or wards to house pneumonic plague patients.

Fortunately in Japan, disaster-based hospitals were set up in large population centers following the Great Hanshin-Awaji Earthquake in 1995. These hospitals allow for surge capacity to care for infected patients and support a stock of antibiotics and other medical supplies. Specifically, they could also allow for triaging certain patients who fit into categories of the highly and moderately infectious diseases to specifically designated hospitals.

In the U.S., a national program is being developed for hospital preparedness that encourages regional collaboration related to epidemic response much like the regional trauma systems, in which one dominant hospital covers a wide region of the city or country. The Greater New York Hospital Association (GNYHA) preparedness effort predates the U.S. government's effort and has been reviewed at length. This collaboration brings together public and private hospitals in the New York area in coordination with local response officials who work to provide a model regional network for emergency and disaster response. Besides providing a link between clinical and public health authorities through integration with the local and state health departments, this organization also provides training in risk communication and the development of an emergency contact directory. Most participants agreed that the Gnyha is, without a doubt, relevant to wider U.S. preparedness activities, as well to Japan.

Medical readiness is strongly related to training. Few participants were convinced that clinicians today were adequately trained to recognize critical biological agents related to bioterrorism. Much of the discussion pointed to the need for health professionals to learn more about emergency management and the roles of other responders. For example, knowledge concerning health officer roles and responsibilities in a community operations center were thought to be lacking for most health personnel currently in leadership positions. In addition, there was thought to be a critical need for some degree of standardized training among first responders —law enforcement, public health, the medical community, transportation and public officials related to bioterrorism. Through a nationwide effort, the U.S. is beginning to address the issues of training and education through its professional guilds, medical schools and schools of public health.

Both American and Japanese participants agreed on the importance of planning at the local level to ensure readiness for bioterrorism.

Such an effort would necessarily include traditional first responders. Special areas for planning cited by virtually all participants included the need for maintaining and distributing a pharmaceutical stockpile at the local level that can fulfill the needs of the local medical community until additional resources arrive from federal caches. U.S. participants noted the increasing emphasis on regional plans as part of national bioterrorism preparedness. Both the U.S. and Japan are continuing to develop hospital preparedness guidelines in both the private and public sector. It was suggested that a database or central repository of hospital planning guidance from both countries would be extremely useful to those involved in bioterrorism preparedness.

Social and Psychological Issues

Over the past decade, specialized knowledge about bioterrorism and its effects has increased dramatically among the health and public policy community. One previously understudied area in which great strides have been made is that of social and clinical psychology. It has become apparent that the mental health emergency response is underdeveloped in both countries. Short-term mental health issues associated with bioterrorism included concern for managing acute situational stress among victims as well as responders. During the recent U.S. anthrax attacks, the lack of knowledge about how anthrax would behave when released within buildings contributed to additional stress and uncertainty. Workers in post offices were unsure about where to obtain information or whom to believe during the critical initial days after the announcement of the attacks. This lack of access to timely and accurate information greatly increased apprehension and concern for personal safety, and ultimately made it difficult for people to determine their own actual risk of contracting anthrax.

Psychological effects can also present themselves later as Post-Traumatic Stress Disorder (PTSD). In Japan, people historically do not seek psychological help because of the stigma associated with mental diseases. Public education is necessary to help encourage those suffering from PTSD to seek help.

In the U.S., the opposite problem seems to exist, in which mental anguish is considered acceptable and is often rewarded in lawsuits. Both the Japanese and the American participants agreed that emergency mental health measures need to be included in the planning process and instituted immediately after an attack. Such activities should include the deployment of counseling centers and the activation of telephone hotlines for people to call and receive guidance. It was noted that one year after the *anthrax attacks* in the U.S., some buildings are still closed, the economy has stagnated, and many people are suffering psychologically from the loss of loved ones as well as from anxiety about new dangers in the workplace. Participants felt that we must expect an increase in personnel problems related to substance abuse, fractured interpersonal relations and depression, following a bioterrorism attack, and that we must therefore include plans for services that will help these people as part of a comprehensive approach to bioterrorism preparedness.

Specific Areas for Potential Collaboration

Preparedness

The U.S. and Japan have already begun to work together on bioterrorism preparedness through such venues as the G7 plus Mexico health security forums. However, there is still much to do to ensure the safety of our populations, and much of this preparedness planning will develop outside of official governmental channels. The following areas were noted by participants as special areas for bilateral collaboration between the U.S. and Japan: joint U.S.-Japan planning and exercises, particularly between the health and medical communities; smallpox and other bioweapon preparedness; and a follow-up lesson featuring the anthrax response in the U.S. It was noted that each U.S.-Japan conference on terrorism promoted an expanded interest in national preparedness, but that something was needed to sustain interest and inform participants in the intervals between meetings. The establishment of a "*bulletin board*" with message capacity devoted to terrorism or bioterrorism preparedness was proposed to fulfill this need. This kind of information exchange is critical to maintaining up-to-date public health information related to bioterrorism preparedness between the two countries.

Biosensor Technology

It was proposed that Japan and the U.S. pool their scientific resources into some key projects related to bioterrorism preparedness. Most participants expressed the desire to establish a joint effort to develop biosensor technology, which is extremely important in the rapid detection of a bioterrorism attack in urban environments. Currently, biosensors are not very accurate and return many false positives. This technology is improving, however, and is definitely an area where collaboration could directly increase the safety of large urban centers while serving to focus attention on issues related to bilateral science and technology collaboration.

Vaccine Development

There are few specific vaccines available for mass vaccination of populations in response to a major bioterrorism threat. Many of these vaccines have no specific market to spur their development or to ensure profit in the commercial sector. Other vaccines, such as those for *smallpox*, are being developed unilaterally by the developed countries. No sharing agreement or pooled technology exchange is in place. Unfortunately, smallpox remains a global threat and will not respect borders if it is again released into the population. After addressing each nation's individual needs for smallpox vaccine, Japan and the U.S. could work closely together to share their expertise with lesser developed countries to further the humanitarian components of bioterrorism preparedness.

Training and Education

Training and education is an area where the U.S. and Japan already collaborate but only on a sporadic basis. It was proposed that the two countries continue to develop and refine curriculum specifically related to bioterrorism preparedness. This activity would have a high preparedness value and would avoid issues related to individual national priorities. In addition, a similar training doctrine for bioterrorism readiness may have additional benefits to each country in a crisis if mutual aid or international assistance is needed. Currently, many prestigious institutions in both countries participate in this activity. One method to ensure continuity and ongoing progress in this area would be to develop an intensive training and curriculum development program between a Japanese and an American university.

Laboratory Research

Participation in a global effort to enhance early disease detection and response around the world would be important as part of a larger international laboratory-based *bioterrorism* response network. Although each nation would maintain and develop its own internal capacities for early detection, there are certainly areas where each nation has a relative advantage. Since this is a highly technical domain of expertise, a separate "*summit*" for laboratory technicians and researchers familiar with the issues of bioterrorism preparedness would be a more appropriate forum to hone the details of such an initiative.

Surveillance

Surveillance was mentioned as one critical area for international collaboration between Japan and the U.S. Sentinel surveillance, the tracking of exotic diseases and laboratory monitoring are all extremely important as means of alerting authorities to bioterrorism or emerging infectious diseases. Specific bilateral collaborations related to promoting global surveillance, perhaps under the aegis of the WHO, would be beneficial to both countries' national bioterrorism readiness plans.

Health Information Exchange

Information on best practices, existing training exercises and relevant literature already exist in both countries. It would be advantageous to both countries if an organized effort could be made to properly identify and ensure appropriate shared database access to this type of information. This would be very beneficial to those officials at the local level engaged in bioterrorism preparedness who live far from institutions of higher learning.

Alternatives to Biological Weapons

The issue of compliance to or support for the BWC was beyond the scope of this forum. However, if an alternative to the BWC is developed in the near future it will rely on site monitoring, early detection, laboratory evaluation and global surveillance activities. In the context of working with other countries, the U.S. and Japan could further this effort with model teams or field technology appropriate to this task.

Conclusion

The threat from bioterrorism is so manifold and scientifically challenging that no country can maintain excellence in all academic areas. Therefore, although it is true that both Japan and the U.S. place a high premium on self-reliance and independent policymaking as part of their respective national preparedness efforts, collaboration in certain key areas would certainly improve their capabilities overall to respond to bioterrorism. Further, if we are not maximally prepared, the potential consequences to our populations could be staggering. For example, it is estimated that smallpox could kill up to 30 percent of the susceptible population in our two countries. As we learned from the anthrax attacks in the U.S. in the fall of 2001, bioterrorism is a real and urgent threat to society. With communicable agents such as smallpox, a threat is posed to all nations since global travel can quickly result in further dissemination. Closer collaboration between the U.S. and Japan is particularly useful, not only because of the two countries' recent histories of bioterrorism, but because of their *de facto* leadership positions in the world.

To that end, there needs to be a better system in place to share critical public health information between Japanese and U.S. officials at the time of crisis, particularly at the most senior levels. We should also look for ways to leverage bioterrorism preparedness investments in both countries and work together to help solve gaps in the international emergency response fabric. Some roundtable participants said our countries should look at existing defense and security relations to further this bilateral preparedness effort related to bioterrorism rather than develop brand new systems. All participants urged the two countries to work to develop an international standard for consequence management that is specifically tailored to this threat. Such an effort would no doubt rest heavily upon the medical and public health communities.

Japan Society has made an important first step in creating a bilateral dialogue on the specific issue of bioterrorism preparedness and consequence management. It is imperative that this dialogue be taken further, beyond this forum, into the policymaking quarters of the respective governments of the U.S. and Japan.

INDEX